Short Takes
Model Essays for Composition

Fourth Edition

Elizabeth Penfield
University of New Orleans

 **HarperCollins*CollegePublishers***

Acquisitions Editor: Patricia Rossi
Developmental Editor: Hope Rajala
Project Editor: Susan Goldfarb
Design Supervisor: Mary Archondes
Cover Design: Mary Archondes
Production: Kathleen Donnelly
Compositor: American–Stratford Graphics Services, Inc.
Printer and Binder: R. R. Donnelley & Sons Company
Cover Printer: The Lehigh Press, Inc.

For permission to use copyrighted material, grateful
acknowledgment is made to the copyright holders on pp. 315–318,
which are hereby made part of this copyright page.

Short Takes: Model Essays for Composition, Fourth Edition

Copyright © 1993 by HarperCollins College Publishers

Library of Congress Cataloging-in-Publication Data
Penfield, Elizabeth, 1939-
    Short takes : model essays for composition / Elizabeth Penfield. —
4th ed.
        p.   cm.
    Includes index.
    1. College readers.   2. English language—Rhetoric.   I. Title.
PE1417.P43   1993
808′.0427—dc20   92-22100
                                                                      CIP

ISBN (Student Edition): 0-673-46598-5
ISBN (Instructor's Edition): 0-673-46599-3

    93   94   95   9   8   7   6   5   4   3   2

Contents

 **Description** 11

"Over the past twelve years I have learned that a tree needs space to grow, that coyotes sing down by the creek in January, that I can drive a nail into oak only when it is green, that bees know more about making honey than I do, that love can become sadness, and that there are more questions than answers."

"From the center of downtown Tucson the ground slopes gently away to Main Street, drops a few feet, and then rolls to the banks of the Santa Cruz River. Here lies the section of the city known as El Hoyo."

"Widowed, alone, children and grandchildren flung wide from California to New England, she fills her days with little things."

"By my fifth ride, my heart was leaping at the onset of each segment as at the approach of a dear old friend, and melting with instantaneous nostalgia for each at its finish."

2 Narration   36

3 Example 60

4 Division and Classification 92

5 Comparison and Contrast   115

6 Analogy   137

10 Argument   243

Yesterday's Drug War Daniel Lazare **288**

"Sidewalk dealers, suddenly legitimized, would have no more reason to settle their disputes with Uzis than do liquor salesmen."

Handgun Control: Pro Pete Shields **291**

"Twenty thousand Americans were killed with handguns last year. Hundreds of thousands more were injured. One child a day dies in a handgun accident."

Handgun Control: Con J. Warren Cassidy **295**

"But gun control, whether it be in the form of registration, licensing, waiting periods, background checks or outright bans, is no joke to the more than 60 million law-abiding gun owners, sportsmen and gun collectors in this country."

Thematic Guide

*P*eople

The Individual

Groups

Occupations

Scenes and Places

*I*deas and Issues

Education

Language

Science and Technology

Society

Preface

T his fourth edition of *Short Takes* remains a collection of short, readable essays, and the commentary continues to focus on how to interrelate reading and writing and how to write various kinds of essays. But much is new. The initial essay, "Freeze Frame: Reading and Writing," has been expanded for a fuller discussion of what is involved in the activities of reading and writing, setting out an interactive model that is reinforced in each chapter's introduction and apparatus. The overall organization of the book remains the same. The chapters are sequenced so that the more accessible patterns of development come first, with each chapter building on the previous one and leading to the one that follows. Within each chapter, the essays are presented in order of difficulty. In keeping with the emphasis on active reading and writing, however, throughout *Short Takes* more attention has been devoted to process.

The Essays

To write is to choose among alternatives, to select the most appropriate organization, persona, diction, and techniques for a given audience and purpose. Each of the essays included in this edition was chosen because it exemplifies the author's choices, and the apparatus emphasizes those choices and alternatives. Thus the essays serve as illustrative models of organization and stylistic techniques available to the writer. The essays were also chosen because their authors represent different genders, ages, and cultures; as a result, subjects of the essays are accessible and their perspectives are lively, qualities that also allow them to serve as sources of invention, as jumping-off places for students to develop their own ideas in their own styles.

The number of essays in this edition has been raised from 56 to 58, and 32 are new. All are indeed short—about 1000 words at most—and as such should easily lend themselves to scrutiny and emulation, since most of the papers assigned in composition courses fall in the 400- to 1000-word range. With one exception, the essays are complete pieces, not excerpts. They represent the basic aims of discourse and illustrate the standard rhetorical modes.

Rhetorical Modes and the Aims of Discourse

Yet anyone who has used a reader with essays arranged by mode has likely run into two problems: first, few essays are pure examples of a single mode; second, most collections of essays treat argument—an aim of writing—as though it were the equivalent of description, comparison/contrast, and so on. *Short Takes* addresses these inconsistencies by emphasizing the difference between mode—how an essay is organized—and purpose—how an essay is intended to affect the reader—and by pointing out how essays frequently blend two or more modes.

Because essays usually employ more than one mode, the essays here are grouped according to their *primary* rhetorical pattern; the questions that follow each essay go on to point out the subordinate modes. As for the aims of discourse, the essays represent the various purposes for writing. The writer's self-expressive, informative, and persuasive purposes are underscored in the discussion questions. In addition, connections between academic writing and the kinds of writing one finds outside the classroom walls are emphasized.

Example, description, or other standard modes are used to develop all kinds of nonfiction prose—self-expression, exposition, and argument. Of those three types of writing, self-expression is the easiest and argument the most difficult. For that reason argument has its own special chapter, and in this edition that chapter has been expanded.

Of the 14 essays in the chapter on argument, 8 focus on different topics, and 4 address the same problem but from very different perspectives, arguing for or against a particular position. And while Chapters 1–9 contain some essays that are intended to persuade, those in Chapter 10 exemplify the classical appeals: to reason, to emotion, and to the writer's ethical values.

Apparatus for Reading and Writing

The apparatus is designed to make full use of the essays. Each chapter begins with a brief introduction that depicts the mode or purpose under discussion, showing how it can be used in formal essays and in practical, everyday writing situations. The introductions go on to point out specifically how the modes can be shaped by considerations of audience, purpose, particular strategies, thesis, and organization. Each of the essays is preceded by a short explanatory note. Following each essay are two sets of questions, one under the heading "Thesis and Organization" and the other under the heading "Technique and Style," followed by "Suggestions for Writing." At the end of each chapter is a list of pointers under the categories "Exploring the Topic" and "Drafting the Paper."

This division of the writing process approximates the classic one of invention, arrangement, and style, and is not intended to imply that the act of writing is a recursive act. As one writes, one constantly invents, organizes, and revises; the lines between those activities are fine if not downright blurry.

The suggestions for writing following each essay contain a number of options related by theme, organization, or ideas to the work the writer has just read. The assignments allow a good deal of flexibility: some lend themselves to open general information or personal experience essays, some to research papers, and some to the classical technique of imitation. Once the writer selects a subject, *exploring the topic* is the next step; the questions in that category are shaped so that no matter what type of paper may be involved, the writer can generate information about it. *Drafting the paper* then helps organize the material and points out some of the pitfalls and advantages inherent in the particular mode. Throughout, the end-of-chapter material emphasizes both the process of writing and flexibility of the model and mode.

Acknowledgments

For their help in bringing this book to publication, I have many to thank. Hope Rajala, as usual, provided some excellent essays as well as good advice, encouragement, and friendship. I am, as always, most grateful. In addition, Theodora Hill assisted with sound suggestions and helped with even the more boring aspects of preparation such as proofreading and setting up tearsheets. Professor Mary Boyles, Pembroke State College; Professor Beverly Cotton, Cerritos College; Professor Catherine Essinger, Edison State Community College; Professor Rodney D. Keller, Ricks College; and Professor Sandra Macphee, Fashion Institute of Design and Merchandising, all provided guidance and advice that improved the manuscript. And, as usual and most of all, I wish to thank my own students, who have taught me at least as much as I have taught them.

ELIZABETH PENFIELD

Short Takes

Freeze Frame:
Reading and Writing

*I*n filmmaking, a "short take" is a brief scene filmed without interruption. Short essays are similar in that they move quickly, without interruption, toward their conclusions. And if you were editing a short take, you might "freeze" a frame, stopping the film on one particular shot to get a better look at the details. That's just what this essay will do, stop and take a close-up look at what goes on when you read and when you write.

Essays, like most written work, are deceptive. What you see on a printed page resembles the writer's work about as much as a portrait photograph resembles the real person. What you don't see when you look at printed pages are all the beginnings and stops, the crumpled paper, the false starts, the notes, the discarded ideas, the changed words. Instead, you have a finished piece—the result of the writer's choices. Don't let that result intimidate you. The process most writers go through to produce their essays is very like your own. The writer Andre Dubus puts it another way: "There is something mystical [about writing] but it's not rare and nobody should treat it as though this is something special that writers do. Anybody born physically able in the brain can sit down and begin to write something, and discover that there are depths in her soul or his soul that are untapped."

Both writers and readers tap into those depths, depths that help make meaning of the world we live in. The essays contained in this book, together with its explanations, questions, and suggestions for writing, reinforce a basic assumption: reading and writing are highly individual processes that are active, powerful, and interrelated ways to discover *meaning*. To check out that statement, think of one day within the last week when something memorable happened to you. Isolate that incident so it's clear in your mind. Now think of all the other details of the day, from the time your eyes opened in the morning to the time they closed at night. That's a lot of detail, and most of it insignificant, meaningless. Those are the bits and pieces of information you would probably discard if you were to write about that day. What you would be left with is that memorable thing that occurred and a few details directly related to it, some preceding it, a few following. In writing about that day, you would reshape events, evaluating, selecting, and re-creating what happened so that what was most meaningful comes through clearly. As a result, someone reading your description would be able to experience at a distance what you experienced firsthand. To write, then, is to create and structure a world; to read is to become part of someone else's. And just as reading makes a better writer, writing makes a better reader.

4   What's a good reader? Someone who interacts with the words on the page. Just as the writer reshapes, evaluates, selects, and re-creates events, so too the reader reshapes, evaluates, selects, and re-creates the text on the page. After all, as a reader you have your own world, one made up of your experiences, family, culture—all of which you bring with you to what you read. An essay about why people love to walk on beaches, for example, will remind you of any beaches you know, and your associations will probably be pleasurable. As you begin the essay, you discover that the writer's associations are also pleasant ones, and they in turn reinforce yours. You read on, constantly reassessing your ideas about the essay as you add more and more information to your first impression. Now and then, you may hit a sentence that at first doesn't make much sense, so you stop, perhaps to look up an unfamiliar word, perhaps to go back and review an earlier statement, then read on, again reevaluating your ideas about what the author is saying and what you think of it. The result is analytical, critical reading—not critical in the sense of being a harsh judge but critical in the sense of questioning, weighing evidence, evaluating, comparing your world to the one the writer has created on the page.

5   If you've done much writing, the process summarized above must sound familiar. Most people find that writing is a form of discovery, that writing about an idea helps clarify it. In your own experience, you have probably found that you usually don't have a clear grasp of your thesis until you've written your way into it. Odds are you start with an idea, a general focus, but that focus becomes clearer as you rethink your choice of a particular word or reread

what you've put on the page to get a sense of what should come next. And on you go, sometimes speeding, sometimes creeping, constantly revising, until you finish. Even the idea of finishing is a shaky notion; many writers will continue to revise right up to their deadlines. This idea of revising and tinkering seems natural to writing but less so to reading. Yet just as you tinker and wrestle with your own writing, you should do the same with what you read. You should scribble, underline, question, challenge. Reading in this way, reading critically with pen or pencil in hand, will give you a fuller appreciation of what you read and a better understanding of how to write.

If you're not used to reading in this manner, it may seem foreign to you. After all, what's printed on the page should be easy enough to understand. But because words only stand for things and are not the things themselves, different readers find different meanings. If, for instance, your only memory of a beach was of nearly drowning in the Atlantic Ocean, then you would have to suspend that association when you read an essay that praises beach walking. And if also your skin turns bright red at the mere mention of the sun, that adds one more obstacle to understanding why others enjoy the seashore. How then can a reader comprehend all that an author is saying? More specifically, how can a reader go about reading an essay critically? 6

It helps to know what different kinds of writing have in common. Whether business letter, lab report, journal entry, news story, poem, or essay, all focus on a subject, address a reader, and have a point. And, too, all have a purpose and a style; they are written for specific reasons and in a certain way. These shared elements are perhaps more familiar as questions used to spark ideas for writing, the familiar journalistic *who? what? where? when? how? why?* 7

Yet these questions can be equally useful for reading. To whom is an essay addressed? What is the writer's main point? How is the piece organized? Why is it structured that way? Where and when does the action take place? Many, many more inquiries can be spun off those six simple words, and they are useful tools for exploring an essay. The kind of analysis they lead to not only contributes to the pleasure you derive from an essay, it makes you more aware of how to address similar concerns in your own writing. No one ever learned to write only by reading, but good writers are also good readers. 8

Detecting the Thesis

9   In most of the reading we do, we are looking for information. The election coverage reported in the newspaper, the syllabus for a course, a set of directions all exemplify this kind of reading, but reading for information and reading for comprehension are as different as a vitamin pill and a five-course dinner. To understand not only what a writer is saying but its implications and also why that writer might have chosen to say it that way isn't easy.

10   The title of an essay is a good place to start, for most titles tip you off not only about the subject of the piece but also the author's stand. You don't need to turn to the essay titled "Legalize Drugs? Not on Your Life" in the section on argument to figure out you will be reading an essay against legalizing drugs. Other essays, such as "The Vibram Stomp," just imply a subject and raise your curiosity. What's a Vibram stomp? Still other titles tip you off to the author's tone, the writer's attitude toward the subject: "The Roots of Rock" is an informative but humorous account of singers' hairstyles; "Fight! Fauna Fight!" explores the eccentric names that schools and colleges give their athletic teams, from Buckeye to Banana Slug.

11   Knowing or at least having a hint about the subject is the first step to discovering an essay's thesis, the assertion the author is making about that subject. The first paragraph or set of paragraphs that act as an introduction will also help you form a tentative thesis. Sometimes, the writer will place the thesis in the first paragraph or introduction. In this essay, for example, the thesis appears in the last sentence of paragraph 5: "Reading critically with pen or pencil in hand, will give you a fuller appreciation of what you read and a better understanding of how to write." But sometimes a bare-bones version of the thesis will appear in the title. If you see it, you should mark it. If you don't see a thesis, you should still jot down a tentative version of your own so that you have a focus for what is to follow, an idea that you can test other ideas against.

12   The obvious comparison here is your own writing. Many writers start with a general idea that then gets refined into a thesis as they write. Once that thesis is clear, then the writer must decide where to place it for the greatest effect. Some opt for the introduction, others choose the conclusion, and still others decide on a more subtle solution by weaving bits and pieces of the thesis into the essay as a whole.

If you are reading the essay, this last choice can give you a challenge. You must create the thesis by identifying key sentences and then mentally composing a statement that covers those ideas, a process that often takes more than one reading but is made easier if you underline the important sentences.   13

Sometimes writers set traps, making it easy to mistake a fact for a thesis. If you keep in mind that a thesis is both a sentence and an assertion—a value judgment—those traps can be avoided. "The average American watches a lot of TV" states a fact that most readers would shrug off with a "So what?" On the other hand, "Television rots the minds of its viewers" takes a stand that will probably raise hackles and a "Hey, wait a minute!"   14

When you read an essay that has a thesis that you must put together from several sentences, you may well find that someone else who reads the essay may come up with a different thesis statement. And you both may be right. What's happening here? If you think about how slippery words are and the different experiences that different readers bring to an essay, you can begin to see why there's more than one "correct" thesis.   15

If you were to give the same essay to ten critical readers, you might find that their versions of the thesis differ but overlap. Their readings would probably cluster around two or three central ideas. If an eleventh person read the essay and came up with a thesis that contradicted the ten other readings, that version would probably be off base. Perhaps that was the reader who almost drowned and can't take the sun.   16

For instance, Tania Nyman's "I Have a Gun" (pages 49–51) tells of the author's fear of urban violence and her ambivalent feelings about owning a handgun. After reading the essay, you may decide that Nyman's subject is handguns and that she is asserting that they are a necessary precaution in an urban environment. Another reader might focus on fear of violence as the subject and come up with a thesis that deciding to buy a handgun has made clear that most urban residents, black and white together, are bound by a net of fear. Both readings would be "correct" in that you can find adequate textual support for both versions of the thesis. Yet a reading that proposed "Everyone should buy handguns" won't work because little if any evidence in the text supports that conclusion.   17

Recognizing Patterns of Development

18   Once you've nailed down a thesis, go a step further to examine how that thesis is developed. Writers depend on various patterns of thought that are almost innate. To tell a joke is to *narrate*; to convey what a party was like is to *describe* and to use *examples*; to jot down a grocery list is to *divide and classify*; to figure out which car to buy is to *compare and contrast* (if you think of your old car as a peach or a lemon, you are drawing an *analogy*); to give directions is to use *process*; to consider how to improve your tennis game is to weigh *cause and effect*; to explain how you feel is to *define*. Narration, description, example, division and classification, comparison and contrast, analogy, process, cause and effect, and definition are the natural modes of thinking that writers rely upon.

19   Used singly and in combinations, these modes provide the structure of the essay, the means by which the author conveys the major point, the thesis. The qualification *in combinations* is an important one, for rarely does an essay rely solely on one pattern of development. So far, for instance, the essay you are now reading has used definition (paragraph 4), cause and effect (paragraph 6), process (paragraph 3), and description (paragraph 4), and will use analogy (paragraph 31), and, most of all, example (virtually every paragraph). The other essays that you will read in this book also employ more than one mode, but each has been placed in a category according to the primary means of development. In fact, the whole textbook can be thought of as organized by division and classification: the essays are first divided into primary purpose—to explain or to argue—and then classified according to primary mode.

20   When you are writing, however, these modes provide ways to think about your topic as well as ways to organize your essay. With practice, they become as much second nature as shifting gears in a manual-transmission car. At first you might be a bit tentative about knowing when to shift from first to second, but with time you don't even think about it. Similarly, you might wonder if your point is clear without an example; in time, you automatically supply it.

Identifying the Purpose

21   Why would you want to tell a joke, describe a party, jot down a grocery list, compare one car to another, give directions, analyze a

tennis stroke, define a feeling? That *why* is your purpose: to entertain, to inform, to persuade, to vent your feelings.

In writing, as in speech, your purpose determines the relation-   22
ship among your subject, yourself, and your reader. Most of the
writing you will be doing in college, for instance, is intended to
inform. For that reason, most of the essays included in this book are
expository; their purpose is to explain a subject, to inform the reader.
In most of your other courses, you will find that your reading fits
into this category, one occupied by stacks of textbooks. As for your
writing, when you write a lab or book report, a précis, or an essay
exam, you focus on your subject so that you explain it to your
readers. How you feel about what was at the opposite end of the
microscope or the article you are abstracting is not pertinent to your
purpose; nor are you trying to persuade your reader that the essay
you are writing a précis of is the best you have ever read.

As for the essay exam, the only persuading you are trying to do   23
is to convince your reader that you know what you are writing
about—again, the focus is on your subject. Think of textbooks,
news articles, business letters, manuals, how-to books, and you will
find that as you read, you are not very conscious of the writer or the
style. What you are dealing with is expository writing.

If you do find yourself responding to the writer's personal reac-   24
tion to a subject, you are probably reading a journal or diary entry,
a personal letter, an opinion piece in the newspaper, or a meditative
essay. In this kind of writing, the focus is on the writer. If, for
example, your teacher asks you to keep a journal in which you
respond to what you read, your responses may range from fury over
an opinion you disagree with to mild musings on what you think
about the author's subject. What is important is what you feel, and
your writing expresses those feelings by communicating them
clearly to your reader.

Conveying what you feel about a subject and persuading your   25
reader to share your opinion, however, are two different aims. Consider the difference between a letter to the editor and an editorial,
both on the 55 mph speed limit. The letter to the editor may rage
against the idiots who came up with the idea and describe how
stupid it is to be required to drive 55 for 150 back-country Montana
miles when there isn't another car on the road. The editorial, however, considers the larger context for the law—the lives saved, the
accidents avoided—and concludes that what is a minor inconve-

nience for some makes roads safer for many. While the writer of the letter may feel better for having let off some steam, no minds will have been changed. In fact, probably the only readers who finished that letter were those who agreed to begin with. The editorial writer, however, is careful to address a multiple audience of readers who agree, who disagree, and who have no opinion. The author's intent is to change minds, and the argument's appeal rests primarily on reason, not emotion.

26   That is also your goal when you are given a writing assignment that asks you to take a stand and defend it. You must know your audience and rely on authority, on reason, and to a lesser extent on emotion to win over those readers. Blatant persuasion hawks products on television commercials, sells political candidates, and begs you to support various causes; the more subtle variety appears in college catalogs, public debates, and the editorial pages. All ask you to consider a certain stand, adopt a given opinion, or take an action: the writer focuses primarily on the reader.

27   Recognizing valid evidence, separating emotional appeals from appeals to reason, and spotting logical fallacies can protect you in a world of contradictory claims and high-powered propaganda. In the newspapers, on the television set, in the halls of Congress, and in your living room, issues are debated and opinions voiced. Sorting through them takes the kind of concentrated thought that reading and writing argumentative essays requires. Whether the argument is blatant or subtle, being able to recognize the techniques at work, the purpose, and the intended audience helps you evaluate assertions and illuminate their validity, whether debating a point in class or at home or reading or writing an essay for class.

Refining the Purpose

28   Just as few essays depend solely on one pattern of organization, few depend on only one purpose, so that more often than not the reader, like the writer, will have to work at determining the primary purpose behind a piece. An effective description of an unusual scene such as a giant feedlot, for example, will not only explain what it looks, smells, and sounds like but also convey how the author feels about it and perhaps imply a need for change. While basically expository, such an essay also incorporates self-expression and persuasion. And other motives and audiences lie beneath the surface. A

student, for instance, may write a paper for the simple reason that it is assigned or to get a good grade; but successful essays go beyond those immediate goals to change both reader and writer. The author learns from the act of writing because it forces the writer to examine the subject closely, to explore it, and to communicate something of interest about it. So, too, the reader learns from a good essay, perhaps finding a fresh perspective on a familiar topic or discovering information about the unfamiliar. Both reader and writer work to create meaning out of what is on the page. The result is not just sweat and knowledge, but pleasure. Good prose delights.

And as all who write can attest, meaning can be elusive. Knowing   29
what one wants to write and having a fair idea of how it should be organized still does not necessarily help shape individual sentences so that they convey the desired tone. That requires draft after draft.

Hemingway rewrote the last page of *A Farewell to Arms* 39 times,   30
and Katherine Anne Porter spent 20 years writing and rewriting *Ship of Fools*. Writing nonfiction doesn't make the process any easier. Wayne Booth, a distinguished essayist and scholar, speaks for most writers: "I revise many, many times, as many times as deadlines allow for. And I always feel that I would have profited from further revision." Poet, novelist, essayist, journalist, student, or professional, all continue in the tradition expressed in the eighteenth century by a fellow writer, Samuel Johnson, who said: "What is written without effort is in general read without pleasure." Pleasurable reading derives from a pleasing writing style, and though some writers strive for elegance as well as clarity, most readers will happily settle for clarity.

Writing—the Challenge

Far from following a recipe, writing an essay is like driving a car   31
while at the same time trying to impress the passengers, read a road map, recognize occasional familiar landmarks, follow scrawled and muttered directions, and watch for and listen to all the quirks of the car. You know vaguely where you are going and how you want to get there, but the rest is risk and adventure. With work and a number of dry runs, you can smooth out the trip so that the passengers fully appreciate the pleasure of the drive and the satisfaction of reaching the destination. That is the challenge the writer faces, a challenge that demands critical reading as well as effective writing.

Pointers for Reading

1. **Get settled.** Gather up a good dictionary and whatever you like to write with, and then find a comfortable place to read.

2. **Think about the title.** What sort of expectations do you have about what will follow? Can you identify the subject? A thesis? Can you tell anything about the writer's tone?

3. **Look for a specific focus.** Where is the essay going? What appears to be its thesis? At what point does the introduction end and the body of the essay begin? What questions do you have about the essay so far? Is the essay directed at you? If not, what is the intended audience?

4. **Look for a predominant pattern of organization.** What are the most important ideas in the body of the essay? Note the modes the writer uses to develop those ideas. Note those you disagree with or question.

5. **Identify the conclusion.** Where does the conclusion begin? How does it conclude the essay? What effect does it have on you?

6. **Evaluate the essay.** Did the essay answer the questions you had about it? How effective was the support for the main ideas? Did the writer's choice of words fit the audience? What effect did the essay have on you? Why?

1

Description

Description turns up in various guises in all types of prose, for it is the basic device a writer uses to convey sense impressions. For that reason, it is as essential to objective writing as it is to subjective prose, and of course to everything in between. A quick sketch of a family gathering that you might include in a letter to a friend draws upon the same skills as a complex report on the effectiveness of a new product. Both rely on the ability to observe, to select the most important details, to create a coherent sequence for those details, and then to convey the result by appealing to the reader's senses. To describe something, then, is to re-create it in such a way that it becomes alive again, so that the reader can see and understand it. Prose that depends heavily on description invites the reader to share the writer's initial sense of vividness and perception.

The role description plays in writing will vary. Personal narratives depend heavily on description to bring scenes and actions to life, to depict an outdoor wedding, for instance, or to convey what it feels like to have a toothache. Other types of expository essays use description in a less obvious role, perhaps to clarify a step in a process or make vivid an example. And persuasion often gets its punch from description, for it enables the reader to see the prisoner on death row or the crime that led to the death sentence. In each of the essays that follow, however, description dominates the structure. The essays' general subjects are familiar—a place, a person, an object, an event—but by selecting details, each author tailors description uniquely.

AUDIENCE AND PURPOSE   Most writers start with a general sense of purpose and audience. Berger, for instance, assumes his reader is familiar with the distinctive print left by the Vibram sole of a hiking boot, but he goes on to develop his own ideas about what those prints mean. J. Merrill-Foster, however, writes to an audience that may know little of the details of the subject—old age—and that leads the author to heap detail upon detail, to contrast past with present, and to make the reader see and feel what it is to be old. Because the audience is somewhat distant from that topic, Merrill-Foster keeps the readers on the outside, looking in.

Sue Hubbell, on the other hand, wants her readers right beside her. Although most people can identify with the idea of a farm, Hubbell creates a relationship with her audience that is intimate, describing her setting so that she places the reader in it to see with her eyes and share her thoughts. But placing the reader on the scene is a more difficult task if the scene is not part of the reader's world, and that is the problem Mario Suarez faces when he writes of "El Hoyo," a Chicano neighborhood in Tucson. To make the unfamiliar familiar, he must choose his details carefully, present them in a memorable sequence, and use what his readers know as points of comparison.

Hubbell, Suarez, Merrill-Foster, Schjeldahl, and Berger all inform their readers, but self-expression and persuasion also enter in. The reader shares the quiet pleasure that Hubbell feels and recognizes Merrill-Foster's sense of admiration and Suarez's fondness for their subjects. Schjeldahl's exhilaration also comes through loud and clear. So, too, the reader senses an argumentative edge behind Merrill-Foster's brief character sketch of an old woman; Berger's argumentative stand is unmistakable.

SENSORY DETAIL   No matter what the purpose or audience, descriptive essays are characterized by their use of detail, particularly detail that appeals to the senses. Bruce Berger's account of "deer paths, coyote prints, javelina pocks, the great peace signs of heron tracks" allows us to see what he sees, and it is vision that description appeals to most frequently. But vision rarely stands alone. Sue Hubbell's "swift, showy river to the north and a small creek to the south, its run broken by waterfalls" evokes our sense of hearing as well.

Hearing also brings Peter Schjeldahl's roller coaster to life as it rides a track with "dips, humps, dives, and shimmies that roar, chortle, cackle, and snort." Appeals such as these to the senses not only help the reader fix the picture in time and space but bring the scene to life so that the reader can hear, see, smell, touch, and taste it.

DICTION   The words a writer chooses determine whether the description is more objective or subjective, whether its tone is factual or impressionistic. Although total objectivity is impossible, description that leans toward the objective is called for when the writer wants to focus on subject as opposed to emotional effect, on what something *is* rather than how it felt. Compare, for example, two descriptions by J. Merrill-Foster, both on the same subject, an 85-year-old woman:

> She is frightened and distressed by letters from retired military men. They write that unless she sends $35 by return mail, the Russians will land in Oregon and take over America. The arrival of the daily mail looms large in her day. Once, every few weeks, it contains a personal letter. The rest is appeals and ads. She reads every item.
>
> I watch the woman—my mother—walking carefully down the frozen, snow-filled driveway to the mail box. She is a photograph in black and white, which only loving memory tints with stippled life and color.

The first description reports the unnamed woman's feelings and the facts that give rise to them, and then generalizes on the importance of the daily mail, noting what it contains and the attention the woman gives it. The second description uses first person and identifies the woman as the author's mother, the words *I* and *mother* forming an emotional bond between reader and writer, overlaying with feeling the picture of the woman walking to the mailbox. What then follows is the author's direct and personal comment, phrased as metaphor and signifying the mother's loss of power, energy, life. On finishing the first passage, the reader understands the role an everyday event—the arrival of the mail—plays in the life of an old woman; on finishing the second, the reader knows and feels how old age has diminished a once vital person.

COMPARISON   Comparisons also enrich description. Like details, they vitalize, and they can produce an arresting image, explain the unfamiliar, make a connection with the reader's own experience, or reinforce the major point in the essay. That reinforcement is what Berger is after in his comparison of animal and bird tracks to those of humans. Schjeldahl, however, turns to metaphor to extol the virtues of a roller coaster, which to him is a "poem . . . in parts or stanzas, with jokes" that he then goes on to enumerate and describe. Metaphor caps Suarez's essay as he stretches it to its limit with a closing analogy, comparing El Hoyo's Chicanos to the local dish capirotada.

THESIS AND ORGANIZATION   All the details, all the comparisons are presented according to a pattern so that they add up to a single dominant impression. In descriptive essays, this single dominant impression may be implicit or explicit, and it stands as the thesis. An explicit thesis jumps off the page at you and is usually stated openly in one or two easily identifiable sentences. An implicit thesis, however, is more subtle. As reader, you come to understand what the thesis is even though you can't identify any sentence that states it. If that process of deduction seems mysterious, think of reading a description of the ultimate pizza, a description that details its aroma, taste, texture. After reading about that pizza you would probably think to yourself, "Wow, that's a really good pizza." And that's an implied thesis.

Whether implicit or explicit, the thesis is what the writer builds the essay upon. The writer must select the most important details, build sentences and paragraphs around them, and then sequence the paragraphs so that everything not only contributes to but also helps create the thesis. In description, paragraphs can be arranged by modes, such as process and definition, and according to spatial, temporal, or dramatic relationships. Like Peter Schjeldahl, the writer can describe a scene so that the reader moves from one place to another, from the time the roller coaster starts its initial climb, through its drops, turns, dips, and into its final glide back into its shed. Schjeldahl's essay also takes the reader from one point in time to another, using chronology to guide the essay's organization. Hubbell, Suarez, and Merrill-Foster, however, organize their paragraphs according to a dramatic order, moving from the physical to the emotional. So, too, Peter Schjeldahl's essay relies on dramatic order, culminating in "a warm debriefing." Bruce Berger uses a different kind of order, moving from the concrete to the abstract.

Where I Live

Sue Hubbell

This essay appeared as the foreword to Sue Hubbell's book A Country Year: Living the Questions (*HarperCollins, 1987*), *an account of her year on her farm, raising bees and gathering honey. The questions she explores in that book are those mentioned at the end of the essay. A self-taught naturalist, Hubbell has an acute eye for detail.*

There are three big windows that go from floor to ceiling on the south side of my cabin. I like to sit in the brown leather chair in the twilight of winter evenings and watch birds at the feeder that stretches across them. The windows were a gift from my husband before he left the last time. He had come and gone before, and we were not sure that this would be the last time, although I suspected that it was. 1

I have lived here in the Ozark Mountains of southern Missouri for twelve years now, and for most of that time I have been alone. I have learned to run a business that we started together, a commercial beekeeping and honey-producing operation, a shaky, marginal sort of affair that never quite leaves me free of money worries but which allows me to live in these hills that I love. 2

My share of the Ozarks is unusual and striking. My farm lies two hundred and fifty feet above a swift, showy river to the north and a small creek to the south, its run broken by waterfalls. Creek and river join just to the east, so I live on a peninsula of land. The back fifty acres are covered with second-growth timber, and I take my firewood there. Last summer when I was cutting firewood, I came across a magnificent black walnut, tall and straight, with no jutting branches to mar its value as a timber tree. I don't expect to sell it, although even a single walnut so straight and unblemished would fetch a good price, but I cut some trees near it to give it room. The botanic name for black walnut is *Juglans nigra*—"Black Nut Tree of God," a suitable name for a tree of such dignity, and I wanted to give it space. 3

Over the past twelve years I have learned that a tree needs space to grow, that coyotes sing down by the creek in January, that I can drive a nail into oak only when it is green, that bees know more 4 about making honey than I do, that love can become sadness, and that there are more questions than answers.

Thesis and Organization

1. *Setting* is a term that includes time, place, and objects. Given that definition, what is the setting in paragraph 1?
2. What else do you learn about the setting in paragraph 2?
3. Paragraph 3 begins with a topic sentence. List the details that support the idea that the particular setting is "unusual and striking."
4. Given the setting in paragraphs 1–3 and the topic sentence you would provide for paragraph 4, what is the essay's thesis?

Technique and Style

1. Hubbell often uses an adjective that she then fleshes out with details. Cite one or two examples. Are the details sufficient? How or how not?
2. What emotion does the essay convey? Is the author sad, happy, resigned, triumphant, or what?
3. What do the thesis and tone lead you to expect in the pages that followed this foreword? Would you like to read on? Why or why not?
4. Draw a map of the farm based on the description in paragraph 3. How precise is the description?

Suggestions for Writing

Using Hubbell's essay as a close model, write your own "Where I Live." Describe where you usually sit or spend most of your time, what you see from that perspective, the immediate area around your house or apartment, the length of time you've lived there, and then list selectively what you've learned.

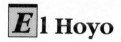l Hoyo

Mario Suarez

In "El Hoyo," Mario Suarez faces a problem common to many writ-
ers: how to describe something so that readers who have little knowl-
edge of a subject will nonetheless be able to see and understand it.
Suarez's problem is double, for most of his readers will not only be
unfamiliar with barrios but also with Latino culture. The neighbor-
hood Suarez describes existed in 1947, but since then many similar
ones have sprung up all over the United States. The essay was origi-
nally published in the Arizona Quarterly *(1947).*

From the center of downtown Tucson the ground slopes gently   1
away to Main Street, drops a few feet, and then rolls to the banks of
the Santa Cruz River. Here lies the section of the city known as El
Hoyo. Why it is called El Hoyo is not very clear. In no sense is it a
hole as its name would imply; it is simply the river's immediate
valley. Its inhabitants are chicanos who raise hell on Saturday night
and listen to Padre Estanislao on Sunday morning. While the term
chicano is the short way of saying Mexicano, it is not restricted to the
paisanos who came from old Mexico with the territory or the last
famine to work for the railroad, labor, sing, and go on relief. Chicano is the easy way of referring to everybody. Pablo Gutíerrez
married the Chinese grocer's daughter and now runs a meat department; his sons are chicanos. So are the sons of Killer Jones who
threw a fight in Harlem and fled to El Hoyo to marry Cristina Men-
dez. And so are all of them. However, it is doubtful that all these
spiritual sons of Mexico live in El Hoyo because they love each
other—many fight and bicker constantly. It is doubtful they live in El
Hoyo because of its scenic beauty—it is everything but beautiful. Its
houses are simple affairs of unplastered adobe, wood, and abandoned car parts. Its narrow streets are mostly clearings which have,
in time, acquired names. Except for some tall trees which nobody
has ever cared to identify, nurse, or destroy, the main things known
to grow in the general area are weeds, garbage piles, dark-eyed
chavalos, and dogs. And it is doubtful that the chicanos live in El
Hoyo because it is safe—many times the Santa Cruz has risen and
inundated the area.

2   In other respects living in El Hoyo has its advantages. If one is born with weakness for acquiring bills, El Hoyo is where the collectors are less likely to find you. If one has acquired the habit of listening to Octavio Perea's Mexican Hour in the wee hours of the morning with the radio on at full blast, El Hoyo is where you are less likely to be reported to the authorities. Besides, Perea is very popular and sooner or later to everyone "Smoke in the Eyes" is dedicated between the pinto beans and white flour commercials. If one, for any reason whatever, comes on an extended period of hard times, where, if not in El Hoyo, are the neighbors more willing to offer solace? When Teofila Malacara's house burned to the ground with all her belongings and two children, a benevolent gentleman carried through the gesture that made tolerable her burden. He made a list of 500 names and solicited from each a dollar. At the end of a month he turned over to the tearful but grateful señora $100 in cold cash and then accompanied her on a short vacation. When the new manager of a local store decided that no more chicanas were to work behind the counters, it was the chicanos of El Hoyo who, on taking their individually small but collectively great buying power elsewhere, drove the manager out and the girls returned to their jobs. When the Mexican Army was en route to Baja California and the chicanos found out that the enlisted men ate only at infrequent intervals, it was El Hoyo's chicanos who crusaded across town with pots of beans and trays of tortillas to meet the train. When someone gets married, celebrating is not restricted to the immediate friends of the couple. Everybody is invited. Anything calls for a celebration and a celebration calls for anything. On Memorial Day there are no less than half a dozen good fights at the Riverside Dance Hall. On Mexican Independence Day more than one flag is sworn allegiance to amid cheers for the queen.

3   And El Hoyo is something more. It is this something more which brought Felipe Suarez back from the wars after having killed a score of Vietnamese with his body resembling a patchwork quilt to marry Julia Armijo. It brought Joe Zepeda, a gunner, . . . back to compose boleros. He has a metal plate for a skull. Perhaps El Hoyo is proof that those people exist, and perhaps exist best, who have as yet failed to observe the more popular modes of human conduct. Perhaps the humble appearance of El Hoyo justifies the indifferent shrug of those made aware of its existence. Perhaps El Hoyo's simplicity motivates an occasional chicano to move away from its nar-

row streets, babbling comadres and shrieking children to deny the bloodwell from which he springs and to claim the blood of a conquistador while his hair is straight and his face beardless. Yet El Hoyo is not an outpost of a few families against the world. It fights for no causes except those which soothe its immediate angers. It laughs and cries with the same amount of passion in times of plenty and of want.

Perhaps El Hoyo, its inhabitants, and its essence can best be   4 explained by telling a bit about a dish called capirotada. Its origin is uncertain. But, according to the time and the circumstance, it is made of old, new or hard bread. It is softened with water and then cooked with peanuts, raisins, onions, cheese, and panocha. It is fired with sherry wine. Then it is served hot, cold, or just "on the weather" as they say in El Hoyo. The Sermeños like it one way, the Garcias another, and the Ortegas still another. While it might differ greatly from one home to another, nevertheless it is still capirotada. And so it is with El Hoyo's chicanos. While being divided from within and from without, like the capirotada, they remain chicanos.

Thesis and Organization

1. Examine the essay using the standard journalistic questions. Which paragraph describes *where* El Hoyo is? What paragraphs describe *who* lives there? What paragraph or paragraphs describe *how* they live? *Why* they live there?
2. All of the questions above lead to a larger one: *What* is El Hoyo? Given the people and place, and how and why they live there, what statement is the author making about El Hoyo?
3. The essay ends with an analogy, and toward the end of paragraph 4, Suarez spells out some details of the analogy. What other characteristics of capirotada correspond to those of chicanos? Where in the essay do you find evidence for your opinion?
4. How would you describe the movement in the essay? Does it move from the general to the particular? From the particular to the general? What reasons can you give for the author's choice of direction?
5. In one sentence, state Suarez's opinion of El Hoyo.

Technique and Style

1. The introductory paragraph achieves coherence and cohesion through the author's use of subtle unifying phrases. Trace Suarez's use of "it is

doubtful." How often does the phrase occur? Rewrite the sentences to avoid using the phrase. What is lost? Gained?'

2. What key words are repeated in paragraph 2? Why does he repeat them?
3. Paragraph 2 gives many examples of the advantages of living in El Hoyo. List the examples in the order in which they appear. The first two can be grouped together under the idea of El Hoyo as a sanctuary, a place where people aren't bothered. What other groupings does the list of examples suggest? What principle appears to have guided the ordering of the examples?
4. Why might the author have chosen not to use either first or second person? What is gained by using "one?"

Suggestions for Writing

If you live in an ethnic neighborhood, you can adopt the essay as a close model. If you do not, however, you can still use the essay as a general model by choosing a topic that combines people and place, such as a characteristic family ritual at Christmas or Hanukkah or Thanksgiving, or a representative time at the university student center or neighborhood restaurant.

*F*rightened by Loss

J. Merrill-Foster

By combining the objective with the subjective, the particular with the general, and the past with the present, the author sets out a compelling picture of old age. The essay was published in the New York Times *in 1988.*

Her walk is slow, hesitant, leaning slightly forward from the waist. Her hands, swollen and misshapen with arthritis, have traceries of blue veins across the back. They are never still. 1

She often interrupts to ask what we are talking about. The telephone seems to confuse her; she thinks the ringing is on the television. She calls us to report that she has lost her Christmas card list. It turns up on her desk, hidden under a pile of appeals. She is on every mailing list there is, and is constantly importuned to "Save the whales" and "Stop the Japanese slaughter of dolphins." 2

She is frightened and distressed by letters from retired military men. They write that unless she sends $35 by return mail, the Russians will land in Oregon and take over America. The arrival of the daily mail looms large in her day. Once, every few weeks, it contains a personal letter. The rest is appeals and ads. She reads every item. 3

Her checkbook is a constant puzzle of missing entries and double deposits of retirement checks. She goes out to do an errand and cannot find the place—a place she's frequented for years. She telephones to say the furnace door has exploded open; the kindly repair man arrives at 10 P.M. to check and assure her that all is well. She tells you about it, not because there is anything needing to be done. She tells you in order to make you understand that life is out of control—that there is a conspiracy of inanimate objects afoot. 4

Often, if you suggest this or that solution, she is annoyed. She wasn't asking for a solution. She was merely reporting disaster. She sits down to read and falls asleep. 5

America's life style prepares us well for our first day at school, for adolescence, for college, for matrimony, for parenthood, for middle age, for retirement. But it prepares us not at all for old age. Busy and active until her seventy-eighth year, the woman, now 85, is frightened by her own loss of power. 6

7   "Why am I so tired all the time?" she asks.

8   "I couldn't figure out how to turn on the dashboard lights."

9   "I look at the snow and wonder how I'll live through the winter."

10   "I think I must light the wood stove. I'm so cold."

11   I do not see the woman as she is today. I look at her familiar face and see her on a stage, floating up a flight of stairs in *Arsenic and Old Lace,* with that skilled power in her knees that made her seem to glide from one step to another. I hear her speak and remember her light but lovely contralto singing Katisha in *The Mikado.*

12   I watch her sleeping in her chair, her head on her chest, and remember her pacing up and down an English classroom, reading aloud from Beowulf, bringing to life the monster Grendel for a class of 16-year-olds. I remember late winter afternoons, fortified with hot cocoa, sitting on the floor at her feet, listening to "The Ballad of the White Horse," *Don Quixote* and *King Lear.*

13   I remember her as a young widow, coming home from school and pulling three children through the snow on a sled. I remember always the summer jobs when school was let out, selling life insurance or encyclopedias, or studying remedial reading at New York University. I remember her as a bride the second time, and the second time a widow. Hers was the home the family came to, a place of books, a big, old house where civility was spoken.

14   There is some rage in aging—a disbelief that one's life has rounded its last curve and this stretch of road leads to death. She has always been a woman of strong faith, and it seems that faith at last has failed her. She quotes Claudius in *Hamlet:*

15   "My words fly up, my thoughts remain below;

16   Words without thoughts never to heaven go."

17   Widowed, alone, children and grandchildren flung wide from California to New England, she fills her days with little things. Socializing fatigues her. She withdraws from the intense conversational jousting that used to delight her.

18   I watch the woman—my mother—walking carefully down the frozen, snow-filled driveway to the mail box. She is a photograph in black and white, which only loving memory tints with stippled life and color.

Thesis and Organization

1. Paragraph 1 describes the woman physically, and paragraphs 2–5 describe her psychologically, both leading up to the concluding sentence of paragraph 6. What details in paragraphs 1–5 relate to the idea of being "frightened by her own loss of power"?

2. Test out the assertions in the first two sentences of paragraph 6. To what extent do they hold true in the experience of you and your family? Are the assertions valid?

3. Paragraphs 7–10 use quotations from the present to illustrate the generalization that ends paragraph 6 and to set up the shift to the past that takes place in paragraphs 11–13, while paragraphs 14–18 return to the present. Do you find the essay's chronology effective or ineffective? How so?

4. How would you characterize the author's feelings for the old woman? What evidence can you cite to support your ideas?

5. Where in the essay do you find the author generalizing upon old age? What generalization is being made about the author's mother? About old age? Putting the two generalizations together, how would you express the thesis of the essay?

Technique and Style

1. The author alludes to a play and an operetta (11) and to an epic, a poem, a novel, and a play (12). What do these allusions imply about the author's mother? What do they contribute to her characterization—the person she was then and the person she is now?

2. In a standard dictionary, look up *pity* and *empathy*. Which does the author feel for the old woman? Which does the writer evoke in you? Cite examples to support your opinion.

3. You will note that throughout the essay the author never refers to the old woman by name. What is the effect of using a pronoun instead? What effect is achieved by holding off identifying her as "my mother?"

4. Examine paragraph 13 for details. What do they imply about the author's mother? How do those characteristics compare with those you can deduce from paragraphs 7–10? What does this contrast achieve?

5. The essay concludes with a metaphor. Rephrase the metaphor into your own words and explain how that statement supports the thesis of the essay.

Suggestions for Writing

Think of someone you know who typifies a certain age, occupation, or region. In a character sketch, describe that person so that you report the qualities that make up the individual and also generalize about the larger category that the person represents. Rely on quotation as well as description to create the overall impression you wish to make.

Cyclone: Rising to the Fall

Peter Schjeldahl

Terror, exhilaration, despair, wonder, anguish, and relief ride the rails of Coney Island's Cyclone, a roller coaster to remember. Schjeldahl's description was published in Harper's *in 1988.*

The Cyclone is art, sex, God, the greatest. It is the most fun you can have without risking bad ethics. I rode the Cyclone seven times one afternoon last summer, and I am here to tell everybody that it is fun for fun's sake, the pure abstract heart of the human capacity for getting a kick out of anything. Yes, it may be anguishing initially. (I promise to tell the truth.) Terrifying, even, the first time or two the train is hauled upward with groans and creaks and with you in it. At the top then—where there is sudden strange quiet but for the fluttering of two tattered flags, and you have a poignantly brief view of Brooklyn, and of ships far out on the Atlantic—you may feel very lonely and that you have made a serious mistake, cursing yourself in the last gleam of the reflective consciousness you are about, abruptly, to leave up there between the flags like an abandoned thought-balloon. To keep yourself company by screaming may help, and no one is noticing: try it. After a couple of rides, panic abates, and after four or five you aren't even frightened, exactly, but *stimulated,* blissed, sent. The squirt of adrenaline you will never cease to have at the top as the train lumbers, wobbling slightly, into the plunge, finally fuels just happy wonderment because you can't, and never will, *believe* what is going to happen. 1

Every roller coaster has that first, immense drop. In practical terms, it provides the oomph for the entire ride, which is of course impelled by nothing but ecologically sound gravity, momentum, and the odd slingshot of centrifugal force. The coaster is basically an ornate means of falling and a poem about physics in parts or stanzas, with jokes. The special quality of the Cyclone is how different, how *articulated,* all the components of its poem are, the whole of which lasts a minute and thirty-some seconds—exactly the right length, composed of distinct and perfect moments. By my fifth ride, my heart was leaping at the onset of each segment as at the ap- 2 proach of a dear old friend, and melting with instantaneous nostalgia for each at its finish.

3   I think every part of the Cyclone should have a name, the better to be recalled and accurately esteemed. In my mind, the big drop is Kismet—fate, destiny. I can't think of what to call the second, a mystery drop commenced in a jiffy after we have been whipped around, but good, coming out of Kismet. (Someday soon I will devote particular attention to the huge and violent but elusive second drop.) I do know that the third drop's name can only be Pasha. It is so round and generous, rich and powerful, looking like a killer going in but then actually like a crash landing in feathers that allows, for the first time in the ride, an instant for luxuriating in one's endorphin rush.

4   This brings me to another important function of the first drop, which (I firmly contend) is to trigger the release of endorphins, natural morphine, into the bloodstream by persuading the organism that it is going to die. I know all about endorphins from reading the *New York Times* science section, and from an accident a few years ago. I broke my elbow, which is something not to do. It hurts. Or let me put it this way: in relation to what I had previously understood of pain, the sensation of breaking an elbow was *a whole new idea,* a new continent suddenly—whole unknown worlds of pain out there over the horizon. I was aghast, when I broke my elbow, at the extent of my naïveté about pain—but only for a second. Then I was somewhere else, pain-free, I think it was a cocktail party, but confusing, I didn't recognize anybody. On some level I knew the party wasn't real, that I was in another, real place which had something unpleasant about it that made me not want to be there, but then I began to be afraid that if I stayed at the party I would be unable ever to be real again, so with an effort of will I returned to my body, which was sitting up with family members leaning over. The pain returned, but muffled and dull, drastically lessened. Endorphins.

5   Other things than breaking an elbow can give you an endorphin high, and one of them is suddenly falling ninety-some feet, seeing the ground charge directly at you. I think the forebrain, loaded with all sorts of chemical gimmicks we don't suspect, just there for special occasions, registers the situation, and, quick, pours a last-minute, bon voyage endorphin highball: "Hey, [*your name here*], this one's for you!" That's why it's important to ride the Cyclone many times, to comb out the distraction of terror—which gradually

yields to the accumulating evidence that you are not dead—in order to savor the elixir for its own sake and for the sake of loving God or whatever—Nature—for cunningly secreted kindnesses. But Kismet is such a zonk, and the anonymous second drop is so perplexing and a zonk, too, that it isn't until mid-Pasha, in great fleshy Pasha's lap, that consciousness catches up with physiologic ravishment. Some part of my soul, because of the Cyclone, is still and will remain forever in that state, which I think is a zone of overlap among the heavens of all the world's mystic religions, where transcendent swamis bump around with freaked Spanish women saints. Blitzed in Pasha permanently, I have this lasting glimpse into the beyond that is not beyond, and you know what I'm talking about, or you don't.

Rolling up out of Pasha, we enter the part of the Cyclone that won't quit laughing. First there's the whoop of a whipping hairpin curve, which, if someone is sitting with you, Siamese-twins you. (Having tried different cars in different company, I prefer being alone at the very front—call me a classicist.) The ensuing dips, humps, dives, and shimmies that roar, chortle, cackle, and snort continue just long enough to suggest that they may go on forever—as worrisome as the thought, when you're laughing hard, that maybe you can never stop—and then it's hello, Irene. Why do I think Irene is the name of the very sharp drop, not deep but savage, that wipes the grin off the laughing part of the Cyclone? (Special about it is a crosspiece, low over the track at the bottom, that you swear is going to fetch you square in the eyebrows.) Irene is always the name—or kind of name, slightly unusual but banal—of the ordinary-seeming girl whom a young man may pursue idly, in a bored time, and then *wham!* fall horribly in love with, blasted in love with this person he never bothered to even particularly look at and now it's too late, she's his universe, Waterloo, *personal* Kismet. This is one good reason I can think of for growing older: learning an aversion reflex for girls named something like Irene. In this smallish but vicious, sobering drop, abstract shapes of my own youthful romantic sorrows do not fail to flash before my inner eye . . . but then, with a jarring zoom up and around, I am once more grown-up, wised-up me, and the rest of the ride is rejoicing.

The Cyclone differs from other roller coasters in being (a) a work of art and (b) old, and not only old but old-looking, decrepit, rusting in its metal parts and peeling in its more numerous wooden parts, filthy throughout and jammed into a wire (Cyclone!) fence abutting

6

7

cracked sidewalks of the Third World sinkhole that Coney Island is, intoxicatingly. Nor is it to be denied or concealed that the Cyclone, unlike newer coasters, tends to run *rough*, though each ride is unique and some are inexplicably velvety. One time the vibration, with the wheels shrieking and the cars threatening to explode with strain, made me think, "This is *no fun at all!*" It was an awful moment, with a sickening sense of betrayal and icy-fingered doubt: was my love malign?

8   That was my worst ride, which left me with a painfully yanked muscle in my shoulder, but I am glad to say it wasn't my last. I got back on like a thrown cowboy and discovered that the secret of handling the rough rides is indeed like riding a horse, at trot or gallop—not tensing against it, as I had, but posting and rolling. It's all in the thighs and rear end, as I especially realized when—what the hell—I joined pimpled teenagers in the arms-raised *no hands!* trick. I should mention that a heavy, cushioned restraining bar locks down snugly into your lap and is very reassuring, although, like everything upholstered in the cars, it may be cracked or slashed and leaking tufts of stuffing from under swatches of gray gaffer's tape. One thing consistently disquieting is how, under stress, a car's wooden sides may *give* a bit. I wish they wouldn't do that, or that my imagination were less vivid. If a side did happen to fail on a curve, one would depart like toothpaste from a stomped-on tube.

9   I was proud of braving the *no hands!* posture—as trusting in the restraining bar as a devout child in his heavenly Father—particularly the first time I did it, while emerging from the slinging turn that succeeds Irene into the long, long career that bottoms out at absolute ground level a few feet from the fence where pedestrians invariably gather to watch, transfixed. I call this swift, showy glide Celebrity: the ride's almost over, and afflatus swells the chest. But going *no hands!* soon feels as cheap and callow as it looks, blocking with vulgar self-centeredness the wahoo-glimmering-away-of-personality-in-convulsive-Nirvana that is the Cyclone's essence. A righteous ride is hands on, though lightly, like grace. The payoff is intimacy in the sweet diminuendo, the jiggling and chuckling smart little bumps and dandling dips that bring us to a quick, pillowy deceleration in the shed, smelling of dirty machine oil, where we began and will begin again. It is a warm-debriefing, this last part: "Wasn't that *great?*" it says. "Want to go again?"

10   Of course I do, but first there is the final stage of absorption,

when you squeeze out (it's easy to bang a knee then, so watch it) to stand wobbly but weightless, euphoric, and then to enjoy the sensation of walking as if it were a neat thing you had just invented. Out on the sidewalk, the object of curious gazes, you see that they see that you see them, earthlings, in a diminishing perspective, through the wrong end of the telescope of your pleasure, and your heart is pitying. You nod, smiling, to convey that yes, they should ride, and no, they won't regret it.

Thesis and Organization

1. What paragraph or paragraphs introduce the essay? What expectations does the introduction set up in the reader?
2. Trace the chronology that runs through the essay. Explain whether the author organizes his material by depending primarily on temporal, spatial, or dramatic order.
3. What effects does the roller coaster ride have on the author? How does the pattern of cause and effect that interweaves the essay relate to your idea of the essay's organization as you outlined it in question 2?
4. If you have ridden on a roller coaster, how well does the author evoke that ride? If you have not had that experience, does Schjeldahl's description persuade you to try it? How so?
5. Given the effect the Cyclone has on Schjeldahl and the impression his description has on you, state the author's thesis in your own words.

Technique and Style

1. Who is the *you* Schjeldahl refers to in the second sentence of paragraph 1? Where else in the essay does he use second person? What effect does he achieve by his choice of pronoun?
2. The names the author gives the various parts of the ride are unusual: Kismet, Pasha, Irene, Celebrity. What reasons can you find for his choices? What other names might work in their place and why?
3. Schjeldahl's diction ranges from slang to stuffy—for instance, "righteous" and "afflatus" in paragraph 9—with various stops in between. What other categories of diction can you discover? What does the range of diction imply about the essay's audience?
4. In what ways is the writer's description negative? Why might he have included these negative details? Do they tend to make his description more objective or less so?
5. Schjeldahl's essay gives the reader a sense of immediacy. Other than the choice of second-person pronoun, what technique does the author use to give the reader this impression?

Suggestions for Writing

Remember an event that affected you in complex, even contradictory ways, and then analyze the elements of the event and the effects they had on you. Consider, for instance, a crucial few minutes in a football game or awaiting a surprise party; or think of walking up the aisle at a wedding, getting your first traffic ticket, going through registration, or applying for your first job.

*T*he Vibram Stomp

Bruce Berger

Almost everyone enjoys hiking, but Bruce Berger points out that we pay a price for our enjoyment. The essay, one of many that focus on humans and nature, appears in Berger's collection, The Telling Distance *(Breitenbush Books, 1990).*

The bootprint is a device for turning the human foot into an abstraction. One sees them trailing across the sands—baroque soles with their sunbursts of stars and bars, deck shoe treads like postage cancellations, sneakers like eyes through Sevillian windows. The foot, like other human extremities, is self-expressive and meets the world with a personal touch. In a large party there are seldom two prints alike. The marks of any two persons are distinct and become known, by some unbreakable back-country code, as Bigfoot and Littlefoot. By size, configuration and placement, footprints acquire personalities, humanize one's predecessors. One trails like a sleuth, strewing ciphers of one's own.

But for all their suggestiveness, bootprints are not always welcome. Deer paths, coyote prints, javelina pocks, the great peace signs of heron tracks all indicate wild sensibilities. The S-curve of sidewinders returns one to Eden, among the unfallen. But Vibram soles are born in factories. They conspire in closets, foster corns, devour moleskins, demand to be replaced. They are about as alluring as waffle irons. The tread of man, the most dangerous beast of all, paradoxically lessens the shiver of adventure.

Until recently the preferred extension of the human personality was the machine; it still is for a majority. The extension of the foot is the wheel, says Marshall McLuhan, and the woods and dunes are quite full of feet multiplied by wheels. But the romance of the machine is wearing off and the hangover has set in. Most contemporary wilderness travelers wish to banish the machine, to recover their individuality in the age of cybernation. That means getting back to the unaided foot. Unaided, that is, except for the friendly boot.

So today's rebel laces up and sets out to outwalk technology. He seeks a canyon unviolated by previous contemplation, a mesa where original response can flower. He reaches a plateau of windswept contours, embroidered by jackrabbits, stitched by lizards. The shadows of hawks disturb no sand. Suddenly a pair of alien Vibrams stomps to the horizon. Eden is gone; the sons of Euclid are back. Even here, at the last outpost, is the assembly line foot, logo of the human will.

5   Some objections, of course, are less metaphysical. Hikers trudging through shale and packed mud set off gullies and slides that continue on their own. Vegetation in narrow desert canyons can be mashed wall-to-wall. Public campsites are being chafed into mudflats. School groups and conservation organizations with the noblest intentions can defoliate through sheer numbers, and private parties are close behind. Wind, rain and occasional flooding may erase the rubber stamps, but revegetation is unlikely in areas that cannot be roped off like city parks.

6   The juniper and piñon country of the Colorado Plateau adds a further problem. Its lumpy red earth, seemingly shaped by the last rain, is actually held in place by microscopic plants called cryptogams. As wind sweeps over the ground it lifts the loose particles, leaving a complex of algae, fungi, lichens, molds and other small growths on tiny pillars, giving the soil a darkish cast. Cryptogams increase the organic carbon content of crust soils, reduce runoff, heighten fertility and keep it all from blowing away. Deer, the only native large animals, file through it on thin trails beaten hard. But campers unaware of its presence scuff it loose at random, and campsites abolish it completely. Of course any damage done by the human foot is negligible compared to meandering cattle which have overgrazed the region for a century. But the cattle know not what they do, while human beings could remove their cows and walk single file, if they so chose.

7   As we hike from our machines it would be liberating for man and plant if we could simply quit our bodies and explore like wraiths, filling canyons with the sheer enthusiasm of disembodied senses, leaving no local trace even of thought. Realistically, the most we can look forward to is air-cushion shoes. For all our abstraction we are gross mammals, possessed of mass like everything else on this planet. Our hearts are full of adventure but our feet are killing us. This is the price of self-awareness—for the farther we range in search of adventure, the faster we stamp it out.

Thesis and Organization

1. Reread the first and last paragraphs. Does the essay progress from the general to the specific or the reverse? Trace its development.
2. What is the function of paragraph 3? What does it add?
3. Paragraphs 4–7 describe some of the effects of Vibram. What effects does each paragraph emphasize?
4. Based on these effects, what conclusion does the author reach in paragraph 7? In your own words, state the thesis.
5. What is being compared in paragraph 2? How does that paragraph prepare you for the thesis?

Technique and Style

1. The third sentence of paragraph 4 uses an implied metaphor. What is the metaphor based on? Given the thesis, in what way is the metaphor appropriate or inappropriate?
2. The effect of paragraph 3 depends in part on the author's choice of verbs. Choose one example and try several alternatives. Which is better and why?
3. Paragraph 6 describes the process by which cryptogams hold earth in place. What does this somewhat technical description add to the essay?
4. Paragraph 4 uses the pronoun *he* and paragraph 7 uses *we*. What justification can you find for the change?
5. In the last paragraph the author employs a cliché that becomes a pun. To what extent is the pun effective?

Suggestions for Writing

Pick an object that has had an impact on your environment. If you live in a city, you might notice the number of cars, the lineup of garbage cans, the litter on the streets. If you live in the suburbs or the country, you may notice the noise of lawn mowers, the smell of burning leaves, the sight of a landfill, a gravel pit, or junked cars. Using Berger's essay as a model, describe the object, the environment, and the effects. If you like, reverse Berger's idea by choosing something that has had a positive effect.

Exploring the Topic

1. **What distinguishes your topic?** What characteristics, features, or actions stand out about your subject? Which are most important? Least important?
2. **What senses can you appeal to?** What can you emphasize about your subject that would appeal to sight? Smell? Touch? Taste? Motion?
3. **What concrete details can you use?** What abstract words do you associate with each of the features or events you want to emphasize? How can you make those abstractions concrete?
4. **How can you vary your narrative?** Where might you use quotations? Where might you use dialogue?
5. **What can your audience identify with?** What comparisons can you use? What similes, metaphors, allusions come to mind?
6. **What order should you use?** Is your description best sequenced by time? Place? Dramatic order?
7. **What is your tentative thesis?** What is the dominant impression you want to create? Do you want it to be implicit? Explicit?
8. **What is your relationship to your subject?** Given your tentative thesis, how objective or subjective should you be? Do you want to be part of the action or removed? What personal pronoun should you use?

Drafting the Paper

1. **Know your reader.** If you are writing about a familiar object, ask yourself what your reader might not know about it. If you are writing about an unfamiliar subject, ask yourself what your reader does know that you can use for comparison.
2. **Know your purpose.** If you are writing to inform, make sure you are presenting new information and in enough detail to bring your subject to life. If you are writing to persuade, make sure your details add up so that the reader is moved to adopt your conviction. Keep in mind that your reader may not share your values and indeed may even hold opposite ones.
3. **Pile on sensory detail.** Don't settle for vague adjectives such as "tall"; replace them with sharper details such as "6 feet 7 inches." Emphasize important details by appealing to the senses.
4. **Show, don't tell.** Avoid abstract terms (funny, beautiful) in favor of concrete details, quotations, dialogue.
5. **Use comparisons.** Make your description vivid with an occasional met-

aphor or simile. If you are writing about something quite unfamiliar, use literal comparison to make your description clear.

6. **Arrange your details to create a single dominant impression.** If you are writing descriptive paragraphs, check the order of your sentences to make sure they follow each other logically and support the impression you wish to create. If you are writing a descriptive essay, check for the same points. Is your topic sentence or thesis implicit or explicit? For a descriptive essay, reexamine your first paragraph. Does it establish the scene? The tone?

Narration

Whether prompted by the child's "Tell me a story" or the adult's "What happened?" narration supplies much of our entertainment and information. But anyone who has asked "What happened?" only to be overwhelmed with every detail knows that telling everything can blunt the point and bore the listener. To use narration effectively takes more than telling a story; it calls for compressing and reshaping experience so that the listener or reader relives it with you and is left with a particular point. Shaping narrative draws upon some of the same skills used in description: keen observation, careful selection of details, and coherent sequencing. But with a narrative you must go a step further: you must present a conflict and its resolution. A story with no point is a shaggy-dog story; one with no conflict is no kind of story at all.

Often the narrative and the subject are the same: if you are writing about what happened to you when lightning struck your house, what happened is the subject of your narrative. Frequently, however, a writer chooses narrative to introduce or to conclude an essay or perhaps to do both, which sets up a narrative framework. Or perhaps you would opt for narrative to emphasize a particular point. An essay that explains the dangers of toxic waste may be made more effective if it starts with a brief narrative of what happens at a place where pollution threatens the area and its residents, such as Los Angeles and its smog. So, too, a paper on the same subject that argues for stricter federal and state controls may end by predicting what might happen without tougher regulation. The essays in this chapter, however, rely on narration for their primary structure. All present conflicts, build to a point, and spring from personal experience, from the something that happened.

AUDIENCE AND PURPOSE   Roger Starr's "Tale of the Rodent" first appeared in the *New York Times,* and perhaps because of that context Starr assumes the reader will know the narrative is set in New York. He does give the story a particular setting, Seventh Avenue and Forty-fourth Street, but only readers familiar with New York would be able to make sense out of those clues. Even though Starr assumes his readers know the setting, he nonetheless describes the crowds on the sidewalk and the "torrent of cars" to make an informative point.

"Living an Adventurous Life" and "I Have a Gun" are written for an audience composed of specific and general readers. Some, like Nancy Mairs, know the difficulty of trying to lead a life of adventure within circumstances that forge a new definition of *adventurous,* but other readers need to know more about the difficulties she faces. So too in "I Have a Gun," some readers feel the same mixture of shame and fear as the author; others may not know the shame but know too well the atmosphere of violent crime. The narratives of Calandra and Martinez, however, focus more squarely on the general reader.

WHO, WHAT, WHERE, WHEN, HOW, WHY   Most narratives set out these elements (*who, what,* etc.) early in the story. In "Angels on a Pin," Calandra establishes them within the first two paragraphs; Mairs and Starr do the same in their essays. From that point on, however, the essays focus on what happened: Starr's rodent seeks shelter, Calandra's student seeks answers, Mairs seeks adventure; the rodent fails, the student and Mairs succeed.

CONFLICT   Narratives begin at a certain time, establish the nature of the conflict, and move toward a point that resolves the conflict. But conflict can be many-layered. In "Angels on a Pin," the conflict is not only between the instructor and the student but also between the student and the educational system. "Tale of the Rodent" presents conflicts between the animal and people and the animal and the city; on a broader scale, the conflict is between the vulnerable and the unfeeling. Some essays, such as "I Have a Gun," suggest internal conflict as well.

POINT OF VIEW   By deciding who tells the story and from what perspective, the author selects a point of view that controls how the story is told and how the reader responds to it. "Bad Luck Bob," for instance, is told in the third person by a narrator who isn't part of the action. As a result, the reader, like the narrator, remains an observer of the action so that the narrative's amusing and ironic point receives maximum emphasis. Just as third-person pronouns serve to distance the reader from the story, the word *I* usually enlists the reader's identification. Note, though, that a story can be written in the first person yet have a narrator somewhat removed from the action. "Tale of the Rodent" and "Angels on a Pin" are both written as first-person narratives, but the narrator, though part of the action, is more observer than actor. And in "Living an Adventurous Life" and "I Have a Gun," the line between action and narrator disappears. The narrator and action are one.

Within a narrative's chronology, the sequence of events can be shaped to emphasize different elements. "Tale of the Rodent" emphasizes place: the sidewalk, an entrance to a building, the street. So, too, Nyman stresses setting and atmosphere. Sometimes chronology is disrupted, as in "I Have a Gun," where the author uses flashbacks. In all the essays, the events, both in their chronology and in the principle behind their presentation, lead the reader to the author's point. In "Living an Adventurous Life," the author's point is easy to identify, but in the other essays, it is more subtle. Starr, in "Tale of the Rodent," is content to hint at his thesis, leaving the reader to deduce what it was that was "supremely serious." Calandra, Nyman, and Martinez are more overt. Like Starr, they reserve their points for the last paragraphs.

*T*ale of the Rodent

Roger Starr

A good narrative may be found in a seemingly insignificant event, as Roger Starr illustrates in "Tale of the Rodent." While both the action and plot are simple, the essay's meaning is complex. The scene is New York City.

The startled movement of a young woman in one corner of the bus shelter indicated that something was wrong. She moved again, a gesture of discomfort, even fear. Then I saw what troubled her: an infant rodent—perhaps mouse, perhaps rat—a small ball of brown cotton, with a toothpick for a tail. It had somehow crossed Seventh Avenue, climbed the curb and was moving through the shelter and across the sidewalk. 1

I say moving rather than running because the creature was too compact to reveal legs. Its speed was so erratic, and its direction so changeable, that it could have been a battery-driven toy riding on a hidden eccentric wheel. Another woman gasped at the sight of the little thing, children pointed, men went out of their way to avoid it. 2

To me it seemed more incongruous than scary, not merely outnumbered by people but intimidated by the hardness of the world into which it had suddenly emerged. From where? In what soft place on the other side of this busiest highway had its mother gnawed a nest in a fortress of brick and concrete, glass and steel? 3

Between the legs of pedestrians, the animal darted to the door of a candy store. Its feeding instincts were sound, although it could not poke through the slit between the bottom of the glass door and the sill. The instinct that had taken it to that store made its adult role obvious. It abandoned the candy store for the adjacent entrance to a large office building. 4

The superintendent, a bundle of keys hanging from his belt, was standing at the door. Rodent and superintendent vanished into the lobby, only to emerge moments later, animal first. 5

The superintendent kicked at it, driving the animal back to the sidewalk. Then he looked at me almost regretfully. Whatever the rodent might sometime become, the keeper of the keys knew it was not yet a fair match for the guardian of an office building. 6

7   The superintendent's kick must have hurt the animal; its movements became even more erratic than before. But to my astonish-
ment, it crossed the curb and darted into the street, the traffic light
in its favor. Unthinkingly wishing it safe passage, I saw it disappear
beneath each passing car, then emerge again and move erratically
onward.

8   The game—if game it was—was not to last. The light changed,
releasing a torrent of cars across Forty-fourth Street, and when they
had gone, the animal was left motionless on the pavement. No
blood, no gore, just a tiny dead thing, hardly bigger than a large
beetle, in the middle of the avenue, invisible to any passing motorist. Moments later my bus came and took me home to my apartment
house.

9   I felt I had witnessed something small, but supremely serious.

Thesis and Organization

1. The story is presented chronologically, starting at the author's first sight-
   ing of the rodent and concluding with its death and the author's comment on the narrative. Examine the paragraphs in between to determine
   why the author breaks his paragraphs where he does.
2. Conflict is a key element in narrative. What is the nature of the conflict
   in this essay? If the subject is the rodent, who or what is the rodent in
   conflict with? What role does the narrator play in that conflict?
3. At what point in the essay does Starr bring in his attitude toward the
   rodent? To what extent does the narrator experience inner conflict? How
   would you describe it?
4. Starr ends the essay with a statement that can be phrased as a question.
   What does the narrative suggest in answer to the question, "What is it
   about the tale of the rodent that is 'supremely serious'?" The answer is
   the essay's implied thesis.

Technique and Style

1. What sentences rely heavily on description to paint a picture of the
   rodent? What is the effect of that description? What emotions do you feel?
   Why? What specific words or phrases can you cite to support your
   opinion?
2. The reader never does find out whether the rodent was a mouse or a rat.
   Why might Starr have chosen to be vague on this point? How does his
   choice relate to the emotions he wishes to evoke from the reader?

3. Paragraphs 7 and 8 illustrate Starr's careful choice of details to include in the narrative. Choose three of the following details and explain what each contributes to the story's plot, conflict, and thesis: the superintendent's kick, the green traffic light, the "wishing [the rodent] safe passage," the rodent's crossing, the change of light, the description of the body, its invisibility "to any passing motorist," the bus.

4. Several times the author characterizes the rodent's movement as "erratic." Where in the essay does he use the word? How does its choice support the attitude the author is trying to elicit toward the animal? The word Starr chooses to convey his attitude toward the rodent is "incongruous." How does that word choice relate to the essay's thesis?

5. Many people frown upon one-sentence paragraphs. Is Starr's last paragraph effective or not? Why?

Suggestions for Writing

If you cannot think of an incident to relate, set yourself up in a likely place as an observer. Pick a busy spot that may lead to action. For instance, post yourself near a broken vending machine or a busy fast-food line. Go to a large supermarket at a popular time, select an interesting customer, and unobtrusively observe the person from the time of entering to the time of leaving the store; watch a sports event from an unlikely perspective, that of an assistant trainer or a player who never gets into the game.

Bad Luck Bob and His Dog

Al Martinez

Bad luck comes and goes, but with some people it just sticks, or so Al Martinez tells us in his essay from his 1989 collection Ashes in the Rain. *As the length of the paragraphs suggests, Martinez is a newspaper columnist. His work is published in the* Los Angeles Times *and deals with everyday events in some not so everyday lives, including his own.*

1   Bob Greene is the kind of guy who, if there were one hole in the ground within a 10,000-mile radius, would fall into it and break his leg. Then, when he got out of the hole and sued the hole owner, he would lose the case and be successfully countersued for falling into an unauthorized hole.

2   Later he would suffer a deadly deep-hole virus that would cause his hair, his teeth and his fingernails to fall out. He would lose his home and his life savings to medical bills and legal costs, his wife would run off with the hole owner and his carnivorous plant would try to eat him.

3   Believe me when I tell you that misfortune sticks to the man like drool to a baby.

4   For those who may not recall Robert Alan Greene, he was arrested last March in Laurel Canyon Park for walking his dog.

5   Forget that the park was probably the worst place on earth to be at the time. Dog owners were battling with children owners over the question of who ought to be leashed, the dogs or the kids, and Animal Regulation Cops were swarming over the hills like Jewish commandos at an Arab outpost.

6   Dogcatchers, as a police friend pointed out, are usually people who cannot qualify to be *real* policemen and take out their career frustrations on whoever happens to be in the vicinity during periods of high tension.

7   Bob Greene, of course, was the one strolling by.

8   The way Bob tells it, his dog Princess was on a leash. The way the animal cops tell it, Princess was walking next to him *unleashed* and was snarling and looking around for babies to kill.

9   An officer shouted for Greene to stop, but Bob said he had

witnessed the "Gestapo tactics" of the animal cops before and was not about to submit to their torture and humiliation and gruesome death. So he told them that and kept going.

Bad news. Bob fell into the hole again.   10

"I probably shouldn't have done that," he reflected during a more   11
reasonable moment the other day. "I have a big mouth."

The animal cops thought so, too. Greene says they waited in the   12
bushes, jumped him, beat him and booked both him and the dog.
The dog was later o.r.'d, but Greene was charged with resisting
arrest and failing to keep his pet on a leash.

He requested a jury trial, acted as his own attorney and, of course,   13
lost.

"I was a fool," Bob lamented.   14

Somewhere along the way, incidentally, he had mortgaged his   15
house in Laurel Canyon to buy a sign-making business. The business naturally failed and he lost the house.

But wait. We're not finished.   16

Bob was arrested that first time on March 31. He remembers it   17
because it was Palm Sunday, but that didn't do him any good at all.
And it didn't improve his luck or his judgment. Four months later, he
went back to the park and this time, he admits, was walking Princess
without a leash.

"Bob," I asked him as gently as I could, "why in the dog-walking   18
hell did you go *back* to Laurel Canyon after that first incident and
not even put the dog on a leash this time?"

He thought about that for a moment, then shook his head sadly.   19

"I don't know," he said. "I guess it was just bad timing on my   20
part."

Greene is 55 and, as one might expect, divorced. We met in the   21
West Hollywood sign-making shop he once owned and now works
for. He sleeps in a tiny room adjacent to the office. Princess and a
stray called Barney sleep in the room with him when they are not
out hunting babies.

"I'd do some things all over again now if I could," he said. I hope   22
to God he would.

Sparing you the strange details of that second encounter at Laurel   23
Canyon Park, Bob was subsequently charged with abandoning a
pet, interfering with a dog officer and threatening a dog officer.

He is to appear in Municipal Court on those charges unless he is   24
already in jail after sentencing on the first set of convictions.

25   "When I was found guilty," Greene remembered, "the judge gave me a choice of being sentenced right away or of waiting until October. I asked him what he would suggest and he said, 'Well, if I sentence you now, you'll go straight to jail.' So I said I'd wait until October."

26   Greene and others involved in the Laurel Canyon Park mess insist that he is being punished not for crimes he committed but for twice testifying before the Animal Regulation Commission on the excesses of the dog cops.

27   Maybe so, but if bad judgment were a felony, Bob Greene might be sitting on Death Row today.

28   As a final example of his synaptic lapses, I asked if he were going to appeal the first conviction.

29   "I sure am," he said. "A friend of mine is going to show me how to fill out the papers. I'm doing it myself."

30   *Oh my goodness, oh my soul, there goes Robert down the hole.*

31   Again.

Thesis and Organization

1. Because the essay was written for a newspaper, the paragraphing is designed to fit a column rather than a book page. As a result the paragraphing is rather arbitrary. What paragraphs would you put together as an introduction?
2. Trace the chronology of the story. What is gained or lost by placing the action within a framework?
3. Outline the conflict involved in the first incident. What is the effect of the incident on Bob?
4. Outline the conflict involved in the second incident. What is its effect on Bob? On the narrator?
5. What did Bob learn from his experiences? What is Martinez's point? Given your answers, what do you deduce to be the thesis?

Technique and Style

1. In an unabridged dictionary, look up *irony*. To what extent can you characterize the tone of the essay as ironic?
2. Exaggeration is often used in humorous writing. Find an example in Martinez's essay and try an ordinary word in its place. What is lost or gained?
3. Martinez uses dialogue in his narrative. What effect does it have?

4. Several of the words Martinez chooses fall into the category of slang. What is the effect of this diction choice?

5. Although some of the short paragraphs can be explained by the essay needing to fit newspaper columns and others by Martinez's use of dialogue, some paragraphing is short for rhetorical effect. What paragraphs fall into that category? What kind of rhetorical effect do they have?

Suggestions for Writing

Often people are known for a particular characteristic. Bob is bad news, but others might be lucky, accident prone, gloomy, funny, boring, or any number of things. Think about the people you know to see who might earn a label. Once you have selected someone, think of two or more examples that typify the person.

*L*iving an Adventurous Life

Nancy Mairs

Adventure and adventurer *evoke images of heroic feats, exotic places, and daring people, but Nancy Mairs makes us reconsider our ideas and give new meaning to what it takes to be heroic and daring. The essay first appeared in 1985 in* Kaleidoscope, *a journal published by United Cerebral Palsy and Services for the Handicapped. The piece was reprinted in the* Utne Reader *in 1990.*

1   Nearly ten years ago, I was told that I had a brain tumor, and this experience changed my attitude about adventure forever. I thought that I was going to die and that all my adventures were over. I did not have a brain tumor, it turned out, but rather multiple sclerosis, which meant that, although they were not over, the nature of my adventures would have to change.

2   Each morning that I wake up, that I get out of bed, is a fresh event, something that I might not have had. Each gesture that I make carries the weight of uncertainty, demands significant attention: buttoning my shirt, changing a light bulb, walking down stairs. I might not be able to do it this time. Inevitably the minutiae of my life have had to assume dramatic proportions. If I could not delight in them, they would likely drown me in rage and in self-pity.

3   I admire the grand adventures of others. I read about them with zest. With Peter Matthiessen I have trekked across the Himalayas to the Crystal Mountain. One blistering July I moved with John McPhee to Eagle, Alaska, above the Arctic Circle. I have trudged with Annie Dillard up, down, into, and across Tinker Creek in all seasons. David Bain has accompanied me along 110 miles of Philippine coast, and Ed Abbey has paddled me down the Colorado River. I've ridden on the back of Robert Pirsig's motorcycle, climbed 95 feet to George Dyson's tree house, and grown coffee in Kenya with Isak Dinesen. I relish the adventures of these rugged and courageous figures, who can strike out on difficult trips—2 miles, 250 miles, 3000 miles—ready to endure cold, fatigue, human and natural hostility—indeed not just to endure but to celebrate.

4   But as for me, I can no longer walk very far from the armchair in which I read. I'll never make it to Tibet. Maybe not even to Albu-

querque. Some days I don't even make it to the backyard. And yet I'm unwilling to forgo the adventurous life: the difficulty of it, even the pain, the suspense and fear, and the sudden brief lift of spirit that graces a hard journey. If I am to have it too, then I must change the terms by which it is lived. And so I do.

I refine *adventure,* make it smaller and smaller. And now,   5
whether I am feeding fish flakes to my bettas or crawling across the dining room helping my cat Burton look for his blind snake, lying wide-eyed in the dark battling yet another bout of depression, cooking a chicken, gathering flowers from the garden at the farm, meeting a friend for lunch, I am always having the adventures that are mine to have.

Thesis and Organization

1. How does paragraph 1 answer the old questions of *who, where, what, when, how,* and *why?*
2. Reread paragraph 2. Which sentence functions as the paragraph's topic sentence? What reasons can you find for its placement?
3. Paragraphs 3 and 4 use comparison and contrast. Trace what is being compared. What is the point of the comparison?
4. How has Mairs "refined" adventure? Why is *refine* an appropriate word?
5. Consider the last sentence of the essay together with its title. What is the thesis?

Technique and Style

1. Try to separate your later impressions of the essay from your first response to its title. Given that title, what expectations did you have of the essay? To what extent were they fulfilled? How or how not?
2. What is the central conflict of the essay? What sort of person is Mairs? Given that impression and the conflict, what is the tone of the essay?
3. *Denotation* refers to the literal meaning of a word, what you would find in a dictionary. *Connotation* takes in the emotional aspect of a word, the associations it has built up over the years. What associations do you ordinarily have with the word *adventure?* To what extent does Mairs play on the connotation of the word in her essay?
4. Paragraph 3 uses allusion, referring to adventurers and the places they have explored. Assuming you may not be familiar with all the names Mairs mentions, how effective or ineffective is her use of allusion?
5. Good writing depends in part on the writer's use of details. To what extent does Mairs use detail? What effect does it have?

Suggestions for Writing

Think of a physical challenge you have had. Perhaps it involved a sport, an illness, an accident, a dare, a catastrophe. Think about the challenge in terms of a conflict. The external conflict is the most obvious, but internal conflict was probably involved as well. Think also about what details are the most significant ones.

I Have a Gun

Tania Nyman

Sometimes being able to defend yourself can be as frightening as being defenseless, a paradox sharply felt by Tania Nyman, who wrote this essay her sophomore year at the University of New Orleans. At the time, 1989, New Orleans was fast becoming the murder capital of the United States, a fact that the editors of the local newspaper, the Times-Picayune, *were well aware of. Urban violence makes many people feel the way Tania Nyman does, which is one reason the* Times-Picayune *published her essay as an opinion piece.*

I have a gun, a .38 caliber that holds five bullets. It is black with a brown handle and it stays by my bed. 1

I don't want a gun. I don't even like guns. But it seems I need one. 2

I've always believed in gun control, and the funny thing is I still do. But my gun is loaded next to my bed. 3

It wasn't ignorance of crime statistics that previously kept me from owning a gun. Nor was it the belief that I was immune to violence. 4

I thought that because I didn't believe in violence, that because I wasn't violent, I wouldn't be touched by violence. I believed that my belief in the best of human nature could make it real. 5

I want to believe in a world where people do not need to protect themselves from one another. But I have a gun, and it stays by my bed. 6

I should carry the gun from my house to my car, but I don't. What the gun is capable of, what the gun is for, still frightens me more than what it is supposed to prevent. 7

If I carry my gun and I am attacked, I must use it. I cannot shoot to injure. I must shoot to kill. 8

I have confronted an attacker not in reality but in my imagination. The man is walking down the street. To prove I am not paranoid, I lock my car and walk to my door with my house key ready. 9

Before I reach the steps, I think I hear a voice. "Money." Before I open the door I hear a voice. "Money." I turn to see the man with the gun. 10

11   He is frightened. I am frightened. I am frightened that I will scare him and he will shoot. I am frightened that I will give him my money and he will shoot.

12   I am frightened, but I am angry. I am angry because there is a gun pointed at me by someone I've never met and never hurt.

13   There is something that bothers me about this robbery I have created in my head. It is something that makes me uncomfortable with myself. It is something I don't want to admit, something I almost intentionally omitted because I am ashamed.

14   I guess I understand why I imagine being robbed by a man. They're physically more intimidating and I've never heard of anyone being robbed by a woman, though I'm sure it happens. But I'm being robbed by a man.

15   But why is he a black man? Why is he a black man with a worn T-shirt and glassy eyes? Why do I not imagine being robbed by a white man?

16   I am standing in a gas station on Claiborne and Jackson waiting to pay the cashier when a black man walks up behind me. I do not turn around. I stare in front of me waiting to pay. I try not to admit that I am nervous because a black man has walked up behind me in a gas station in a bad neighborhood and he does not have a car.

17   There is another scenario I imagine. I am walking to my door with my gun in my hand and I hear the voice. The man mustn't have seen my gun. I get angry because I am threatened, because someone is endangering my life for the money in my pocket.

18   I turn and without really thinking, angry and frightened, I shoot. I kill a man for $50. Or it could be $100. It does not matter that he was trying to rob me. A man has died for money. Not my money or his money, just money. Who put the price on his life, he or I?

19   I remember driving one night with my friend in her parents' car. We stop at a red light at Carollton and Tulane and a black man is crossing the street in front of us. My friend quickly but nonchalantly locks the doors with the power lock.

20   I am disgusted that she sees the man as a reminder to lock her doors. I wonder if he noticed the two girls nonchalantly lock their doors. I wonder how it feels to have people lock their doors at the sight of you.

21   I imagine again a confrontation in front of my house. I have my gun when the man asks for money. I am angry and scared, but I do not use the gun. I am afraid of what may happen to me if I don't use

it, but I am more afraid of killing another human being, more afraid of trying to live with the guilt of murdering another person. I bet my life that he will take my money and leave, and I hope I win.

I am in a gas station on St. Charles and South Carollton near my house and there is a black man waiting to pay the cashier. I walk up behind him to wait in line and he jumps and turns around. 22

When he sees me, he relaxes and says I scared him because of the way things have gotten in this neighborhood. 23

"Sorry," I say and smile. I realize I am not the only one who is frightened. 24

Thesis and Organization

1. Like the Martinez essay, the paragraphs here conform to newspaper columns. If you were reparagraphing for a regular page, what paragraphs would you use to make up an introduction? What reasons do you have for your decision?
2. List the three imaginary incidents. What do they have in common? How are they different?
3. List the real incidents. What do they have in common? How are they different?
4. What is the point of the last narrative?
5. What is the author's attitude toward violence? Toward having a gun? Toward race? Combine your answers into a thesis statement.

Technique and Style

1. How would you describe the *I* in this essay? Is this the kind of person you would like to know? Why or why not?
2. The author uses repetition intentionally. Find an example and describe its effect.
3. What effects are achieved by mixing real and imagined situations?
4. How would you describe the various conflicts in the narrative? Which is the most important and why?
5. The author depends heavily on the first-person singular, *I*. Explain whether or not she overuses the pronoun.

Suggestions for Writing

Think of a time when your action or actions contradicted your values. Perhaps you were forced to lie to protect a friend, perhaps you kept silent at a time when you should have spoken up, or perhaps pressure from others pushed you into doing something you knew you shouldn't do. What were your values? What situation or action conflicted with those values? Perhaps you will want to develop how the conflict made you feel, how it affected others, and how you either resolved the conflict or learned to live with it.

Angels on a Pin

Alexander Calandra

"Angels on a Pin" was first published in the Saturday Review *in 1968 in the wake of the United States' push to surpass Russia's strides in scientific technology strides that led to Sputnik, the first artificial earth satellite. Sputnik was launched in 1957. Now, some 35 years later, we no longer have "Sputnik-panicked classrooms," but we are still trying to come to terms with our educational system.*

Some time ago, I received a call from a colleague who asked if I would be the referee on the grading of an examination question. He was about to give a student a zero for his answer to a physics question, while the student claimed he should receive a perfect score and would if the system were not set up against the student. The instructor and the student agreed to submit this to an impartial arbiter, and I was selected.

I went to my colleague's office and read the examination question: "Show how it is possible to determine the height of a tall building with the aid of a barometer."

The student had answered: "Take the barometer to the top of the building, attach a long rope to it, lower the barometer to the street, and then bring it up, measuring the length of the rope. The length of the rope is the height of the building."

I pointed out that the student really had a strong case for full credit, since he had answered the question completely and correctly. On the other hand, if full credit were given, it could well contribute to a high grade for the student in his physics course. A high grade is supposed to certify competence in physics, but the answer did not confirm this. I suggested that the student have another try at answering the question. I was not surprised that my colleague agreed, but I was surprised that the student did.

I gave the student six minutes to answer the question, with the warning that his answer should show some knowledge of physics. At the end of five minutes, he had not written anything. I asked if he wished to give up, but he said no. He had many answers to this problem; he was just thinking of the best one. I excused myself for interrupting him, and asked him to please go on. In the next minute, he dashed off his answer which read:

6   "Take the barometer to the top of the building and lean over the edge of the roof. Drop the barometer, timing its fall with a stopwatch. Then, using the formula $S = 1/2at^2$, calculate the height of the building."

7   At this point, I asked my colleague if *he* would give up. He conceded, and I gave the student almost full credit.

8   In leaving my colleague's office, I recalled that the student had said he had other answers to the problem, so I asked him what they were. "Oh, yes," said the student. "There are many ways of getting the height of a tall building with the aid of a barometer. For example, you could take the barometer out on a sunny day and measure the height of the barometer, the length of its shadow, and the length of the shadow of the building, and by the use of a simple proportion, determine the height of the building."

9   "Fine," I said. "And the others?"

10   "Yes," said the student. "There is a very basic measurement method that you will like. In this method, you take the barometer and begin to walk up the stairs. As you climb the stairs, you mark off the length of the barometer along the wall. You then count the number of marks, and this will give you the height of the building in barometer units. A very direct method.

11   "Of course, if you want a more sophisticated method, you can tie the barometer to the end of a string, swing it as a pendulum, and determine the value of g at the street level and at the top of the building. From the difference between the two values of g, the height of the building can, in principle, be calculated."

12   Finally he concluded, there are many other ways of solving the problem. "Probably the best," he said, "is to take the barometer to the basement and knock on the superintendent's door. When the superintendent answers, you speak to him as follows: 'Mr. Superintendent, here I have a fine barometer. If you will tell me the height of this building, I will give you this barometer.' "

13   At this point, I asked the student if he really did not know the conventional answer to this question. He admitted that he did, but said that he was fed up with high school and college instructors trying to teach him how to think, to use the "scientific method," and to explore the deep inner logic of the subject in a pedantic way, as

is often done in the new mathematics, rather than teaching him the structure of the subject. With this in mind, he decided to revive scholasticism as an academic lark to challenge the Sputnik-panicked classrooms of America.

Thesis and Organization

1. In a narrow sense, the essay focuses on the question, "What is the correct answer to the examination question?" But paragraphs 8–13 take up a broader point, and there the essay concentrates on the question, "What is the purpose of education?" How do the three participants answer this question?
2. At first, the conflict arises between the instructor and the student. What larger conflict is involved in their dispute? What paragraph serves as a transition between the smaller and larger conflicts?
3. Does the author intend the essay primarily to inform, persuade, or entertain? What evidence can you cite to support your view?
4. The subject of the essay is education. What statement is the author making about education? Where in the essay does he put forth his assertion? Is the essay's thesis expressed in one of Calandra's sentences? Which one? Or do you find that the thesis is composed of several ideas? Where are they expressed?
5. What principle guides the order in which the paragraphs are presented? What words or phrases does the author use to bring out that principle?

Technique and Style

1. To show how "to determine the height of a tall building with the aid of a barometer," the student depends on process analysis. How many processes does he provide in answer to the examination question? Why might the student have saved his "best" answer for last?
2. In every example the student gives, the barometer plays a role that belies its most important function. What roles does it play? How do these roles subvert the instructor's questions?
3. What is the relationship of the narrator to the story? What is the narrator's point of view? Given the information in paragraph 4, what impression of the narrator is conveyed to the reader? Does the narrator take sides? What evidence can you find to support your opinion?
4. Use your library to find out about *scholasticism* (13) and the allusion to "angels on a pin." How does the author's choice of title relate to his thesis?

Suggestions for Writing

Recall an incident in which you were the victim of education. Perhaps a teacher falsely accused you of cheating or plagiarizing or of receiving help on a paper. Perhaps you did something to embarrass the teacher or vice versa. Perhaps you were not allowed to make up a test when you had a doctor's excuse for missing it. Perhaps a teacher lost your paper and gave you a zero for it. On the other hand, perhaps one of these instances or something similar happened to a friend. Make up what you cannot remember and embroider the details to suit your purpose.

▩ POINTERS FOR USING NARRATION

Exploring the Topic

1. **What point do you want to make?** What is the subject of your narrative? What assertion do you want your narrative to make about the subject? Is your primary purpose to inform, to persuade, or to entertain?
2. **What happened?** What are the events involved in the narrative? When does the action start? Stop? Which events are crucial?
3. **Why and how did it happen?** What caused the events? How did it cause them?
4. **Who or what was involved?** What does the reader need to know about the characters? What do the characters look like? Talk like? How do they think? How do others respond to them?
5. **What is the setting for your story?** What does the reader need to know about the setting? What features are particularly noteworthy? How can they best be described?
6. **When did the story occur?** What tense will be most effective in relating the narrative?
7. **What was the sequence of events?** What happened when? Within that chronology, what is most important: time, place, attitude, what?
8. **What conflicts were involved?** What levels of conflict exist? Is there any internal conflict?
9. **What is the relationship between the narrator and the action?** Is the narrator a participant or an observer? What is the attitude of the narrator toward the story? What feelings should the narrator evoke from the reader? What should be the attitude of the reader toward the narrative? What can be gained by using first person? Second person? Third person?

Drafting the Paper

1. **Know your reader.** Try to second-guess your reader's initial attitude toward your narrative so if that attitude is not what you want it to be, you can choose your details to elicit the desired reaction. A reader can be easily bored, so keep your details to the point and your action moving. Play on similar experiences your reader may have had or on information you can assume is widely known.
2. **Know your purpose.** If you are writing to inform, make sure you provide enough information to carry your point. If you are writing to persuade, work on your persona so that the reader will be favorably inclined to adopt your viewpoint. If you are writing to entertain, keep

your tone in mind. A humorous piece, for instance, can and probably will vary from chuckle to guffaw to belly laugh. Make sure you're getting the right kind of laugh in the right place.

3. **Establish the setting and time of the action.** Use descriptive details to make the setting vivid and be concrete. Keep in mind the reaction you want to get from your reader and choose your details accordingly. If, for instance, you are writing a narrative that depicts your first experience with fear, describe the setting in such a way that you prepare the reader for that emotion. If the time the story took place is important, bring it out early.

4. **Set out the characters.** When you introduce a character, immediately identify the person with a short phrase such as "Anne, my sister." If a character doesn't enter the narrative until midpoint or so, make sure the reader is prepared for the entrance so that the character doesn't appear to be plopped in. If characterization is important to the narrative, use a variety of techniques to portray the character but make sure whatever you use is consistent with the impression you want to create. You can depict a person directly—through appearance, dialogue, and actions—as well as indirectly—through what others say and think and how they act toward the person.

5. **Clarify the action.** Narration is set within strict time limits. Make sure the time frame of your story is set out clearly. Within that time limit, much more action occurred than you will want to use in your narrative. Pick only the high points so that every action directly supports the point you want to make. Feel free to tinker with the action, sacrificing a bit of reality for the sake of your point.

6. **Sharpen the plot.** Conflict is essential to narration, so be sure your lines of conflict are clearly drawn. Keeping conflict in mind, review the action you have decided to include so that the plot and action support each other.

7. **Determine the principle behind the sequence of events.** Given the action and plot you have worked out, set up an order. Now determine what principle should guide the reader through the events. Perhaps time is the element you want to stress, perhaps place, perhaps gradual change. No matter what you choose, make sure that the sequence has dramatic tension so that it builds to the point you want to make.

8. **Choose an appropriate point of view.** Your choice of grammatical point of view will depend on what attitude you wish to take toward your narrative. If you can make your point more effectively by distancing yourself from the story, you will want to use the indefinite pronouns associated with an objective point of view. If you want to get a little closer, use a limited omniscient point of view. On the other hand, if you can make your point most effectively by being in the story, use first

person. Then decide whether you want to be *I* the narrator or *I* the narrator and character. You should shape your persona to elicit the desired reaction from your audience.

9. **Make a point.** The action of the narration should lead to a conclusion, an implicit or explicit point that serves as the thesis of the piece. If explicit, the thesis can appear in a single sentence or it can be inferred from several sentences. Ask yourself if everything in the narrative leads up to this conclusion and if the conclusion resolves the conflict.

3

Example

*A*ny time you encounter *for instance, such as,* or *for example,* you know what will follow: an example that explains and supports the generalization. Used with general statements, examples fill in the gaps. If you write "Many people believe most crime is violent and that crime is increasing" and then only support the statement by citing statistics to show that the rate of crime peaked in the seventies but then ceased to rise in the eighties and actually fell in the nineties, you would have supported your second assertion, but the first would still be up in the air. Readers also need to know what evidence supports your claim that crime, to many people, means violent crime. An example, then, is an illustration that clarifies or develops a point, and for the essay it is the most basic building block of all. Example pins down generalizations, supporting them with specifics.

To use examples well, you first need to know when to use them, then what ones to select, and finally, how to incorporate them. If you read actively, responding to the words on the page as you would to a person talking to you, odds are you will spot where examples are needed. On reading the sentence above about crime, you might think to yourself, "Hey, wait a minute! How about that violent crime statement?" Often it helps to read your own work belligerently, ready to shoot down any generalization with a "Says who?" The response to "Says who" will vary according to your

Example   **61**

audience. A sociology paper will call for statistics; a personal narrative will draw on your own experience. Other good sources are the experience of others and that of authorities. The skill here is to match the example not only to the generalization it supports but to the readers to whom it is addressed.

After you have found good examples, you need to sequence them logically, while at the same time you avoid overusing terms such as "for example." Where you use multiple examples, you can use transitions that signal addition (*and, again, besides, moreover, next, finally,* etc.); where you use examples that compare, opt for transitions that indicate a turn (*but, yet, however, instead, in contrast,* etc.). And you can usually find a key word in the last part of a sentence that you can repeat or refer to to introduce the new example. Used often, appropriately, and smoothly, examples enlarge meaning by weaving the particular into the general.

AUDIENCE AND PURPOSE   Analyzing the audience often helps a writer select examples. William Lutz, for instance, writes for general readers for whom "revenue enhancement" and "user fees" are such familiar synonyms for taxes that similar euphemisms go by largely unnoticed. Undertakers become funeral directors and graveyards turn into memorial gardens. We barely notice. Working on that assumption, Lutz goes on to discuss the euphemisms used by the military and points out the dangers of having them become familiar. The wonders of modern technology as brought to us on the television screen are also very familiar, but Kathleen J. Turner shows us how that same technology can give us an incomplete and even distorted view of a serious event, the Gulf War. Both Lutz and Turner use examples to support and clarify their argumentative points, though the readers they address are neither the producers of news shows nor the inventors of euphemisms.

If the reader is part of the problem you are addressing, however, the essays by Martin Gottfried and Michael Gorra will serve as good examples. Although they write about very different subjects—Ramboesque drivers and gender-related roles—both authors assume that their readers are uninformed of the situations they describe and thus, unwittingly, may contribute to them. Both must avoid alienating the very people they want to inform. Anna Quindlen has a similar problem. Her general subject is abortion, an issue on which almost everyone has a strongly held opinion. To communicate her ideas, she must be sensitive to those views and try to avoid alienating those whose views represent opposing sides of the issue.

And then there's Angus McGill, whose views are intended only to entertain and inform. He assumes his readers will find his subject—the seemingly obscure research carried out by summer students in exotic places—as amusing and intriguing as he does. Who would have thought that the Brazil nuts we know so well come from "rock-hard" pods "the size of very large oranges" that the tree "sends . . . hurtling down like cannonballs."

TYPES OF EXAMPLES   Examples generally fall into two types, extended and multiple. An essay that rests its assertion on only one example is relatively rare, but Michael Gorra's use of extended example is more typical. He uses his own experience—a man teaching at a women's college—as an extended example of how gender affects teaching and learning, and then cites multiple examples within that broader one. Multiple examples add clarity, support, and emphasis, and thus are the most frequent type found in essays. A writer who builds example on example provides a firm foundation for generalizations.

Whether you are looking for multiple or extended examples, you can draw them from sources close to you, from your own experience, and the experiences of others, which is what Gottfried does in his essay; or you can opt for outside sources, from books, magazines, interviews, reports, and so on. Or you can quote people, which is Anna Quindlen's technique.

No matter what the source, however, the example should be representative and fitting. Quindlen, for example, gives meaning to a recent Supreme Court ruling by giving it a face, an example drawn from the experience of a "frightened 15-year-old." Drawing upon her own general experience, common to us all, as an adolescent "private as a safe-deposit box" and her recent conversation with the woman who runs the abortion clinic in Duluth, Quindlen cites examples to support her point about the complexity of a Supreme Court ruling.

DETAILS   In presenting an example, the writer uses many of the same techniques that come into play in description. Descriptive details enter into Angus McGill's "Here Be Beasties" with his amused account of the expeditions sent out to study glaciers and how they

Example   **63**

affect our climate. "What news," he asks, "from the Bakaninbreen glacier, said to be coming on at 1 km a year at least? Twelve hardy British students spent the summer measuring its reckless advance." On a more immediate subject, Anna Quindlen uses details to make an abstract decision into a concrete reality. To illustrate the effect of the law requiring that parents grant permission for an abortion, Quindlen cites two detailed examples: "The best case is the daughter who decides, with supportive parents, whether to end a pregnancy or have a baby. The worst case . . . is Becky Bell, a 17-year-old Indianapolis girl who died after an illegal abortion. She could not bear to tell her parents she was pregnant."

THESIS AND ORGANIZATION   Whether the essay is developed by multiple examples or a single extended example, it has a major assertion. Often, as in the case of "Here Be Beasties," "Mom, Dad and Abortion," "The Gulf War as Miniseries," "Rambos of the Road," and "Learning to Hear the Small, Soft Voices," the major assertion comes from the ideas contained in several key sentences, but sometimes the thesis appears in a single sentence, as in "No Ordinary Nut." Although all the essays that follow have a thesis developed by examples, the examples themselves often cross over into other categories. The example that opens Gottfried's essay is both an example and a narrative, or put more precisely, it is a narrative that functions as an example. So, too, descriptions, causal relationships, comparisons, processes, and the like can serve as examples. As you read the essays that follow, be on the lookout for the kinds of examples that writers use, but keep in mind that it is the example, not the type, that counts.

No Ordinary Nut

William Lutz

A stroll down a supermarket aisle will reveal that "giant" may be the smallest size of all. Such is doublespeak, a term first used by George Orwell in his novel 1984. *As William Lutz points out, doublespeak is now not only a part of our lives but a military specialty. The essay appeared in* Common Cause (*1990*), *a publication of the nonprofit group of the same name that is dedicated to improving the quality of federal and state governments.*

1   Administrations come and go but government doublespeak grinds on. A few examples: The Reagan administration didn't propose any new taxes, just "revenue enhancement" through new "user fees." There are no more poor people, just "fiscal underachievers." The U.S. Army doesn't kill the enemy anyone, it just "services the target."

2   Doublespeak—whether jargon, euphemisms or bureaucrat-ese—is not a slip of the tongue but a conscious use of language as both a tool and a weapon. It is language that conceals or manipulates thought. It makes the bad seem good, the negative appear positive, the unpleasant appear attractive or at least tolerable.

3   There is doublespeak in everyday life ("nondairy creamer"), business ("nonperforming assets") and government (the Internal Revenue Service). But when it comes to doublespeak, the military has a way with words that is unmatched. Only the military could call a tent a "frame-supported tension structure"; a parachute an "aerodynamic personnel decelerator"; and a zipper an "interlocking slide fastener."

4   Others may call it a bomb, but to the Army it's a "vertically deployed anti-personnel device."

5   Military doublespeak starts at the top. From the founding of our republic, there has been a Department of War. Until 1947, that is, when the military pulled off the doublespeak coup of the century. On July 27 President Harry S. Truman signed the National Security Act of 1947, an act that completely reorganized the armed forces. Section 202 establishes the post of secretary of Defense, while Section 205(a) eliminates the Department of War. Thus, war became "defense."

At first glance this change might not seem all that significant, but   6
examine the implications. Now members of Congress campaign to
spend more on "defense." Candidates for public office charge their
opponents with wanting to cut the $300 billion defense budget, not
the $300 billion war budget. And in 1982 Secretary of Defense Cas-
par Weinberger could say that the "defense" budget was "the most
important social welfare program for which the federal government
must be responsible."

Doublespeak also is useful when the Pentagon wants expensive   7
items to sound very complicated and worth their high price. It's not
an ordinary steel nut; it's a "hexiform rotatable surface compression
unit," which is why it cost $2,043 for just one of them. This little
piece of doublespeak also allows the military to say that the equipment "suffered dramatically degraded useful operational life owing
to the fact that a $2,000 hexiform rotatable surface compression unit
underwent catastrophic stress-related shaft detachment," which
sounds a lot more impressive than saying it won't work because a
13-cent nut broke.

Some penny-pinchers may think that $31,672 is a lot to pay for a   8
couch, a love seat, and 20 dining room chairs (or almost $1,500 for
each piece of furniture), but not if you think of it the way the Navy
does. All that money was spent on "habitability improvements" for
the destroyer *USS Kidd*.

Nothing is ever simple with the Pentagon. Even a newly designed   9
bayonet becomes a "weapons system," while the smoke used in
smoke bombs becomes a "universal obscurant." Even that favorite
of the GI, field rations or C-rations, has now become MRE or "meal
ready to eat," though changing the name won't make it taste any
better.

Then there is the "survivable enduring shelter," or SES, designed   10
by Goodyear Aerospace to be placed on an existing truck chassis.
Equipped with a 5,000-pound-plus payload, armor-plated shielding
capable of stopping .30 caliber "projectiles" (Pentagon doublespeak
for bullets) and an "intrusion detection system" (meaning a burglar
alarm), the SES is designed "to meet the most stringent technical
requirements for survival during a nuclear event," meaning it's supposed to be able to survive a nuclear bomb attack. Some have called
the SES the Pentagon's atomic-bomb-proof camper. Exactly what it's
supposed to do wandering over a nuclear-ravaged landscape is
never quite explained by the Pentagon, even in doublespeak.

11   With doublespeak, weapons never fail. The Pentagon can explain that the cruise missile didn't fly out of control and crash in three pieces during a test flight in Canada. According to the Air Force, the missile merely "impacted with the ground prematurely." Not to be outdone by their U.S. counterparts, an official of the Canadian forces said the test flight was simply "terminated five minutes earlier than planned." When an unarmed Minuteman III intercontinental ballistic missile developed problems after launch and had to be destroyed by commands radioed from the ground, the U.S. Air Force announced, "An anomaly occurred during the flight which caused the early termination." Although the Bigeye aerial nerve gas bomb has been on the drawing boards for more than 20 years, it still doesn't work and, during one test drop in 1982, the bomb malfunctioned, producing what the Pentagon called "a forcible ejection of the internal bomb components." In other words, the bomb blew up.

12   With doublespeak, the missile can miss the target but the test can still be a success. "We did acquire the target, but we did not hit it. . . . We achieved our objectives," said Jim Kittinger, an official in the air-to-surface guided weapons office at Elgin Air Force Base.

13   Because it avoids or shifts responsibility, doublespeak is particularly effective in explaining or at least glossing over accidents. An Air Force colonel in charge of safety wrote in a letter that rocket boosters weighing more than 300,000 pounds "have an explosive force upon surface impact that is sufficient to exceed the accepted overpressure threshold of physiological damage for exposed personnel." In English: if a 300,000-pound booster rocket falls on you, you probably won't survive. In 1985 three American soldiers were killed and 16 were injured when the first stage of a Pershing II missile they were unloading suddenly ignited. There was no explosion, said Maj. Michael Griffen, but rather "an unplanned rapid ignition of solid fuel."

14   You might think it reasonable to say that the helicopter crashed during a training exercise at Camp Lejeune in 1984. After all, 6 marines were killed and 11 were seriously injured. To military officials, however, it was not a crash but a "hard landing." When a seriously ill sailor was transferred to another ship for medical attention, the Navy doctor noted the sailor's condition as "not salvageable."

15   Using doublespeak, the military avoids discussing the unpleasant

realities of war and its consequences. When John Lehman was secretary of the navy, he promoted a strategy that in case of war called for U.S. aircraft carriers to sail near the Soviet Union in order to strike that country's ports. Undersecretary of Defense Richard De Lauer said that such a strategy would place the carriers in a "target-rich environment."

During the Vietnam war we learned that refugees were "ambient   16
noncombatant personnel" and enemy troops who survived bombing were "interdictional nonsuccumbers." Poisoning thousands of acres of vegetation with Agent Orange was a "resources control program" that produced "defoliation." American planes conducted "limited duration protective reactive strikes."

The 1983 invasion of Grenada produced more doublespeak.   17
What started as an invasion became a "rescue mission" and ended up being, in those immortal words of the Pentagon, a "pre-dawn vertical insertion."

Military doublespeak that calls chewing out somebody "verbal   18
counseling" isn't all that misleading. But a lot of the other doublespeak the military uses can have serious consequences. We laugh and dismiss doublespeak as empty or meaningless at our own peril.

The "MK-12A reentry system" is really the nuclear warhead on an   19
ICBM missile, and the "physics package" former Secretary of Defense Frank Carlucci talked about is the nuclear warhead on an intermediate range ballistic missile. The Pentagon tried to slip funding for the neutron bomb into an appropriations bill in 1977 by calling it a "radiation enhancement device."

In 1982 a meeting was called in the White House to find a new   20
and appealing name for the MX missile. When someone suggested calling it the Peacemaker, the name that was finally selected, Robert McFarlane, then national security adviser, said, "I suppose Widowmaker wouldn't do?"

Later, President Reagan mistakenly called the missile the Peace-   21
keeper, a name that it still has today.

Thesis and Organization

1. Which paragraph or paragraphs serve as the introduction to the essay?
2. Paragraph 2 defines the essay's central term. What are the effects of doublespeak?
3. What paragraphs make up the body of the essay? Group those para-

graphs into paragraph blocks and identify the topic sentence for each block.
4. Paragraph 18 functions as a transition. What new point does it introduce?
5. Considering the topic sentences you have identified, what do you conclude is the thesis of the essay?

Technique and Style

1. Lutz does not define his central term until his second paragraph. What does he gain or lose by that placement?
2. Think about the terms Lutz identifies as doublespeak. How many do you find in your dictionary? As words, what do these terms have in common?
3. Select a group of examples Lutz cites to support one of his points. Explain the effectiveness of his examples.
4. How would you characterize the level of diction Lutz uses for his "translations" of doublespeak phrases? Is his diction casual, slangy, formal, stuffy, what?
5. If you assume that paragraphs 18–21 function as the essay's conclusion, how effective do you find Lutz's final example? His last paragraph? Explain your opinion.

Suggestions for Writing

Look and listen for the euphemisms about you. Figure out the various categories they fit. Some, for example, will be job related, and others may represent the language of advertising; janitors can turn into sanitary engineers as quickly as fat can become cellulite. Select one category and find as many examples as you can. Then look up each euphemism in an unabridged dictionary, noting its etymology. Figure out what changes have occurred and why and then use the resulting generalization as a working thesis, selecting the examples most appropriate to your point and tone.

Rambos of the Road

Martin Gottfried

In Martin Gottfried's essay, a little bit of Rambo steps down from the screen and slips behind the steering wheel of many an American vehicle, be it hot rod or family sedan, pickup truck or tractor trailer. The essay was published in the "My Turn" column of Newsweek *in 1986. Driving etiquette has not improved.*

The car pulled up and its driver glared at us with such sullen intensity, such hatred, that I was truly afraid for our lives. Except for the Mohawk haircut he didn't have, he looked like Robert DeNiro in *Taxi Driver,* the sort of young man who, delirious for notoriety, might kill a president.

He was glaring because we had passed him and for that affront he pursued us to the next stoplight so as to express his indignation and affirm his masculinity. I was with two women and, believe it, was afraid for all three of us. It was nearly midnight and we were in a small, sleeping town with no other cars on the road.

When the light turned green, I raced ahead, knowing it was foolish and that I was not in a movie. He didn't merely follow, he chased, and with his headlights turned off. No matter what sudden turn I took, he followed. My passengers were silent. I knew they were alarmed, and I prayed that I wouldn't be called upon to protect them. In that cheerful frame of mind, I turned off my own lights so I couldn't be followed. It was lunacy. I was responding to a crazy *as* a crazy.

"I'll just drive to the police station," I finally said, and as if those were the magic words, he disappeared.

Elbowing fenders: It seems to me that there has recently been an epidemic of auto macho—a competition perceived and expressed in driving. People fight it out over parking spaces. They bully into line at the gas pump. A toll booth becomes a signal for elbowing fenders. And beetle-eyed drivers hunch over their steering wheels, squeezing the rims, glowering, preparing the excuse of not having seen you as they muscle you off the road. Approaching a highway on an entrance ramp recently, I was strong-armed by a trailer truck so immense that its driver all but blew me away by

69

blasting his horn. The behemoth was just inches from my hopelessly mismatched coupe when I fled for the safety of the shoulder.

6   And this is happening on city streets, too. A New York taxi driver told me that "intimidation is the name of the game. Drive as if you're deaf and blind. You don't hear the other guy's horn and you sure as hell don't see him."

7   The odd thing is that long before I was even able to drive, it seemed to me that people were at their finest and most civilized when in their cars. They seemed so orderly and considerate, so reasonable, staying in the right-hand lane unless passing, signaling all intentions. In those days you really eased into highway traffic, and the long, neat rows of cars seemed mobile testimony to the sanity of most people. Perhaps memory fails, perhaps there were always testy drivers, perhaps—but everyone didn't give you the finger.

8   A most amazing example of driver rage occurred recently at the Manhattan end of the Lincoln Tunnel. We were four cars abreast, stopped at a traffic light. And there was no moving even when the light had changed. A bus had stopped in the cross traffic, blocking our paths: it was normal-for-New-York-City gridlock. Perhaps impatient, perhaps late for important appointments, three of us nonetheless accepted what, after all, we could not alter. One, however, would not. He would not be helpless. He would go where he was going even if he couldn't get there. A Wall Street type in suit and tie, he got out of his car and strode toward the bus, rapping smartly on its doors. When they opened, he exchanged words with the driver. The doors folded shut. He then stepped in front of the bus, took hold of one of its large windshield wipers and broke it.

9   The bus doors reopened and the driver appeared, apparently giving the fellow a good piece of his mind. If so, the lecture was wasted, for the man started his car and proceeded to drive directly *into the bus*. He rammed it. Even though the point at which he struck the bus, the folding doors, was its most vulnerable point, ramming the side of a bus with your car has to rank very high on a futility index. My first thought was that it had to be a rented car.

10   **Lane merger:** To tell the truth, I could not believe my eyes. The bus driver opened his doors as much as they could be opened and he stepped directly onto the hood of the attacking car, jumping up and down with both his feet. He then retreated into the bus, closing the doors behind him. Obviously a man of action, the car driver

backed up and rammed the bus again. How this exercise in absurdity would have been resolved none of us will ever know for at that point the traffic unclogged and the bus moved on. And the rest of us, we passives of the world, proceeded, our cars crossing a field of battle as if nothing untoward had happened.

It is tempting to blame such belligerent, uncivil and even neurotic behavior on the nuts of the world, but in our cars we all become a little crazy. How many of us speed up when a driver signals his intention of pulling in front of us? Are we resentful and anxious to pass him? How many of us try to squeeze in, or race along the shoulder at a lane merger? We may not jump on hoods, but driving the gauntlet, we seethe, cursing not so silently in the safety of our steel bodies on wheels—fortresses for cowards. 11

What is it within us that gives birth to such antisocial behavior and why, all of a sudden, have so many drivers gone around the bend? My friend Joel Katz, a Manhattan psychiatrist, calls it, "a Rambo pattern. People are running around thinking the American way is to take the law into your own hands when anyone does anything wrong. And what constitutes 'wrong'? Anything that cramps your style." 12

It seems to me that it is a new America we see on the road now. It has the mentality of a hoodlum and the backbone of a coward. The car is its weapon and hiding place, and it is still a symbol even in this. Road Rambos no longer bespeak a self-reliant, civil people tooling around in family cruisers. In fact, there aren't families in these machines that charge headlong with their brights on in broad daylight, demanding we get out of their way. Bullies are loners, and they have perverted our liberty of the open road into drivers' license. They represent an America that derides the values of decency and good manners, then roam the highways riding shotgun and shrieking freedom. By allowing this to happen, the rest of us approve. 13

Thesis and Organization

1. Divide the essay into sections. What paragraphs introduce the essay? Which paragraphs comment on the introduction? Which provide the author's major example? Which generalize about it? What paragraph or paragraphs conclude the essay?
2. Gottfried uses both extended and multiple examples in his essay. What, if anything, does this variety add?

3. Trace the cause-and-effect relationships that weave in and out of the essay. In what way is that pattern of organization appropriate for Gott-fried's subject?

4. Reexamine the paragraphs that generalize upon the examples Gottfried uses. List the assertions the author makes, explicitly or implicitly, about the "Rambos of the Road." In your own words, state the thesis of the essay.

5. Obviously, Gottfried reacts negatively to hostile drivers, and, in a way, you can read the piece as his own way of letting out his frustrations and getting even. Where in the essay does he vent those feelings? Where does he inform the reader? To what extent is his thesis argumentative? What is Gottfried's primary purpose: to express himself, to inform the reader, or to persuade his audience?

Technique and Style

1. If Gottfried is correct, there is a bit of the Road Rambo in all of us; we are part of the problem. Given that position, Gottfried can adopt any number of possible rhetorical stances or roles: Lecturer, Policeman, Judge, Social Commentator, Big Brother, Angry Victim. What others can you add? Which term most accurately describes Gottfried?

2. In paragraphs 11 and 12, the author relies heavily on questions. What purpose do they serve? Try restating some as declarative statements. What is lost? Gained?

3. Gottfried is careful to describe both his pursuer and the man who attacked the bus. Why are both of these descriptions important? What do they add to the author's credibility as narrator?

4. What authorities does Gottfried cite to make his points? In what ways are they appropriate? What would the essay have lost without them?

5. Examine the level of the author's diction. What examples can you find of slang? Of formal language? How would you characterize Gottfried's choice of words? What does that choice imply about the essay's readers?

Suggestions for Writing

Any given group of people—be it drivers, joggers, shoppers, sports fans, moviegoers, or fast-food munchers—always has its "types" that may or may not include Rambos. Pick a group that you know about and see if you can come up with one representative and distinctive "type" that you can both illustrate through example and generalize upon.

*H*ere Be Beasties

Angus McGill

McGill describes how various students spend their summer vacations and in doing so explores the ways of camels and cockroaches, among an assortment of other creatures and their countries. His title comes from old world maps, where unexplored countries were labeled with warnings instead of names. McGill is a British columnist, and this essay first appeared in the English newspaper the Evening Standard *in 1990.*

Mark O'Byrne and his friends had a really nice summer. They spent it in Sudan studying diarrhea in camels. Young camels get a lot of diarrhea. So do students visiting camels in Sudan, as Mark's expedition very soon discovered.

Summer expeditions to remote and preferably disagreeable foreign parts, the ones labeled "here be beasties," are a long-established student tradition. The lucky ones get the seal of approval of the august Royal Geographical Society, which is still batting away filling in the global jigsaw. This year it gave 73 expeditions its blessing, which meant 677 young scientists and explorers had the time of their lives.

They sought out parrots in peril in Ecuador, dwarf crocodiles in trouble in Gambia, mollusks having a bad time in Tanzania. They interviewed white-toothed shrews in the Democratic Republic of Sao Tome and Principe and Mongolian hedgehogs in, well, Mongolia actually, and what do you suppose feral goats are up to on the Isla de la Plata? We will soon be told.

The students who explored caves in Russia, Vietnam and Dominica will be reporting back, too, also the ones who checked out reefs in Mexico and the Indian Ocean. Several expeditions surveyed threatened rain-forests and Justin Gerlach of Wadham College, Oxford, led one into a recently discovered mist forest in the Seychelles.

Seven expeditions set off for the Arctic to spend summer on glaciers. The way glaciers are behaving may affect us all. They are indicators of climatic change. What news, then, from the Bakaninbreen glacier, said to be coming on at 1 km a year at least? Twelve hardy British students spent the summer measuring its reckless advance. Michael Fish awaits their findings.

6   More lightly clad, George Beccaloni, Fernley Symons and Magnus Schoeman, third-year students from Imperial College, were to be found in Papua New Guinea studying cockroaches and macrofungi. You can eat macrofungi. Well, you can eat cockroaches, too, come to that. They do in Papua New Guinea.

7   George Beccaloni's private passion is cockroaches. He has done his best to furnish his parents' home in Hanwell with them. Ex-cockroaches are neatly mounted, live ones skitter and scamper in tanks.

8   He has no sympathy for the curious reaction of most of us, which is to go ugh and make a face. The local cockroach, he says, is not actually local but a tropical import and, while he would not wish it to be at large at home, it is a handsome and successful animal that will outlive us all when the bomb falls. To kill it, he says, pop it in the deep freeze.

9   There are 20,000 species of cockroach, apparently, though only 4,000 of them have so far been named. Some, he says, are really pretty. There is the one in the Philippines that mimics ladybirds and the bright green South American kind and a whole designer range of shiny metallic ones. Papua New Guinea has some particularly nice cockroaches.

10   Beccaloni was thrilled to find an amazing subaquatic species that lives under stones on the riverbank and plops into the water at night to feed on algae. Also, and this was a real triumph, he found a genus of cockroach believed to have a mother-infant relationship unique in the insect world.

11   The young are white and have no eyes or mouths. They do have a useful tube and this fits into a hole in their mother's body. They suckle through this. The adults, says Beccaloni, are attractive, shiny black insects that roll into a ball when threatened. He collected 20 adult females and 40 young. The adults were needed for science, I am sorry to say, but the young are at this moment approaching a vigorous, interesting adulthood in a plastic sweet bottle in his mother's airing cupboard.

12   Ben Alexander, of Redhill in Surrey, seems to have missed some good cockroach opportunities in Bolivia. With three other Cambridge students, two Bolivian students, two guides and a driver he spent six weeks in the rain forests of East and West Pando, sleeping

in hammocks by night and collecting data on the Brazil nut tree by day.

The Brazil nut tree is extremely important to the tropical forest ecologically and economically. It is also unusually uncooperative, declining point blank to be cultivated. Its pollination is extravagantly complicated, demanding the combined services of a particular bee, a particular orchid and a taruna tree and it has granted exclusive distribution rights to a rodent called the agouti. The agouti is the only animal that can get into a Brazil nut and that includes us. 13

Furthermore—I'm not finished with Brazil nuts yet—furthermore, this difficult tree declines all assistance with harvesting. There is no climbing it. It goes straight up 100 feet. When it is good and ready, and preferably when you are standing looking up, it sends the pods hurtling down like cannonballs. The pods are the size of very large oranges and they are rock-hard. Inside the nuts cluster like segments. This explains their shape. 14

There is, of course, a famous explanation for the camel's shape: it is a horse designed by a committee. Mark O'Byrne and his 14-strong expedition from the Royal Veterinary College got on with the camels of Sudan very well, and, by and large, with their nomadic herdsmen and with the Sudanese in general, though the soldiers were suspicious. Sudan is, after all, at war with Chad on one border and with Ethiopia on another. It also has a civil war going on in the south, so foreign students in a Land Rover might well set alarm bells ringing. 15

The camels should have been pleased to see them. Diarrhea kills half the calves and the nomads' traditional remedy does not help. What they do is burn holes in the sick calves with hot metal rods. Don't they notice it doesn't work? The veterinary students had a better remedy, the simple sugar and salt solution as used on domestic cattle with diarrhea the world over. They took it themselves when they got diarrhea. They are all right now, thank you. 16

Thesis and Organization

1. Paragraphs 1 and 2 work together as an introduction. What do they imply about the subject? The author's tone?
2. What areas of the globe are covered by McGill's examples? What reasons can you find for his selection?
3. What fields of study are covered by McGill's examples? What reasons can you find for his selection?

4. How does McGill prepare the reader for his example of the cockroaches? For the Brazil nuts? For the camels?

5. Given McGill's subject, tone, and information, what do you find to be the essay's thesis?

Technique and Style

1. How would you characterize McGill's tone? Is he disapproving? Sarcastic? Amused? Outraged? What?

2. McGill places his examples within a frame provided by his first and last paragraphs. Explain whether or not you find the framework effective.

3. Paragraph 12 functions as a transition between the cockroaches and the Brazil nut. Explain whether or not you find the paragraph effective.

4. How detailed are McGill's examples? Are they concrete or abstract? Explain their effect.

5. Given all the examples McGill had to choose from, why do you think he selected the particular three he developed in some detail?

Suggestions for Writing

Whether it's a summer job or a long-term one, an unusual job or a humdrum one, a person can learn more than he or she expected. Consider the jobs you have had, including volunteer or unpaid ones, and what you learned that was not what you expected. Perhaps you learned something about people or about yourself. Perhaps you learned that you didn't want to learn anymore.

The Gulf War as Miniseries

Kathleen J. Turner

Published eight days after the January 15, 1991, deadline for Iraq's withdrawal from Kuwait, this essay explores the television news coverage of the early stages of the Gulf War and just how informative that coverage was. Kathleen J. Turner is in a good position to judge, for she teaches communication at Tulane University. The essay was published in the New Orleans Times-Picayune *as part of a series of views on the war.*

One hundred seventy-six years ago this month, the Battle of New Orleans raged—two weeks after the War of 1812 had been officially concluded. News of the diplomatic agreements did not reach Andrew Jackson and his fellow combatants until much later. Moreover, news of the battle did not reach President Madison until the following month. 1

In contrast, war has raged before our eyes this past week live and direct from the Middle East. We heard the bombs falling in Baghdad as correspondents crept to windows to report what they could see. We watched reporters donning gas masks in the middle of airing their reports. Live satellite coverage has made even the taped television war of Vietnam seem passé. 2

Like weathercasters who can't quite contain their professional excitement about a hurricane even as they report on the destructive capacity of the storm, television news teams have revelled in the story of a lifetime unfolding before them. Operation Desert Shield and the January 15 deadline allowed the networks to prepare to cover the military action. 3

By putting correspondents and camera crews in place in the Middle East, the networks committed themselves to reporting the story in a big way, no matter what happened. Once they learned that Operation Desert Storm had begun, they launched a news offensive of massive proportions. 4

Key to the preparations for coverage were the arrangements for the satellite linkups that have enabled live telecasts. The technological imperative suggests that when you have the technology, you feel a need to use it. 5

6   Because the networks had the capacity to broadcast live, they did
so to demonstrate that they had that capacity. As a consequence, the
news was being reported even as it [was] being gathered, indeed,
even as it was being made. With the live satellite linkage, no one
knew what would happen next—even as it appeared on television
screens in millions of living rooms.

7   As a result, the audience received a barrage of piecemeal information patched together into a telecast that necessarily contained
some speculation that later proved incorrect. A prime example was
the initial report that Thursday night's attack on Israel included
nerve gas.

8   Adding to the patchwork nature of the broadcasts were the traditional techniques of using interviews and multiple correspondents.
The anchors served as traffic cops of sorts, jumping from the Pentagon to the White House to Saudi Arabia to the person on the street
in Olathe, Kansas, and back to the latest of a string of experts in the
studio. Each of these components was constrained by the compressed time of the electronic media: four minutes is considered a
lengthy interview on television, even with the most erudite observer.

9   This pastiche of news sources was especially important given the
constraints on news gathering for this conflict. The Bush administration monitored the news flow from the start, guided partly by
President Reagan's sharp claims on coverage of the Grenada incur-
sion and partly by the traditional constraints on war coverage.

10   Those constraints have been intensified by live television, since
Saddam Hussein watches CNN and the Iraqis can use such coverage
for military reconnaissance.

11   Thus the Pentagon has exhibited more than its usual reticence to
share detailed information. Yet the huge scale of the story, underscored by the keen competition in coverage, has led the networks to
cover the conflict extensively, filling in gaps with opinion polls,
fancy models and snippets of interviews.

12   To provide continuity and flair, the networks have packaged the
story as if it were a miniseries, with titles like "America at War" and
"Showdown in the Gulf." Even the most urgent news is reported in
the context of flashy computer-generated graphics, thrilling theme
music and anchor stars who urge us to stay tuned for the next
installment.

What we don't see is pieces that help us understand the cultural, 13
historical and ideological contexts of this conflict.

Thus we sit before our televisions, along with heads of state and 14
military leaders, watching hour after hour of the war in the gulf. In
spite of all of the coverage, we still know only a small part of the
story, constrained as it is by myriad military, political, economic and
network factors.

Yet the stylishly constructed parade of maps and models, report- 15
ers and professors, data and footage in these Persian Gulf miniseries
masks these limitations.

The technology of contemporary media is light years away from 16
the War of 1812, but the sum total of our knowledge and understanding may not be so different from Andrew Jackson's after all.

Thesis and Organization

1. Paragraphs 1 and 2 set up a comparison. What point is the author
   making with it?
2. Paragraphs 3–6 provide background for the television coverage of the
   war. What are Turner's main points?
3. Paragraphs 7–12 trace how television coverage reported the war. What
   are Turner's main points?
4. Paragraphs 13–15 explain the effect of that coverage. What are Turner's
   main points?
5. Paragraph 16 brings back the comparison between the War of 1812 and
   the Gulf War. What point is Turner making? What is the essay's thesis?

Technique and Style

1. What language does Turner use that is associated with television? What
   sort of person does Turner seem to be? How credible do you find her
   views? To what extent does her choice of words reinforce her credibility?
2. How would you characterize Turner's tone? Is she calm? Angry? Rea-
   soned? Outraged? What?
3. What reasons can you find for Turner's use of the pronoun *we?*
4. Explain the extent to which you find Turner's framework for the essay
   effective.
5. In a way, Turner uses the live television reporting on the Gulf War as an
   example of how style can substitute for substance. Trace her argument
   and the examples she uses to support it.

Suggestions for Writing

Think of an example within your own experience where style obscured substance. Perhaps you bought an expensive piece of equipment or a car that turned out to be a lemon, or perhaps you read a biography that was good reading at the expense of fact. Or think about people or events that turned out to be a disappointment in that the surface led you to expect one thing, yet the reality was another.

Mom, Dad and Abortion

Anna Quindlen

Anna Quindlen's column, "Public & Private," appears regularly in the New York Times. *The title is a particularly appropriate one for an essay about a pregnant minor's right to privacy, the issue she considers in the essay that follows. It was published in 1990.*

Once I got a fortune cookie that said: to remember is to understand. I have never forgotten it.   1

A good judge remembers what it was like to be a lawyer. A good editor remembers what it was like to be a reporter.   2

A good parent remembers what it was like to be a child.   3

I remember adolescence, the years of having the impulse control of a mousetrap, of being as private as a safe-deposit box. If my mother said "How are you?" she was prying.   4

And I've remembered it more keenly since the Supreme Court ruled that the states may require a pregnant minor to inform her parents before having an abortion.   5

This is one of the most difficult of many difficult issues within the abortion debate. As good parents, we remember being teenagers, thinking that parents and sex existed in parallel universes.   6

But as good parents, it also seems reasonable to wonder why a girl who cannot go on a school field trip without our knowledge can end a pregnancy without it.   7

The Supreme Court found succor in a Minnesota law that provides for something called "judicial bypass." If you are 15 and want to have an abortion but cannot tell your parents—for the law provides that both must be informed, not simply one—you can tell it to the judge. You come to the clinic, have an exam and counseling. Then you go to the courthouse, meet with a public defender and go to the judge's chambers, to be questioned about your condition, your family, your plans for the future.   8

If the judge agrees, you can have the abortion.   9

The Court did not find this an undue burden for a frightened 15-year-old.   10

Tina Welsh, who runs the only abortion clinic in Duluth, remem-   11 bers the first girl she took to the courthouse when the law went into effect. The young woman did not want to notify her father; he was in jail for having sex with her sister. Ms. Welsh remembers taking girls up in the freight elevator because they had neighbors and relations working in the courthouse. You can just hear it:

12   "Hi, sweetheart, how are you? What brings you here?"

13   So much for the right to privacy.

14   But Ms. Welsh best remembers the young woman who asked, "How long will the jury be out?" She thought she was going on trial for the right to have an abortion.

15   Much of this debate centers, like the first sentence of *Anna Karenina,* on happy families, and unhappy ones. Abortion rights activists say parental notification assumes a world of dutiful daughters and supportive parents, instead of one riven by alcoholism, incest and abuse. Those opposed to abortion say it is unthinkable that a minor child should have such a procedure without her parents' knowledge.

16   But I remember something between the poles of cruelty and communication. I remember girls who wanted their parents to have certain illusions about them. Not girls who feared beatings, or were pregnant by their mother's boyfriend. Just girls who wanted to remain good girls in the minds that mattered to them most.

17   Ms. Welsh remembers one mother who refused to let her husband know their daughter was having an abortion. "Twenty-five years ago," the woman said, "we made a promise to one another. I would never have to clean a fish, and he would never have to know if his daughter was pregnant."

18   If parental notification laws are really designed to inhibit abortion—and I suspect they are—Ms. Welsh's experience suggests they are not terribly successful. Not one teenager who came to the Duluth clinic changed her mind, even in the face of public defenders and judicial questioning. If the point is to facilitate family communication, that's been something of a failure, too. In the five years the Minnesota law was in effect, 7000 minors had abortions. Half of those teenagers chose to face a stranger in his chambers rather than tell both parents.

19   But perhaps there is another purpose to all this. If adolescents want their parents to have illusions about them, parents need those illusions badly. These laws provide them. They mandate communi-

cation. If she has nothing to tell you, then it must mean nothing is wrong.

Ah, yes—I remember that.   20

These are difficult questions because they involve not-quite   21 adults facing adult decisions. The best case is the daughter who decides, with supportive parents, whether to end a pregnancy or have a baby. The worst case is the girl who must notify the parent who impregnated her. Or the worst case is Becky Bell, a 17-year-old Indianapolis girl who died after an illegal abortion. She could not bear to tell her parents she was pregnant.

In the middle are girls who have been told by the Supreme Court   22 that they must trade. They can keep a good-girl persona at home, but in exchange they must surrender some of their privacy and dignity. That is what adults want, and that is what we will have. We will take our illusions. The teenagers will take the freight elevator.

Thesis and Organization

1. What is the connection between the fortune cookie and the Supreme Court decision?
2. Which paragraphs explain the Supreme Court decision?
3. What paragraphs deal with examples of its effect?
4. What is Quindlen's opinion of the ruling?
5. Considering the ruling, the examples Quindlen provides, and her opinion, what do you find to be the essay's thesis?

Technique and Style

1. How would you describe Quindlen's tone? Is she angry? Calm? Emotional? Logical? Sad? Distressed? What?
2. Now and then, Quindlen sets off a personal comment in a separate paragraph. Do you think this technique strengthens or weakens the essay? Explain.
3. Reread Quindlen's description of adolescence (4). What metaphors can you substitute for the ones she uses? Which do you like best and why?
4. The two sentences of paragraph 2 and the one in paragraph 3 together illustrate the technique of parallelism. Rewrite the sentences so that the parallelism is destroyed. What is lost? Gained?
5. One of the techniques Quindlen uses is to set out two opposing views and then find a middle ground. What examples can you find of this technique? What does it contribute to her tone? Her persona?

Suggestions for Writing

In a way, you can characterize Quindlen's essay as a thinking through of a compromise, which in that case was one reached by the Supreme Court. Think about the compromises in your own life, the times when you or your family found a middle ground. Think too about the compromises that exist in our culture, say the balance between rights and responsibilities, freedom and constraint, individual and group liberty.

*L*earning to Hear the Small, Soft Voices

Michael Gorra

In the essay that follows, Michael Gorra uses the extended example of his own experience to explore the roles of men and women, of students and teachers. The essay appeared in the Sunday edition of the New York Times (*1988*) *as an opinion piece in the gender-oriented "About Men" column, a regular feature that alternates weeks with "About Women."*

"You at a women's college?" a friend said just after I'd been hired to teach English at Smith. "That's a scandal waiting to happen." He never made it clear if I was to be the debaucher or the debauchee. Another friend, a Smith alumna, told me its students saw the young male faculty, married or not, as "fair game." My mother told me to get a heavy doorstop for my office and to keep my wife's picture on my desk.

After three years at Smith, those comments seem far away, though by the time I got here I'd heard enough of them to make me decide I didn't really want to teach *Lolita* to my class of freshmen. And for the first few months I felt a sort of amused uneasiness walking around the place at night, wondering if the women I passed would start at my slouch-hatted shadow, or if campus security would stop me and demand to see an ID.

But the experience of being a man at a women's college is both less lurid and more ambiguous than my friends had half-jokingly predicted. I remember being asked at my interview why I wanted to teach at a women's college. It's a disingenuous question, given the absence of a job market for English professors, particularly because it's hard for a man to have an ideological commitment to women's colleges the way some feminist women do. So I said I wanted good students at a good liberal arts college; and that once you get used to being at the teacher's end of the table, the other people in the room seem simply students, rather than members of one sex or the other. That's partly true.

Most days I don't feel any differently walking into a classroom full

85

of women than I did walking into a coed classroom as a graduate teaching fellow. I don't notice that I'm the only man there. And I did notice my singularity, and felt uneasy with it, when I was an undergraduate myself, taking exchange courses at women's colleges.

5   That suggests I usually think of myself as a teacher rather than a male, that one role supersedes another. But sometimes at Smith College I do feel rather self-consciously male. Those times seem to fall into two categories. One is social—when a student invites me to dinner or a faculty-student tea at her dormitory. (Or when I meet a student at a door and hold it for her. That always seems to surprise and confuse the student, because it makes her see me suddenly as a man, rather than a teacher.)

6   The other is when discussion turns on questions of gender. Looking at posters advertising lectures or workshops—"Women Scholars of Judaism," "Bringing Girls to Math"—I often think that however interesting I might find such talks, I'm not really part of their intended audience. Some of that comes from the natural rift between faculty and student life and some doesn't, but it's not easy to say where the line falls. At a coed school, a workshop on eating disorders sponsored by the health service seems clearly for students; here it appears to be for women. Which makes me momentarily aware of myself as a member of a minority group, and produces some of the wariness that I imagine members of other minority groups feel in bumping against the white male hegemony of which I'm a part.

         Now and then I feel that wariness in my own classroom. I'm
7   preparing to teach Doris Lessing's *The Golden Notebook* for the first time, and am hesitant, nervous—and a bit excited—about how I'll handle it, in a room where some of my students will speak with more authority about it than I can. (I'm also terrified, in much the same way I would be in teaching *Lolita,* that somebody will ask me what Lessing means by equating a woman's orgasm with her integrity.) But I've also sought that wariness, or rather the self-consciousness that's a part of it, by trying to blur my two roles.

         Each year in my freshmen writing class I have my students read
8   Adrienne Rich's essay "Taking Women Students Seriously." There she asks us to "Listen to the small, soft voices, often courageously trying to speak up, voices of women taught early that tones of confidence, challenge, anger, or assertiveness, are strident and unfeminine. Listen to the voices of the women and the voices of the men; observe the space men allow themselves, physically and ver-

bally, the male assumption that people will listen, even when the majority of the group is female."

I ask my students to talk about their own behavior in the class- 9
room, and mine. Most of them have chosen a women's college because they already know what Rich means about the difference between men and women—as students. But few of them have extended the argument to include their male teachers. So they always tell me, at first, that they defer to my opinion because I'm the teacher, not because I'm a man; because they're students, not because they're women. I'm not so sure—and neither, by the end of class, are they.

I'm satisfied when I can get my students to see the issue, but for 10
me that's just the beginning. For I know now that I was naïve when I said at my interview that the students' sex doesn't matter. It matters profoundly, even or particularly when one isn't conscious of it. After a class on Orson Welles's *Citizen Kane* last year, my best student, an articulate and seemingly confident New Yorker, apologized to me for not having spoken that day. "I have a much different view of the movie than everyone else seems to," she said, "and I didn't want to disagree."

Our students still suffer, even at a women's college, from the 11
lessons Rich says women are taught about unfemininity of assertiveness. They are uneasy with the prospect of having to defend their opinions, not only against my own devil's advocacy, but against each other. They would rather not speak if speaking means breaking with their classmates' consensus. Yet that consensus is usually more emotional, a matter of tone, than it is intellectual.

Last week I had two students, both of them bright and one speak- 12
ing right after the other, offer diametrically opposed readings of a W. H. Auden poem. But the second student didn't define her interpretation against her predecessor's, as I think a man would have. She didn't begin by saying "I don't agree with that." She betrayed no awareness that she disagreed with her classmate, and seemed surprised when I pointed it out.

Such incidents have made me question my chief assumption 13
about teaching—that people involved in a discussion will not only disagree with each other, but say so. I think they have made me a better teacher, a better listener, more able to gauge when silence means a real consensus and when it is a question of manners, to anticipate the ways in which a text might trouble my students, in

case those "small, soft voices" can't summon the confidence to challenge it themselves.

14   But they have also made me use Rich's terms to question my own performance. The verbal space I allow myself, my assumption that people will listen—is that the teacher or the man? Does my maleness make me assume what I'm saying is worthwhile, even when it isn't? I don't have any answers to those questions. But I do know that having to ask them makes teaching here both more challenging, and more intriguing, than either my joking friends or I had imagined it could be.

Thesis and Organization

1. Gorra uses paragraphs 1–3 to introduce his essay. Given the information supplied in the introduction, what questions do you expect to have answered in the rest of the essay?
2. In paragraphs 4–12, Gorra cites particular examples to illustrate what he feels as a man teaching in a women's college. What progression do you find in those feelings?
3. Almost all of the essay's readers have never been in the situation Gorra describes. Given that fact, how well does he describe that situation? Select one of his examples and explain how it is or is not effective.
4. The title of the essay alludes to the passage Gorra quotes from Adrienne Rich (8). In your own words, state what Gorra has learned by listening to his students' "small, soft voices."
5. To what extent does Gorra express his personal feelings in the essay? How much of the piece is informative? Persuasive? Make a case for all three purposes being at work.

Technique and Style

1. Gorra mentions a number of works and authors: *Lolita,* Lessing, Rich, *Citizen Kane,* Auden. To what extent do these allusions depend on your familiarity with the works and authors? What attempts, if any, does Gorra make to identify them for you?
2. What sort of person does Gorra appear to be? Would you want him as a teacher? Why or why not?
3. Gorra's essay explores the extended example of his own experience as a man teaching at a woman's college. Examine the assertions he makes in paragraphs 7 and 9–12. Testing those assertions against your own experience, in what ways does the behavior he describes reveal itself in a coeducational setting?

4. Much has been written on the different ways men and women learn, to say nothing of the wealth of research available on gender roles. What would Gorra's essay have gained or lost if he had drawn upon some of this information?

5. Look up *sexist* in an unabridged dictionary and then reread paragraph 1. In what ways are the statements referred to there sexist? Taking the essay as a whole, explain why Gorra's tone is or is not sexist.

Suggestions for Writing

At any given time, each of us is apt to play a number of roles: child or parent, student or teacher, male or female, insider or outsider. Select a time when you became aware of a role you played and then explore what you learned from being aware of that role and how you learned it.

POINTERS FOR USING EXAMPLE

Exploring the Topic

1. **What examples can you think of to illustrate your topic?** Are all of them from your own experience? What examples can you find from other sources?
2. **Check to see that your examples are both pertinent and representative.** Do they fit? Do they illustrate?
3. **Which examples lend themselves to extended treatment?** Which are relatively unimportant?
4. **How familiar is your audience with each of your examples?**
5. **Which examples best lend themselves to your topic?** In what order would they best be presented?
6. **What point do you want to make?** Do your examples all support that point? Do they lead the reader to your major assertion?
7. **What is your purpose behind your point?** Is your primary aim to express your own feelings, to inform, to persuade, to entertain?

Drafting the Paper

1. **Know your reader.** Figure out where your reader may stand in relation to your topic and thesis. It may be that your audience knows little about your subject or that the reader simply hasn't thought much about it; on the other hand, maybe the reader knows a great deal and holds a definite opinion. Once you have made an informed guess about your audience's attitude toward your topic and thesis, reexamine your examples in the light of that information. Some may have to be explained in greater detail than others, and the more familiar ones will need to be presented in a new or different light. Use the techniques you would employ in writing descriptive papers.
2. **Know your purpose.** Self-expressive papers are often difficult to write because you are so close to being your own audience. If you are writing with this aim in mind, try making yourself conscious of the personality you project as a writer. Jot down the characteristics you wish to convey about yourself and refer to this list as you revise your paper. While this is a highly self-conscious way to revise, when it is done well, the result appears natural. You will also need to double-check your examples, making sure that you present them in sufficient detail to communicate fully to your audience. That warning serves as well for informative and persuasive papers. Again, use description to make your examples hit the mark: use sensory detail, compare the unfamiliar to the familiar, be

concrete. If you are writing a persuasive paper, use these techniques to develop your emotional appeal.

3. **Consider extended example.** If an essay rests on one example, that illustration must be chosen and developed with great care. Make sure your example is representative of its class and that you provide all relevant information. Make as many unobtrusive connections as you can between your example and the class it represents. During revision, you may want to eliminate some of these references, but at first it's best to have too many. If you are writing a persuasive paper, you don't want to be found guilty of a logical fallacy.

4. **Consider multiple examples.** Most essays rely on multiple examples to support their points; nevertheless, some will be more developed than others. Figure out which examples are particularly striking and develop them, reserving the others for mere mention. Show how your examples fit your point and stress what is noteworthy about them. To lend breadth and credibility to your point consider citing statistics, quotations, authorities, and the experience of others as well as your own experience. Comment on what you take from other sources in order to make it more your own.

5. **Arrange your examples effectively.** The most frequent pattern of organization moves from the less dramatic, less important to the most, but examples also can be arranged chronologically or in terms of frequency (from the least frequent to the most). Like the essay itself, each paragraph should be developed around a central assertion, either stated or understood. In longer papers, groups of paragraphs will form a paragraph block in support of a unifying statement. These statements guide the reader through your examples and save the paper from turning into a mere list.

6. **Make a point.** Examples so obviously need to lead up to something that it's hard not to make a point in this kind of paper. The only real pitfall is that your point may not be an assertion. Test your thesis by asking whether your point carries any information. If it does, it's an assertion. Say you come up with, "We live in a world of time-saving technology." You can think of lots of examples and even narrow down the "we" to "anyone who cooks today." The setting is obviously the kitchen, but is the revised thesis an assertion? Given the information test, it fails. Your audience already knows what you are supposedly informing them about. But if you revise and come up with "Electronic gizmos have turned the kitchen into a laboratory," you've given the topic a fresher look, one that does contain information.

Division
and Classification

*T*he next time you shop in a supermarket or clean out a closet, think about how you are doing it and you will understand the workings of division and classification. "How often do I wear those shoes?" and "I never did like that sweater" imply that dividing items according to how frequently you wear them would be a good principle for sorting out your bedroom closet. Supermarkets, however, do the sorting for you. Goods are divided according to shared characteristics—all dairy products in one section, meat in another, and so on—and then items are placed into those categories. The process looks easy, but if you have ever tried to find soy sauce, you know the pitfalls: Is it with spices? Sauces? Gourmet foods? Health foods?

To divide a subject and then classify examples into the categories or classes that resulted from division calls for the ability to examine a subject from several angles, work out the ways in which it can be divided, and then discern similarities and differences among the examples you want to classify. A huge topic such as *animals* invites a long list of ways they can be divided: wild animals, work animals, pets; ones that swim, run, crawl; ones you have owned, seen, or read about. These groups imply principles for division—by degree of domesticity, by manner of locomotion, by degree of familiarity. Division and classification often help define each other in that having divided your subject, you may find that once you start classifying, you have to stop and redefine your principle of division. If your division of animals is based on locomotion, for instance, where do you put the flying squirrel?

Division and classification is often used at the level of the paragraph. If your essay argues that a particular television commercial for toilet cleaner insults women, you might want to introduce the essay by enumerating other advertisements in that category—household products—that also insult women's intelligence.

From Julius Caesar's "Gaul is divided into three parts" to a 10-year-old's "animal, vegetable, or mineral," classification and division has had a long and useful history. And, of course, it has a useful present as well. You will see that in each of the essays in this chapter, the system of division and classification supports a thesis, though the essays use their theses for different purposes: to entertain, to explain, to argue.

AUDIENCE AND PURPOSE   Knowing who your readers are and what effect you want to have on them will help you devise your system of classification and sharpen your thesis. If your audience is quite specific, Penelope Green's essay, "The Roots of Rock," should be a useful model, for it is aimed at a specific audience, those who know contemporary rock groups. Drawing on her readers' familiarity with MTV and the visual appearance of rock stars, she invents a system of classification for their hairstyles and then tests it out on experts. Their description, added to hers, allows even those readers who have never watched MTV to follow the principle behind her system and to see the results.

Writers who address a more general audience also need to know their audiences. In Russell Baker's "The Plot Against People," for example, his reader is the average human whose car breaks down, whose keys get lost, and whose flashlight rarely works. Baker proposes a theory that makes sense out of this chaos; he divides objects into three categories: "those that don't work, those that break down, and those that get lost." The principle behind Baker's sorting of inanimate objects is the method each uses to achieve its aim: "to resist man and ultimately to defeat him." Furnaces, pliers, barometers, keys, and various other objects are classified according to their method of waging war. Ostensibly, Baker is writing to inform; but because the reader readily recognizes the absurdity of Baker's system and his ironic tone, his true purpose is to entertain. That, too, is the main purpose behind the essays by Green and Telander, though both also have an informative aim as well. After all, it would be news to many of us that the neo-nihilist look is in and that the Banana Slugs had a bad basketball season.

To explain, however, is the more obvious use of division and classification. Jeff Greenfield informs his readers. In writing about the significance of cable television, however, he also argues that it has become the viewers' first choice.

SYSTEM OF CLASSIFICATION   To work effectively, a system of classification must be complete and logical. The system that governs how goods are arranged in a supermarket needs to be broad enough to cover everything a supermarket might sell, and it needs to make sense. Can openers should be with kitchen implements, not vegetables; cans of peas should be with other canned goods, not milk. Rick Telander, for instance, first divides the nicknames of athletic teams into beasts and non-beasts and then further subdivides the beasts according to the reasons that lie behind the choice of individual names: predators are associated with aggression, unlikely animals can be chosen for their not so obvious qualities, some creatures symbolize a bit of the school's history, and at least one name implies the seriousness with which the school takes sports. Like Telander, you may want to point to a category that doesn't quite fit. Is the golden gopher, the source of nickname for the University of Minnesota team, a fearsome and vicious creature? More likely, however, you will find some overlap among classes. This overlap can be accounted for by explaining it or by adjusting the system of division. Russell Baker, for example, writes of a world of willful inanimate objects and places women's purses in the category of "things that get lost." He notes that although the purse "does have some inherent capacity for breaking down, [it] hardly ever does; it almost invariably chooses to get lost."

Baker's categories exemplify a complete system, though it is humorously exaggerated. Just about all inanimate objects one might care about do have a habit of breaking down, getting lost, or not working. Baker pokes fun at the logic of his system, pointing out that furnaces break down with some frequency, but will never get lost. And just in case the reader may think that breaking down and not working are similar, Baker goes to some trouble to show the difference: the things we expect to work, do, but then break down; the things we expect not to work, don't, except perhaps the first time.

EXAMPLE   Examples are essential to classification, usually in the form of multiple illustrations. To explain why cable TV programming is favored by millions, Greenfield gives examples for each category of cable program. Sports, for instance, becomes "Larry Bird's classic steal of Isiah Thomas's inbounds pass in the fifth game of the Eastern Conference finals"; MTV turns into the "newest offerings of U2, Bryan Adams or Bon Jovi." Rick Telander's examples strike a more humorous note. It's bad enough that the Ohio State team is named after a seed, but how about some of those high school teams—the Teutopolis Wooden Shoes, the Effingham Flaming Hearts, the Centralia Orphans, the Hoopeston Cornjerkers?

THESIS AND ORGANIZATION   Essays structured by division and classification are usually organized simply and have a clear-cut thesis. All the essays use a straightforward pattern of organization. "Fight! Fauna Fight!" takes some liberties with the body of the essay in that Telander devotes the middle to his system of classification but includes some asides; his categories do not receive equal time. "The Plot Against People" and "Life Without Cable? No Way!" follow the classic method of development for division and classification essays, with the body of the paper devoted to developing the various categories involved in the author's system of classification. Two of these essays also have the most easily spotted kind of thesis, one that is made up of various explicit statements contained in the essay.

*F*ight! Fauna Fight!

Rick Telander

What's in a name? A lot if you're an athlete on a team, says Rick Telander, a senior staff writer for Sports Illustrated. *Playing for the Jaguars or the Lions may make you feel fast and strong, but how would you feel if your team were named the Fighting Camels or the Moles? Telander explores the associations behind these names and others in this 1989 essay, which appeared, appropriately enough, in* National Wildlife, *a publication of the National Wildlife Federation.*

1   I started my sports career as a Colt, which seemed fitting to me since I was 11 years old and gawky as a newborn foal. I was a member of the fifth- and sixth-grade basketball team at Kellar Grade School in Peoria, Illinois, and I remember how revved up I'd get in games when the dozen or so Kellar fans in the stands would yell, "Go, Colts, go!"

2   Right then I knew that a school's nickname is more than an arbitrary tag handed down to its teams by bored administrators. A nickname is an identity. I was a Colt. I was frisky and goofy and big-footed. And I sensed that animal nicknames are the most appropriate monikers for sports teams. Why? Because, well, athletes can gain more inspiration from beasts than they can from, say, Wind or Fire or Earthquakes or Hoyas or Hoosiers or Tarheels.

3   When the game's on the line, there's nothing like being an Eagle (the most popular nickname in college sports). Or a Tiger (number two) or a Cougar (number three) or a Bulldog (number four) or Lions, Panthers, or Wildcats. Strong and ferocious, these animals motivate. In the clutch you have to pity the poor jock who is a Rambling Wreck (from Georgia Tech) or a Rambler (Loyola, Chicago) or a Fighting Irishman (Notre Dame). A common Wildcat will eat those dudes up in a flash.

4   As it happened, I was a football Wildcat in college (Northwestern), and we played Notre Dame. And, okay, we had our whiskers handed to us on a platter. But even in defeat I felt pity for those poor victorious, golden-helmeted wretches who were led by a leprechaun. I mean, how tough can you be when your mascot wears tights and buckled shoes?

We Wildcats also played Ohio State. Okay, we lost to them too.   5
But I sneered as we left Columbus. The big, bad Buckeyes? Hah!
Those guys are actually named after a seed.

Members of the animal kingdom are what fascinate and propel   6
us, particularly those predators that embody aggression, pride and
invincibility. Ah, to soar like a Hawk (St. Joseph's University, Philadelphia), to attack like a pack of Wolves (North Carolina State
University). Which makes one wonder about the University of Iowa,
whose teams are called the Hawkeyes. Darwin had a "problem"
with eyes while working out his theory of evolution. How, he wondered, could such a complex instrument, useless unless completely
formed, simply evolve? Moreover, why name your teams after an
organ? What's wrong with the rest of the bird?

And then there are the University of Minnesota Golden Gophers.   7
What's the point here? Does the adjective *golden* somehow make
these burrowing rodents fierce? Or does the school see itself as a
"digger" for knowledge and its teams as relentless destroyers of golf
courses?

When I reached high school, I was stunned by the names of my   8
team's opponents. The Canton Little Giants. The Farmington Farmers. The Morton Potters. We couldn't take any of them seriously, and
we crushed them all. Illinois high schools are rife with oddball
nicknames—the Teutopolis Wooden Shoes, the Effingham Flaming
Hearts, the Centralia Orphans, the Hoopeston Cornjerkers—which
may or may not have something to do with the creativity of folks
staring off at endless fields of grain. But I do know that during my
senior year in high school, the neighboring Pekin Chinks (which
were renamed the Dragons in 1980) played the downstate Cobden
Appleknockers for the state championship.

But back to animals. Teams at both the University of Missouri at   9
Kansas City and Austin (Texas) College are called the Kangaroos.
Most people find this mascot a funny choice, but not me. A healthy
'roo could kick a football through a wall and dunk a basketball with
its tail. And think of the possibilities for school sportswriters: "Kangaroos Bounce Back," "Marsupials Pouch State."

Indeed, the basic animal mascots—usually large, furry carni-   10
vores—can get a little boring. That makes the unusual ones—the
University of Richmond Spiders, the Campbell (North Carolina) University Fighting Camels, the Texas Christian Horned Frogs, for instance—stand out like, well, elephants. Or Jumbos, as they're called

at Tufts University. Why Jumbos? Because P. T. Barnum was a trustee of the college and when his circus pachyderm Jumbo died in 1885, he had it stuffed and put on display at the school. The students took a shine to the critter, adopted its name for their teams and continue to use it even though the beast itself burned in a fire 14 years ago.

11   Other top nicknames include the Bowdoin (Maine) College Polar Bears, Temple University Owls and Pittsburg (Kansas) State Gorillas. A word about the latter two. The owl became the mascot for Temple because the college was started in the late 1800s as a night school. An owl likes the dark, but it also, as the school notes in a press release, "is the symbol of Athena, not only goddess of wisdom, but also goddess of arts, skills and even warfare." Clearly, a well-rounded bird.

12   The gorilla of Pittsburg State, on the other hand, is more of a one-dimensional party animal. It was adopted as the school mascot in 1925 after a group of wild, whooping students led by Harold "Babe" Alyea organized themselves as the Gorillas to "accelerate college spirit and enthusiasm until it shall permeate the State." The gang's motto: "We want PEP and we want it all the time." Get down, Gorillas!

13   You also have to like the Nazareth (Kalamazoo, Michigan) College Moles. The name was adopted because the campus buildings are connected by tunnels. One envisions Nazareth athletes as being nearsighted and not prone to turning little sports problems into, well, mountains.

14   And then there are the Banana Slugs, everybody's favorite gang. The Slugs are the mascot for the University of California, Santa Cruz (UCSC), which adopted the name in 1986, thereby shoving the University of California, Irvine, and its proud Anteaters into nickname shadows.

15   A real banana slug is a small, pale mollusk that lives near redwood trees and eats almost anything. As a rallying point for a team, it ranks right up with the amoeba. UCSC Chancellor Robert Sinsheimer was opposed to the mascot proposal, decrying the animal as "spineless, yellow, sluggish and slimy." Economics professor David Kaun countered by praising the slug as "flexible, golden and deliberate."

16   UCSC students sided with the professor and voted the creature in; once they watched as their NCAA Division III basketball team players crawled onto the court in yellow warmups with antennae pro-

truding from their hoods. At the time, the last member of the team pulled a trail of clear cellophane behind him. That, I assume, represented slime.

The animal kingdom is full of fine and glorious creatures, almost   17
any of which could inspire a team more than a banana slug. But like every beast, the slug has its enviable traits. The slow-moving UCSC hoopsters may have gone 7–19 last season, but consider: is there a team anywhere better at leaving its mark?

Thesis and Organization

1. The essay begins with a brief narrative. What expectations does it set up about the essay that will follow?
2. Paragraph 2 suggests a working thesis. What is it?
3. The last sentence of paragraph 2 provides a division between kinds of names. What is it? What principle is involved?
4. Given that division, what paragraphs cluster around what characteristics
5. The essay concludes with a pun. Consider the tentative thesis you identified and the ending pun. What do you deduce as the thesis of the essay?

Technique and Style

1. How would you further characterize the author's humorous tone? Is he sarcastic? Ironic? Bemused? Is the humor of the giggle or gut-buster variety or somewhere in between? Explain.
2. What examples of slang can you find? Of elevated language? What effects does the author achieve by mixing the two?
3. The essay has a strong sense of voice, which is to say that the personality of the author comes through clearly. What does Telander reveal about himself? Does what he tells you add to or detract from the essay? Explain.
4. Where in the essay do you get a sense that the author separates himself from the reader? What effect does that achieve?
5. Much of the essay's humor depends on contrast. Select several examples for each of Telander's divisions. How effective is the contrast?

Suggestions for Writing

Try taking an unusual topic and dividing it into categories. Suggestions: excuses, blind dates, spaghetti eaters, soft drinks, video game addicts. Assume a definite personality, such as that of a pseudopsychologist, dating-service manager, self-styled gourmet, or Olympic trainer.

The Roots of Rock

Penelope Green

If you've ever wondered about the hairstyles of rock musicians, wonder no more. Penelope Green explains it all. The essay that follows appeared as one of her regular columns, "Beauty," in the New York Times Magazine *(1991).*

1   "Almost cut my hair," David Crosby sang 20 years ago. What a tease: Crosby, albeit a little bigger, a little older, is hanging on to what's left of his hair as if it still meant something. It certainly used to. In the late 1960s, the rocker with hair below the ears was a remarkably effective symbol of dissent against everything from the Tet Offensive to Mom. But these days, Crosby's straggly head is just that: a straggly head, completely devoid of its original social import. For while the hair of a nineties musician is still a kind of political statement, the politics may be a tad closer to Madison Avenue than Kent State. In other words, radical hair sells records.

2   "Hair, image, or an unusual look can certainly draw more attention to an act in this MTV era," says Tim Devine, a vice president at Capitol Records. "But no matter how much time an artist spends in front of the mirror, it doesn't make bad music good." True, Sinead O'Connor and Madonna are more than the sum of their locks—or lack thereof. But, what about Rob Pilatus and Fab Morvan, better known as Milli Vanilli, who scored a Grammy partly on the strength of their hair moves? "When I first saw them I thought, 'Hey, look at the black Bo Dereks!' " says Ademola Mandela, who runs Kinapps, a salon specializing in African-American hair. "They weren't even appropriating an African look." (For the record, those are hair extensions, not dreadlocks.)

3   But they're old news anyway. The current crop of MTV heads breaks down into four distinct (and far more interesting) looks: the neo-nihilist, the glitter-rock, the house-girl and the royal-rapper. We've asked four social commentators—Michael Musto, the night-life columnist for the *Village Voice,* Walter Thomas, a copywriter at the Arnell/Bickford advertising agency, Naomi Wolf, the author of *The Beauty Myth,* to be published by William Morrow in April, and

Ademola Mandela, the hair stylist—to give us their reading on the following headliners.

Robert Smith of the Cure: The neo-nihilist look. We're talking 4 lots of hair spray, lots of angst and a nice model for Edward Scissorhands.

Musto: Oh my God, the lawn mower look. It's everyone's dream 5 to keep your hair the way it looks when you wake up in the morning, and Smith has elevated that to an art form.

Wolf: I like the idea of men playing with gender roles, with 6 makeup. It shows that they are accepting that they are the object of the gaze, be it male or female.

No comment from Thomas and Mandela. 7

Ann and Nancy Wilson of Heart: The time-warp, glitter-rock 8 look. Even if the hair is completely anachronistic, it's got pan-gender appeal that just won't go away. (Look at Whitesnake.)

Musto: Ann's hair is designed to camouflage her face. I think she's 9 lovely, and she should stop doing her hair that way. Nancy's is that 1970s "Charlie's Angels" do, ripe for a comeback.

Wolf: To be a woman musician, especially an older woman, you 10 have to blot out your features, your life experiences and your body type.

Thomas: These two desperately need a seventies bypass opera- 11 tion. Let's give the shag its right to die.

Mandela: I love the commitment of the look. It's old and trying to 12 look young and not really doing the right thing. Somehow, the awkwardness is endearing.

Lady Miss Kier of Deee-Lite: The house girl. If you take the 13 idea of house music into the realm of the visual, Kier's neo-psychedelic look becomes a kind of image sampling of the past 20 years (not just a 1960s rip-off, as some have charged).

Musto: I just worry that the headband is on too tight—not on 14 Kier, but on her followers.

Wolf: This is a look that's about infantilism, about the days before 15 *Roe* v. *Wade*. I see the current retro fad as a way to hold back the implications of women's achievements, to assure the status quo.

Thomas: The whole look—especially the two male accesso- 16 ries—is as fierce as the wigs she lives in.

Mandela: She has a wonderful, strong spirit. I only wish her 17 esthetics were as strong. (Kier, by the way, does her part for conservation, washing her hair just twice a week, to avoid major suds and the solid waste generated by too many empty shampoo bottles.)

18   **Queen Latifah:** The Royal Rapper is giving rap a feministic spin, if you go by such tracks as "Ladies First." Latifah eschews hair altogether, using instead a succession of regal headdresses.

19   Musto: No comment.

20   Wolf: I'm not comfortable speaking about her look, because I'm not black.

21   Mandela: It's not hair, it's a crown. It shows the inherent royalty of the African look. It's quite a responsibility to call yourself a queen, and Latifah is living up to it.

22   Thomas: Forget the hair club, she's the Mad Hatter of rap.

Thesis and Organization

1. Paragraph 1 compares and contrasts the 1960s to the 1990s. What is the point of the comparison? What do you anticipate as the thesis of the essay?
2. What is the relationship of paragraph 2 to the last sentence of paragraph 1?
3. Paragraph 3 sets out the organization of the paragraphs that follow. To what extent does it adequately prepare you for the rest of the essay?
4. Paragraphs 4–22 rely on example and description. What subjects are the paragraphs clustered around?
5. The last paragraph lumps together a continuation of the pattern of organization and a conclusion. To what extent does that last paragraph satisfactorily end the essay?

Technique and Style

1. How would you characterize the author's diction? What examples can you find of varying levels of diction? What effect do they achieve?
2. Green uses direct quotation to present the views of her experts. Is the essay made stronger or weaker by her using only direct quotation? How so?
3. The essay is full of details in the form of names. What does the author achieve by bringing in so many allusions?
4. Consult your handbook to see what it says about the use of parentheses. To what extent does Green's use of parentheses conform? What effect do the parentheses achieve?

5. Green relies upon the same pattern of organization to present her four categories. To what extent do you find that predictability a strength or a weakness? Explain.

Suggestions for Writing

Think of the experts you know, experts on anything from the specialized to the ordinary. Perhaps you work with people who are quite knowledgeable on some aspect of the business, but experts can also be thought of as people who have insight into the ordinary: baby-sitting, shopping, studying, playing a particular sport. Think too of what these people are experts on and how that topic can be broken down into categories.

The Plot Against People

Russell Baker

Russell Baker has discovered the principles behind the continuing battle between humans and inanimate objects. He discusses these principles as he neatly divides things into three categories and then places objects into his classifications. The author of several collections of essays and an autobiography, Russell Baker has a syndicated column that also appears as a regular feature in the New York Times, *where this essay was published in 1968.*

1   Inanimate objects are classified into three major categories—those that don't work, those that break down and those that get lost.

2   The goal of all inanimate objects is to resist man and ultimately to defeat him, and the three major classifications are based on the method each object uses to achieve its purpose. As a general rule, any object capable of breaking down at the moment when it is most needed will do so. The automobile is typical of the category.

3   With the cunning typical of its breed, the automobile never breaks down while entering a filling station with a large staff of idle mechanics. It waits until it reaches a downtown intersection in the middle of the rush hour, or until it is fully loaded with family and luggage on the Ohio Turnpike.

4   Thus it creates maximum misery, inconvenience, frustration and irritability among its human cargo, thereby reducing its owner's life span.

5   Washing machines, garbage disposals, lawn mowers, light bulbs, automatic laundry dryers, water pipes, furnaces, electrical fuses, television tubes, hose nozzles, tape recorders, slide projectors—all are in league with the automobile to take their turn at breaking down whenever life threatens to flow smoothly for their human enemies.

6   Many inanimate objects, of course, find it extremely difficult to break down. Pliers, for example, and gloves and keys are almost totally incapable of breaking down. Therefore, they have had to evolve a different technique for resisting man.

7   They get lost. Science has still not solved the mystery of how they do it, and no man has ever caught one of them in the act of getting

lost. The most plausible theory is that they have developed a secret method of locomotion which they are able to conceal the instant a human eye falls upon them.

It is not uncommon for a pair of pliers to climb all the way from the cellar to the attic in its single-minded determination to raise its owner's blood pressure. Keys have been known to burrow three feet under mattresses. Women's purses, despite their great weight, frequently travel through six or seven rooms to find hiding space under a couch. 8

Scientists have been struck by the fact that things that break down virtually never get lost, while things that get lost hardly ever break down. 9

A furnace, for example, will invariably break down at the depth of the first winter cold wave, but it will never get lost. A woman's purse, which after all does have some inherent capacity for breaking down, hardly ever does; it almost invariably chooses to get lost. 10

Some persons believe this constitutes evidence that inanimate objects are not entirely hostile to man, and that a negotiated peace is possible. After all, they point out, a furnace could infuriate a man even more thoroughly by getting lost than by breaking down, just as a glove could upset him far more by breaking down than by getting lost. 11

Not everyone agrees, however, that this indicates a conciliatory attitude among inanimate objects. Many say it merely proves that furnaces, gloves and pliers are incredibly stupid. 12

The third class of objects—those that don't work—is the most curious of all. These include such objects as barometers, car clocks, cigarette lighters, flashlights, and toy train locomotives. It is inaccurate, of course, to say that they never work. They work once, usually for the first few hours after being brought home, and then quit. Thereafter, they never work again. 13

In fact, it is widely assumed that they are built for the purpose of not working. Some people have reached advanced ages without ever seeing some of these objects—barometers, for example—in working order. 14

Science is utterly baffled by the entire category. There are many theories about it. The most interesting holds that the things that don't work have attained the highest state possible for an inanimate object, the state to which things that break down and things that get lost can still only aspire. 15

16   They have truly defeated man by conditioning him never to expect anything of them, and in return they have given man the only peace he receives from inanimate society. He does not expect his barometer to work, his electric locomotive to run, his cigarette lighter to light or his flashlight to illuminate, and when they don't, it does not raise his blood pressure.

17   He cannot attain that peace with furnaces and keys and cars and women's purses as long as he demands that they work for their keep.

Thesis and Organization

1. In what ways does the introduction, paragraphs 1–2, set up both the system of classification and the major principle at work among inanimate objects?
2. Paragraphs 3–6 explain the first category. What effects does the automobile achieve by breaking down? How do those effects support Baker's contention about "the goal of all inanimate objects"? What other examples does Baker put into his first category? What example does not fit?
3. Paragraphs 7–12 present the second classification. What causes, reasons, or motives are attributed to the examples in this group?
4. Paragraphs 13–16 describe the third group. What are its qualities? Why might Baker have chosen to list it last? What principle of organization can you discern beneath Baker's ordering of the three groups?
5. Consider how each group frustrates and defeats people together with the first sentence of paragraph 2. Combine this information into a sentence that states the author's thesis.

Technique and Style

1. In part, the essay's humor arises from Baker's use of anthropomorphism, his technique of attributing human qualities to inanimate objects. How effectively does he use the technique?
2. Baker has a keen eye for the absurd, as illustrated by paragraph 10. What other examples can you find? What does this technique contribute to the essay?
3. Baker's stance, tone, and line of reasoning, while patently tongue-in-cheek, are also mock-scientific. Where can you find examples of Baker's explicit or implied "scientific" trappings?
4. The essay's transitions are carefully wrought. What links paragraph 3 to paragraph 2? Paragraph 7 to paragraph 6? Paragraph 10 to paragraph 9? Paragraph 12 to paragraph 11?

5. How an essay achieves unity is a more subtle thing. What links paragraph 8 to paragraph 6? Paragraph 9 to paragraphs 3–6? Paragraph 16 to paragraph 2? Paragraph 17 to paragraphs 10–12 and paragraphs 3–5?

Suggestions for Writing

Write your own "plot" essay, imagining something else plotting against people. Suggestions: clothes, food, pets, the weather, plants, traffic. Take a "scientific" stance.

*L*ife Without Cable? No Way!

Jeff Greenfield

For someone who lives in the country without benefit of a satellite dish, the information in Jeff Greenfield's essay may come as a surprise. As for those who are plugged into cable, they may not agree that it has become their "leisure-time lifeline." Jeff Greenfield's essays appear in numerous magazines, but this piece, as you might suspect, appeared in TV Guide. *It was published in 1987, just as cable television started to dominate the airwaves.*

1   Back in 1950, when television was still a new and expensive plaything, America's Television Dealers and Manufacturers Association asked the country's guilt-ridden parents:

2   "Can you deny television to your children any longer? Youngsters today need television for their morale as much as they need fresh air and sunshine for their health."

3   Whether the tube is more comparable to "fresh air and sunshine" or to smog, few would deny that TV today is a necessity rather than a luxury. Bankrupts, families on public assistance, even prisoners are provided access to the tube. The presence of television in a home is no more an indication of affluence than is a telephone or indoor plumbing.

4   Now, it seems, another device may be making a bid for inclusion as one of the necessities of life: cable television. Odd as that may seem to those of us who can remember when cable was just a futuristic promise, the importance of cable—at least, to a household that cares about being plugged into the national conversation—can no longer be denied.

5   First, some basic facts. The A. C. Nielsen Company tells us that, as of last May, 49.2 percent of all TV households were wired for cable; sometime before this year is out, that number is going to pass 50 percent. In other words, by New Year's Eve, cable will be the norm in America.

6   And, because so many cable subscribers have access to so many

channels—62 percent of subscribers get between 30 and 53 of them—it means the *average American TV home now receives 20 channels.*

And what's on these channels? Here's where the impact of cable really becomes telling. For a wide variety of tastes, cable has become not some amusing diversion, but the choice of first resort.

Consider sports, one of the first and most enduring attractions of television. A devoted follower of NBA basketball could have watched regular-season and most of the play-off action on superstation WTBS. If you weren't wired for cable, you probably didn't see Larry Bird's classic steal of Isiah Thomas's inbounds pass in the fifth game of the Eastern Conference finals.

If you wanted to see the live heavyweight boxing duel between Mike Tyson and Tony Tucker, you were out of luck unless you were a Home Box Office subscriber.

If hockey is your glass of iced tea, you didn't see any of the NHL playoffs unless your cable system carried ESPN. (Or unless you lived in a city with a team in contention.) ESPN also carried virtually all the tennis action of the French Open until the finals.

Even baseball, once a staple of broadcast television, has been steadily moving over to the cable arena. Earlier this spring, New Yorkers were shocked to discover that half of the Mets' games, and well over half of the Yankees', were available only on a pay-cable channel. And, beginning this fall, eight Sunday night National Football League games will be telecast on ESPN.

Sports, however, is only one part of the picture. Parental concern over the quality of children's television has been with us since the first cries of "Howdy Doody!" 40 years ago. The commercial broadcast networks now confine their kids' programming to Saturday mornings and occasional afternoon specials, and local stations seem content with "He-Man and the Masters of the Universe" and the like. Public TV has cornered the market on "uplifting" fare such as "Sesame Street" and "Square One TV."

But where do you turn for good, clean kids' entertainment? Nickelodeon is a basic-cable service programming for kids from morning until early evening. The Disney Channel is a pay service from the company that just about invented mass entertainment for kids. And for years the only place to find Jim Henson's "Fraggle Rock" was on HBO.

And what happens when junior turns adolescent? MTV seems to

have taken permanent hold on the affections of the leaders of to-morrow. Thirty years ago, my friends and I did our homework to the sounds of pioneer rock-and-roll disk jockey Alan Freed. Now—if my daughter and her friends are any judges—teenagers' homework is done by the light of music videos, with a telephone nearby to exchange delight over the newest offerings of U2, Bryan Adams or Bon Jovi. Indeed, so instinctive is my daughter's resort to MTV that I have had difficulty convincing her that the network's "24 hours-a-day" operation doesn't mean it has to be on 24 hours a day in *our* house.

15   Of course, once my daughter becomes an adult, she may trade her obsession with rock music for her father's obsession with politics and public policy. In this arena, cable has become even more of a necessity. A news junkie who was home in the middle of the afternoon once had to be content with hourly radio summaries or, possibly, all-news radio. Today, Cable News Network provides two 24-hour-a-day operations: the long-form CNN, and the Headline News service.

16   For the addict of politics, no cable service is more compelling than C-SPAN, the Cable Satellite Public Affairs Network. Apart from its coverage of the House and Senate floors, C-SPAN brings its cameras to just about every committee hearing, press conference, convention and candidate appearance imaginable.

17   For anyone who really wants to keep up with the 1988 presidential campaign, C-SPAN's "Road to the White House" is a pearl of incalculable price: each week, the network runs—complete and uncut—the speeches and appearances of presidential hopefuls across the continent. In one 90-minute chunk, I can watch Bob Dole work the tables at a luncheon in Des Moines, Iowa; Joe Biden answer questions at a kaffeeklatsch in Concord, New Hampshire; and Paul Simon react to Gary Hart's withdrawal on the steps of a town house in Washington, D.C.

18   And for the truly trendy among us, a working familiarity with the latest uncensored comedy routines of a Sam Kinison or a Garry Shandling is as important as it once was to have seen Milton Berle's latest evening gowns.

19   To be sure, there are huge chunks of cable TV programming that most viewers may well classify as unmistakable wastes of time. The vaunted "public access" channels, at least on my system, are programmed mostly by ego-trippers, charlatans, and would-be show-

business personalities whose talents are smaller than their audiences. The explosion in home-shopping channels has already made the cubic zirconia a national laughingstock.

More significantly, the rise of the VCR has made the pay movie   20
channels much less significant as viewer alternatives. With video-
rental stores as commonplace as hamburger joints, a viewer has the choice among hundreds of possibilities, rather than having to rely on whatever HBO or Showtime happens to be airing.

Overall, however, the impact of cable is undeniable. No, it has   21
not revolutionized American TV. Yes, it does offer programming that is more or less more of the same. But in one key sense, it has fulfilled one of its original promises: by providing an abundance of channels, cable has made it possible to deliver fare that could not find a place on broadcast outlets, but that is immensely appealing to minority audiences. Taken together, those minorities add up to mil-lions of viewers for whom cable has become a leisure-time lifeline.

Thesis and Organization

1. Greenfield's introduction (1–7) sets out a number of assertions. What are they? How do the facts he presents relate to them? Which assertion is the most important to the essay?
2. The author divides his subject—TV programming—into cable and non-cable. How does the introduction relate to that division?
3. The body of the essay (8–19) is devoted to categories of programming. What are they? What does Greenfield achieve by providing examples within each category?
4. Although paragraphs 8–11 focus on a type of show, paragraphs 12–17 focus on different audiences. What principle does Greenfield point out that covers both? Argue that he does not change his principle of classi-fication.
5. Consider the last sentence of paragraph 7 and the last sentence of para-graph 21. In your own words, state Greenfield's thesis. How is his system of classification related to that thesis?

Technique and Style

1. Greenfield occasionally uses a question to begin a new paragraph (7, 13, 14). How are those questions linked to the paragraphs that precede them? Does each question receive an answer? What does this use of questions suggest about the author's tone? His sense of audience?

2. Throughout the essay, Greenfield is careful to back up his statements with contemporary examples, thus lending a sense of the present to the essay. This essay was published in 1987, and some of his illustrations are now dated. To what extent does that fact undercut the essay's impact? How would you update it?

3. How would you characterize Greenfield's overall level of diction? What different levels does he use? What does his choice of diction imply about his audience?

4. Jeff Greenfield is both an ABC News analyst and a syndicated columnist. In what ways do those roles match the personality he projects in this essay? How do they differ?

5. Rewrite the second to the last sentence of the essay in two different ways, both of which do not use a colon. What differences do you note? What is better and why?

Suggestions for Writing

Consider other subjects that lend themselves to being divided by changes in technology: kitchen gadgets, automobile accessories, stereo equipment, cameras, sports gear, games, and the like. Select an area you are familiar with and see if you can find a dividing line between the simple and the complex, keeping in mind that that line may be drawn by a technological advance, by popularity, or by time. Next list the items that fall into the contemporary category. The differences and similarities among those items will lead you to the principle behind their groupings.

Exploring the Topic

1. **How can your topic be divided?** What divisions can apply? Of those you list, which one is the best suited?
2. **What examples can you think of?** What characteristics do your examples have in common? Which do you have the most to say about?
3. **Are your categories for classification appropriate?** Are the categories parallel? Do they overlap? Do you need to make any adjustments?
4. **Do your examples fit your categories?** Are you sure the examples have enough in common? Are they obvious? Which are not?
5. **What is your principle for classification?** Have you applied it consistently to each category?
6. **Are your categories complete?** Do they cover the topic? Do they contain enough examples?
7. **How can your categories be sequenced?** From simple to complex? Least to most important? Less to most effective?
8. **What is your point?** What assertion are you making? Does your system of classification support it? Are your examples appropriate?
9. **What is your purpose?** Are you primarily making your point to express your feelings, to inform, to persuade, to entertain?

Drafting the Paper

1. **Know your reader.** Where does your reader fit in relation to your system of classification? Is the reader part of it? If so, how? If the reader is not part of your system, is he or she on your side, say a fellow student looking at teachers? What does your audience know about your topic? About your system of classification? What does the reader not know? Your audience might be biased toward or against your subject and classification system. How can you best foster or combat the bias?
2. **Know your purpose.** If your primary purpose is to express your feelings, make sure that you are not just writing to yourself and that you are not treading on the toes of your audience. Similarly, if you are writing to persuade, make sure you are not convincing only yourself. Check to see that you are using material that may convince someone who disagrees with you—or at the least is either sitting on the fence or hasn't given the matter much thought. Writing to inform is probably the easiest here, for though your subject may be familiar, your system of classification is probably new. On the other hand, writing to entertain is difficult and will require a deft use of persona.

3. **Set up your system of classification early in the paper.** You may find that a definition is in order or that some background information is necessary, but make your system clear and bring it out early.

4. **Explain the principle behind the system.** To give your system credibility, you need to provide an explanation for the means of selection you chose. The explanation can be brief, a phrase or two, but it should be there.

5. **Select appropriate examples.** Perhaps you can best illustrate a class by one extended example, or maybe it would be better to pile on examples. If your examples are apt to be unfamiliar to your audience, make sure you give enough detail so that they are explained by their contexts.

6. **Make a point.** Remember that what you have to say about your subject is infinitely more interesting than the subject itself. So, too, your major assertion is more important than your system of classification; it is what your system of classification adds up to. It's easy, in writing this kind of paper, to mistake the means for the end, so make sure that you use classification to support an overall assertion.

Comparison and Contrast

hat's the difference" gets at the heart of comparison and contrast, and it is a question that can fit into any context. In college, it often turns up in the form of essay questions; in day-to-day life, it implies the process behind most decisions: "What shall I wear?" "Which movie will I see?" "Should I change jobs?" All these questions involve choices that draw upon comparison and contrast. Like description, narration, example, classification, comparison and contrast forces you to observe, but here you are looking for similarities and differences. In a way, comparison and contrast is the simplest form of division and classification in that you are examining only two categories, or perhaps only one example from the two categories. "Which sounds better, tapes or records?" compares two categories; "Which sounds better, compact discs or records?" compares two items in the same category.

No matter what you select, however, you need to be sure that the comparison is fair. Deciding where to go out to dinner often depends on how much you are willing to spend, so comparing a fast-food place to an elegant French restaurant doesn't appear to have much of a point. If neither is worth the money, however, you have an assertion to work from, but you have to work carefully. Sometimes the similarities will not be readily apparent. Huey

Newton and Martin Luther King, Jr., were both African-Americans, and for most of us the similarity ends there. In "Of Prophets and Protesters," however, Robert C. Maynard shows us that many more similarities tie the two together. Both cared deeply about their people and the poor, both were passionate speakers, both affected their generations, both led movements that affected American history, both died violently, both left legacies. There the similarity ends. One was admired, the other despised; one advocated nonviolence, the other violence; one believed in democracy, the other in socialism; one was in the mainstream of the civil rights movement, the other on the radical fringe.

Essays that depend primarily on other modes, such as description, narration, and definition, often use comparison and contrast to heighten a difference or clarify a point, but the pieces in this section rely on comparison and contrast as their main principle of organization, even though their purposes differ.

AUDIENCE AND PURPOSE   If you intend to inform your audience, you'll find the essay that follows by Robert C. Maynard useful. Maynard cannot assume that his audience is as familiar with Huey Newton as they are with Martin Luther King, Jr., so he must spell out some details. In doing so and in pondering the similarities and differences of the two figures, Maynard assumes a thoughtful, meditative tone. He distances himself from the two figures so that he sees them for what they stand for instead of the flesh-and-blood people they were.

Shana Alexander also leaves the reader with much to think about, though her satirical tone tips the essay toward persuasion. Along the way to her final point she needs to fill in a lot of gaps, for the reader is apt to know as little about "new-style" funerals in Nashville as old-style justice in New Guinea. The essays by James Gorman and Suzanne Britt, however, are written primarily to entertain, and both have a satirical edge as well. Gorman compares a cairn terrier to a Macintosh computer and in doing so makes the reader take another look at how the computer industry markets its products. So, too, Suzanne Britt's humorous defense of the fat forces us to think again about the values of our culture, even though her essay is fundamentally humorous. Humor and satire turn to irony in Toni Morrison's essay, for it seems to her that we live in times when the unthinkable can become reality. Morrison has a serious reason to visit Disneyland: there you know for certain what's really unreal; in the world beyond Disneyland, one is not so sure.

METHOD OF COMPARISON Comparison-and-contrast essays group information so that the comparison is made by blocks or point by point. In "Fashions in Funerals," for example, Shana Alexander first discusses a funeral (of sorts) in New Guinea, then the "new-style" funeral that has come to pass in Nashville. Her concluding paragraph brings together the two blocks of information. Robert C. Maynard, however, relies on point-by-point comparison, grouping King and Newton together in paragraphs that make particular points. Outlining an essay readily reveals which type of organization the writer depends on.

OTHER MODES A close look at any of the essays that follow will show how you can use other modes, such as description, narration, and cause and effect, to help flesh out the comparison and contrast. In "On to Disneyland and Real Unreality," Toni Morrison relies heavily on narration and example to clarify and emphasize her comparisons. In "That Lean and Hungry Look," for example, Suzanne Britt relies heavily on description and example to clarify her comparisons, and she adds narration to give credibility to her assertions. On the other hand, Robert C. Maynard's analysis of Huey Newton and Martin Luther King, Jr., employs cause and effect. What was it about these men, Maynard wonders, that so influenced the course of American history? What do their very different lives have in common?

THESIS AND ORGANIZATION The one-sentence thesis placed at the end of an introductory paragraph certainly informs the reader of your subject and stance, but you might find your paper more effective if you treat your thesis more subtly, trying it out in different forms and positions. While some of the essays in this chapter save their major assertion until last, others combine ideas from various points in the essay to form a thesis. In "Fashions in Funerals," "Of Prophets and Protesters," and "On to Disneyland and Real Unreality," each author builds to a final point that is the essay's explicit or implied thesis. Suzanne Britt, however, weaves bits and pieces of thesis throughout her whole essay, although her thesis is implied. As for James Gorman, the reader will have to decide. His essay's organization, however, is clear-cut.

Fashions in Funerals

Shana Alexander

The jungles of New Guinea are a long way from Nashville, Tennessee, but Shana Alexander compares the funeral customs of the two places to show that two different cultures are perhaps not so far apart after all. The piece was included in Alexander's collection of essays, Talking Woman (*1976*).

1   A man in the remote jungles of New Guinea not long ago murdered another man with an ax. Tribal justice ensued. First the murderer was shot and killed with an arrow, and then seven other members of the tribe cut him up and ate him.

2   When word of the feast reached civilization, the authorities concluded that on this occasion justice had literally been served, and perhaps a bit too swiftly, so they hauled the seven cannibals into court, where a wise Australian judge dismissed all the charges, and acquitted the seven men. "The funerary customs of the people of Papua and New Guinea," he explained, "have been, and in many cases remain, bizarre in the extreme."

3   What, I wonder, would the judge have to say about the new, high-rise mausoleum now under construction in Nashville, Tennessee? When completed, this model of modern funerary design will be twenty stories high, fully air-conditioned, and capable of holding 65,000 bodies. A second slightly less deluxe tower on an adjoining site will have facilities to entomb 63,500 more. Nashville's enterprising mortician entrepreneur points out that his high-rise mortuary will be self-contained on only 14 acres, whereas it would require 129 acres to contain all these caskets in the, uh, conventional manner.

4   Well, not exactly caskets. In the new-style funeral, you will be laid out—after embalming, of course—on something called a "repose," described as a "bedlike structure," complete with white sheets, pillow, and blanket. When the ceremonies are ended, bed, pillow, sheet, and blanket are all whisked away; a fiberglass lid snaps down over what remains; and—zap—it's into the wall, stacked seven-high, with a neat bronze marker attached to the face of the crypt.

5   The forward-looking undertaker who thought all this up is al-

ready respected, in the trade, for bringing to Nashville the one-stop funeral.

But the most important advantage of the high-rise mausoleum is that by putting everything-but-everything under one roof you cut down on the high cost of dying. Maybe so, maybe so. But I can't help thinking it would be even cheaper to die in New Guinea, where the funerary customs are certainly no less bizarre, and a lot more practical.   6

Thesis and Organization

1. Which paragraphs emphasize New Guinea? Which emphasize Nashville? What sentence summarizes the point the author wishes to make about New Guinea?
2. What sentence serves as a transition between New Guinea and Nashville? What sentence summarizes the point the author wishes to make about Nashville?
3. What paragraph covers both New Guinea and Nashville? What sentence presents that paragraph's major assertion? Explain how that sentence is or is not the thesis of the essay.
4. What is Alexander's attitude toward "the new-style funeral"? Is she attempting to persuade the reader to adopt that attitude or is she simply informing the reader about the latest fashion in funerals and making a comment about it? What evidence can you find in the essay to support your view? Has she convinced you of anything? Why or why not?

Technique and Style

1. How would you characterize the author's tone? Is it earnest, lighthearted, sarcastic, ironic, tongue-in-cheek, what? What examples can you find to support your answer? Is the tone effective? Why or why not?
2. Where in the essay does the author use narration? Description? How do those modes support the author's use of comparison and contrast?
3. Why might Alexander have chosen to begin the essay in the third person with an objective point of view? Where and why does she introduce first person? Second person? How does her choice of point of view relate to her thesis?
4. How would you characterize the author's level of diction? Is it colloquial? Conversational? Formal? Fancy? What examples support your view? What relationship do you find between Alexander's tone and her level of diction?

5. Where in the essay does Alexander use fragments? What important parts of speech do those sentences lack? Rewrite the sentences as complete sentences. What is lost? Gained?

Suggestions for Writing

Compare and contrast two fads or fancies from different times or cultures: gold-fish swallowing or flagpole sitting in the 20s versus one of the odder pursuits of today; the Icarus myth versus hang-gliding; tattooing in primitive cultures versus nail polish and lipstick in sophisticated societies; killing enemies with primitive weapons versus killing people you don't even know with cars; polygamous marriage versus serial marriage.

That Lean and Hungry Look

Suzanne Britt

Our culture may worship the "lean and hungry look," but the more fools they, Suzanne Britt implies in her point-by-point comparison of thin people and fat ones. The essay appeared in Newsweek's *"My Turn" column in 1976.*

Caesar was right. Thin people need watching. I've been watching them for most of my adult life, and I don't like what I see. When these narrow fellows spring at me, I quiver to my toes. Thin people come in all personalities, most of them menacing. You've got your "together" thin person, your mechanical thin person, your condescending thin person, your tsk-tsk thin person, your efficiency-expert thin person. All of them are dangerous. 1

In the first place, thin people aren't fun. They don't know how to goof off, at least in the best, fat sense of the word. They've always got to be a-doing. Give them a coffee break, and they'll jog around the block. Supply them with a quiet evening at home, and they'll fix the screen door and lick S&H green stamps. They say things like "there aren't enough hours in the day." Fat people never say that. Fat people think the day is too damn long already. 2

Thin people make me tired. They've got speedy little metabolisms that cause them to bustle briskly. They're forever rubbing their bony hands together and eyeing new problems to "tackle." I like to surround myself with sluggish, inert, easygoing fat people, the kind who believe that if you clean it up today, it'll just get dirty again tomorrow. 3

Some people say the business about the jolly fat person is a myth, that all of us chubbies are neurotic, sick, sad people. I disagree. Fat people may not be chortling all day long, but they're a hell of a lot *nicer* than the wizened and shriveled. Thin people turn surly, mean and hard at a young age because they never learn the value of a hot-fudge sundae for easing tension. Thin people don't like gooey soft things because they themselves are neither gooey nor soft. They are crunchy and dull, like carrots. They go straight to the heart of the matter while fat people let things stay all blurry and hazy and vague, the way things actually are. Thin people want to face the truth. Fat 4 people know there is no truth. One of my thin friends is always staring at complex, unsolvable problems and saying, "The key thing is. . . ." Fat people never say that. They know there isn't any such thing as the key thing about anything.

5   Thin people believe in logic. Fat people see all sides. The sides fat people see are rounded blobs, usually gray, always nebulous and truly not worth worrying about. But the thin person persists. "If you consume more calories than you burn," says one of my thin friends, "you will gain weight. It's that simple." Fat people always grin when they hear statements like that. They know better.

6   Fat people realize that life is illogical and unfair. They know very well that God is not in his heaven and all is not right with the world. If God was up there, fat people could have two doughnuts and a big orange drink anytime they wanted it.

7   Thin people have a long list of logical things they are always spouting off to me. They hold up one finger at a time as they reel off these things, so I won't lose track. They speak slowly as if to a young child. The list is long and full of holes. It contains tidbits like "get a grip on yourself," "cigarettes kill," "cholesterol clogs," "fit as a fiddle," "ducks in a row," "organize" and "sound fiscal management." Phrases like that.

8   They think these 2000-point plans lead to happiness. Fat people know happiness is elusive at best and even if they could get the kind thin people talk about, they wouldn't want it. Wisely, fat people see that such programs are too dull, too hard, too off the mark. They are never better than a whole cheesecake.

9   Fat people know all about the mystery of life. They are the ones acquainted with the night, with luck, with fate, with playing it by ear. One thin person I know once suggested that we arrange all the parts of a jigsaw puzzle into groups according to size, shape and color. He figured this would cut the time needed to complete the puzzle by at least 50 percent. I said I wouldn't do it. One, I like to muddle through. Two, what good would it do to finish early? Three, the jigsaw puzzle isn't the important thing. The important thing is the fun of four people (one thin person included) sitting around a card table, working a jigsaw puzzle. My thin friend had no use for my list. Instead of joining us, he went outside and mulched the boxwoods. The three remaining fat people finished the puzzle and made chocolate, double-fudged brownies to celebrate.

10   The main problem with thin people is they oppress. Their good

intentions, bony torsos, tight ships, neat corners, cerebral machina-
tions and pat solutions loom like dark clouds over the loose, comfortable, spread-out, soft world of the fat. Long after fat people have
removed their coats and shoes and put their feet up on the coffee
table, thin people are still sitting on the edge of the sofa, looking
neat as a pin, discussing rutabagas. Fat people are heavily into fits of
laughter, slapping their thighs and whooping it up, while thin people are still politely waiting for the punch line.

Thin people are downers. They like math and morality and rea-   11
soned evaluation of the limitations of human beings. They have
their skinny little acts together. They expound, prognose, probe and
prick.

Fat people are convivial. They will like you even if you're irreg-   12
ular and have acne. They will come up with a good reason why you
never wrote the great American novel. They will cry in your beer
with you. They will put your name in the pot. They will let you off
the hook. Fat people will grab, giggle, guffaw, gallumph, gyrate and
gossip. They are generous, giving and gallant. They are gluttonous
and goodly and great. What you want when you're down is soft and
jiggly, not muscled and stable. Fat people know this. Fat people
have plenty of room. Fat people will take you in.

Thesis and Organization

1. How does the introduction prepare the reader for the essay's pattern of
   organization? Its tone? Its thesis?
2. Paragraphs 2–5 and 8–10 use point-by-point comparison to support the
   essay's thesis. What point or points are raised in each of those paragraphs?
3. Why might the author change her paragraph structure in paragraphs 6
   and 7 and paragraphs 11 and 12? In each pair of paragraphs, which
   paragraph deals with what type of person? Why might the author have
   chosen to present them in that order? How does the order of paragraphs
   11 and 12 affect Britt's thesis?
4. The thesis of the essay is obvious, but its purpose is somewhat complex.
   The humorous tone of the essay and the author's wordplay suggest that
   the essay's purpose is to entertain, but the author's unusual perspective
   provides the reader with a fresh way of looking at a familiar topic; at the
   same time the reader suspects that underneath the humor there may lurk
   a serious point and a persuasive one. Citing evidence from the essay,
   make a case for what you think is the author's main purpose.

Technique and Style

1. The title of the essay is an allusion that is picked up in the first sentence. What is being alluded to? What other allusion can you spot in paragraph1? In paragraph 9? What do the allusions add to the essay's persona?
2. Britt relies heavily on details to make her points vivid. How many specific details can you find in paragraph 10? What assertion about thin people is supported by details? What assertion about fat people is implied by details?
3. Frequently, the author relies on a short declarative sentence to open a paragraph. What effect does this technique have on the paragraph? On the essay as a whole?
4. Britt achieves her comic effect by taking words at their face value, by putting clichés to use as clichés, and by employing alliteration. Where in the essay do you find examples of these techniques? Choose a sentence that uses one of the techniques and analyze its specific effect. What does it contribute to the thesis and purpose of the essay and to its tone and persona?

Suggestions for Writing

Make a humorous or sarcastic case for the villain instead of the hero; the ordinary instead of the beautiful; the poor instead of the rich; the hungry instead of the fed; the loser instead of the winner.

On to Disneyland and Real Unreality

Toni Morrison

Best known as a fiction writer and in particular for her novel Beloved, *Toni Morrison also writes about times when reality and illusion blur, when Disneyland's fantasy is welcome because it is recognizable. In 1973, when this essay was first published, reality wasn't that easy to find. That was the time of Watergate, the Vietnam War, the bombing of Cambodia, and the Oglala Sioux occupation of Wounded Knee. Perhaps the* New York Times *thinks little has changed; the newspaper reprinted the essay in 1990.*

I have to go to Disneyland. For years when my children begged 1
me to take them, I gave them a nice round of "uh huh" designed to
shut them up. I couldn't explain to them that I saw Snow White and
the Cowardly Lion and the alligators every morning. That there were
no fantasies in California that I had not seen in New York.

It was a mistake. This year especially I have regretted it. For this 2
year fantasy itself lost its genuineness. The normal lines of communication between sham and reality had broken down. The world's
best known black writer discussed his relations with his publisher in
the same terms slaves used to describe their owners. Two of the
most liberated and intelligent women I know talked about their
abortions with the same verbs, the same adjectives, the same nar-
cissism, the same fond recollection with which women of another
generation discussed childbirth. I spent months doing (with 24 times
the money) what my father did in 1935: anguish about how to put
meat on the table. I smelled famine in the world's richest country,
and was told by the privileged to tighten my belt. A 10-year-old
French mulatto responded to being called a dirty black with "I'm not
black, I'm Parisian." Apparently Fanon had never lived; I halluci-
nated him.

Nine years after a white boy spit at my son and accused him of 3
being black, this year a white boy accused him of not being black.
He was confused. "Well," I said, "white people complain a lot. They
use blackness for lots of things—for whatever is going on in the

world. Please don't let them define you. And please don't try to
please them. Whatever they want you to be, chances are they want
it for themselves, not for you."

4   He didn't know what I was talking about and, like not going to
Disneyland, I couldn't explain. But I'm going. The reason I had
refused to go is no longer valid.

5   Too tired? I've never been more exhausted in my life. Not just the
weight of old anger, but an inability to contain the new. Mine is a
tiredness of perception, of strafed ganglia. Anchors float. Bread won't
mold. Children's brains splatter on the walls of "very good" homes.

6   So I want to go to Disneyland where the deceptions are genuine,
where I can see constant unreality, steady illusion. I want to see the
real Snow White dancing among the dirty old men. I want to see the
plastic teeth of real alligators snapping at the hull of my boat. I want
to watch real cowboy murderers kill the same number of people at
the same time every day.

Thesis and Organization

1. What does Morrison mean in paragraph 1 when she says, "I saw Snow
   White and the Cowardly Lion and the alligators every morning . . . there
   were no fantasies in California that I had not seen in New York"?
2. Paragraph 2 implies that what should be a fantasy has become reality.
   Cite the examples Morrison gives and what they contrast.
3. Trace the contrasts in paragraph 3.
4. What does Morrison mean in paragraph 6 by stating Disneyland is a
   place "where the deceptions are genuine"? Given your answer and the
   ideas in paragraph 2, what is the essay's thesis?

Technique and Style

1. Morrison tells you that she is weighted down by "old anger" and her
   "inability to contain the new." To what extent does anger represent her
   tone? If she is not writing out of anger, what are the emotions revealed
   in the essay?
2. Look up *irony* in an unabridged dictionary. What examples can you find
   of Morrison's use of this device?
3. Look up *paradox* in an unabridged dictionary. What part does paradox
   play in the essay?
4. How would you describe the Toni Morrison who is revealed in this
   essay? What does her characterization contribute to the essay's point?

Suggestions for Writing

Think of a time in your experience when reality turned into illusion or illusion became reality. If you have witnessed an event and then seen it reported on television, you may find that the television version has replaced the real one. Or perhaps a book you have read you later saw turned into a film that bore no relation to the reality the book had for you. Or perhaps a real event started to take on elements of unreality.

*M*an, Bytes, Dog

James Gorman

Few people would think of evaluating a dog in terms of the charac-teristics of a computer, but that's what James Gorman does to discover which is man's best friend. This unlikely comparison appeared in the New Yorker *in 1984.*

1   Many people have asked me about the Cairn Terrier. How about memory, they want to know. Is it IBM compatible? Why didn't I get the IBM itself, or a Kaypro, Compaq, or Macintosh? I think the best way to answer these questions is to look at the Macintosh and the Cairn head on. I almost did buy the Macintosh. It has terrific graph-ics, good word-processing capabilities, and the mouse. But in the end I decided on the Cairn, and I think I made the right decision.

2   Let's start out with the basics:

Macintosh
Weight (without printer): 20 lbs.
Memory (RAM): 128 K
Price (with printer): $3,090

Cairn Terrier
Weight (without printer): 14 lbs.
Memory (RAM): Some
Price (without printer): $250

3   Just on the basis of price and weight, the choice is obvious. Another plus is that the Cairn Terrier comes in one unit. No printer is necessary, or useful. And—this was a big attraction to me—there is no user's manual.

4   Here are some of the other qualities I found put the Cairn out ahead of the Macintosh.

5   **Portability:** To give you a better idea of size, Toto in *The Wizard of Oz* was a Cairn Terrier. So you can see that if the young Judy Gar-land was able to carry Toto around in that little picnic basket, you will have no trouble at all moving your Cairn from place to place. For short trips it will move under its own power. The Macintosh will not.

Reliability: In five to ten years, I am sure, the Macintosh will be   6
superseded by a new model, like the Delicious or the Granny Smith.
The Cairn Terrier on the other hand, has held its share of the market
with only minor modifications for hundreds of years. In the short
term, Cairns seldom need servicing, apart from shots and the odd
worming, and most function without interruption during electrical
storms.

Compatibility: Cairn Terriers get along with everyone. And for   7
communications with any other dog, of any breed, within a radius
of three miles, no additional hardware is necessary. All dogs share
a common operating system.

Software: The Cairn will run three standard programs, SIT,   8
COME, and NO, and whatever else you create. It is true that, being
microcanine, the Cairn is limited here, but it does load the programs
instantaneously. No disk drives. No tapes.

Admittedly, these are peripheral advantages. The real compari-   9
son has to be on the basis of capabilities. What can the Macintosh
and the Cairn do? Let's start on the Macintosh's turf—income-tax
preparation, recipe storage, graphics, and astrophysics problems:

	Taxes	Recipes	Graphics	Astrophysics
Macintosh	yes	yes	yes	yes
Cairn	no	no	no	no

At first glance it looks bad for the Cairn. But it's important to look   10
beneath the surface with this kind of chart. If you yourself are
leaning toward the Macintosh, ask yourself these questions: Do you
want to do your own income taxes? Do you want to type all your
recipes into a computer? In your graph, what would you put on the
x axis? The y axis? Do you have any astrophysics problems you want
solved?

Then consider the Cairn's specialties: playing fetch and tug-of-   11
war, licking your face, and chasing foxes out of rock cairns (epony-
mously). Note that no software is necessary. All these functions are
part of the operating system:

	Fetch	Tug-of-war	Face	Foxes
Cairn	yes	yes	yes	yes
Macintosh	no	no	no	no

12   Another point to keep in mind is that computers, even the Macintosh, only do what you tell them to do. Cairns perform their functions all on their own. Here are some of the additional capabilities that I discovered once I got the Cairn home and housebroken:

13   **Word Processing:** Remarkably, the Cairn seems to understand every word I say. He has a nice way of pricking up his ears at words like "out" or "ball." He also has highly tuned voice recognition.

14   **Education:** The Cairn provides children with hands-on experience at an early age, contributing to social interaction, crawling ability, and language skills. At age one, my daughter could say "Sit," "Come," and "No."

15   **Cleaning:** This function was a pleasant surprise. But of course cleaning up around the cave is one of the reasons dogs were developed in the first place. Users with young (below age two) children will still find this function useful. The Cairn Terrier cleans the floor, spoons, bib, and baby, and has an unerring ability to distinguish strained peas from ears, nose, and fingers.

16   **Psychotherapy:** Here the Cairn really shines. And remember, therapy is something that computers have tried. There is a program that makes the computer ask you questions when you tell it your problems. You say, "I'm afraid of foxes." The computer says, "You're afraid of foxes?"

17   The Cairn won't give you that kind of echo. Like Freudian analysts, Cairns are mercifully silent; unlike Freudians, they are infinitely sympathetic. I've found that the Cairn will share, in a nonjudgmental fashion, disappointments, joys, and frustrations. And you don't have to know BASIC.

18   This last capability is related to the Cairn's strongest point, which was the final deciding factor in my decision against the Macintosh—user-friendliness. On this criterion, there is simply no comparison. The Cairn Terrier is the essence of user friendliness. It has fur, it doesn't flicker when you look at it, and it wags its tail.

Thesis and Organization

1. Paragraph 1 begins by setting out the answers to some of the standard journalistic points: *who, what, where, when, why,* and *how.* What answers does paragraph 1 provide?
2. Paragraph 2 summarizes the "basics," and paragraph 3 draws a conclusion from them. What is the thesis suggested by paragraphs 1–3?

3. Paragraphs 5–12 compare the Cairn to the Macintosh. What is the basis of comparison in each paragraph? Which paragraphs focus on the Cairn, the Macintosh, both? Which pattern of comparison dominates, the point-by-point or block?

4. What sentence introduces paragraphs 13–18? Which paragraphs focus on the Cairn, the Macintosh, both? Which pattern of comparison dominates, the point-by-point or block?

5. Reconsider the thesis of the essay from a broader perspective by summarizing what the dog can do that the computer cannot. What comment might the author be making about dogs? Pets? Computers? Machines? About their relative worth? Consider the essay as a satire, and state its thesis.

Technique and Style

1. Explain how the author's use of punctuation and spelling in the title establishes the tone of the essay.

2. Humor often stems from improbable juxtapositions. Given that the fundamental comparison fits that idea, what other examples can you find of Gorman's using this technique?

3. What effect does the author achieve by including the two charts? What do the charts contribute to the satire?

4. The tone of the essay is at times informal, almost as though the author were talking to the reader. How is that tone reinforced by point of view? By diction? By the examples Gorman includes? Why did he choose his tone?

5. In paragraphs 5, 8, and 16, Gorman relies on the short sentence. Choose an example from one of those paragraphs and rewrite it, combining the sentence with another. What is gained? Lost?

Suggestions for Writing

Compare two quite dissimilar subjects in order to make a satiric point about one of them. Suggestions: going to a party versus studying, raising a garden versus children, owning a bicycle versus a car, eating junk food versus cooking, playing poker versus football. Of if you prefer, write a serious paper evaluating two products to determine which is better.

Of Prophets and Protesters

Robert C. Maynard

At first thought, the lives of Huey Newton and Martin Luther King, Jr., would seem to have more differences than similarities. After all, Newton epitomized a radical approach to asserting one's civil rights while King espoused nonviolence. Robert Maynard, however, finds some significant commonalities: concern, passion, charisma, and—unhappily—violent death. Maynard's essay was published in 1989, appearing in his syndicated column carried by the Times-Picayune *of New Orleans.*

1   If Huey Newton and Martin Luther King, Jr., ever met, they certainly formed no bond. They are bound nonetheless today by the common threads of how they lived and how each died. In one of history's curious accidents, their deaths help tell the tale of their times.

2   Dr. King and Huey Newton shared a deep concern for their people and for the plight of the poor. They aroused the passions of their generations. They were charismatic figures whose words were remembered and repeated. In different ways, the movements they led helped change America.

3   Dr. King was gunned down in Memphis, probably at the instigation of a hate group. Newton was gunned down in West Oakland, probably the victim of criminal street activity. The full extent of his own criminal involvement is not altogether clear.

4   What is clear in the first half-light of history is how the two men differed. The work of one is revered in much of the nation, yet the activity of the other was reviled.

5   Newton was representative in the sixties and seventies of sharp and chic radical diversion from the mainstream of the civil rights movement.There were others, such as Stokely Carmichael and H. Rap Brown. Their criticism of Dr. King and the nonviolent movement was that it was too passive, even "Uncle Tom."

6   I covered many of those leaders before and after the split in the movement. I found the differences fascinating. So were some of the similarities. All agreed on one basic tenet: Racism was destroying black lives by the millions.

Newton, Carmichael, and Brown, though all critics of Dr. King, differed in their styles and approaches. They shared with each other and with Dr. King a great talent at articulating the nature of the inequities in our society.   7

The radicals differed among themselves and with Dr. King in the solutions they advocated. Newton and the Panthers were socialists and allied themselves with other fringe groups in the white community. Carmichael and Brown preached black nationalism and racial separation.   8

Dr. King preached democracy. He resisted those who would change ours to a socialist system. He also had no patience for those who advanced the idea that black people should have a state of their own. Dr. King believed black Americans contributed mightily to the shaping of America and were entitled to their fair share of the American dream.   9

The struggle of differing views did not die with Dr. King in 1968. Some of those arguments went full force into the decade of the seventies. By then, the Voting Rights Act and other reforms of the nonviolent movement began showing tangible results.   10

The fringe movements died. Their leaders had their 15 minutes of fame. H. Rap Brown took a Muslim life-style and name, and leads a very low-profile life. Stokely Carmichael pops up now and again, but he has a small following.   11

Dr. King, even in death, continues to command the conscience of the nation. This is so because his choice of a remedy was to resort to basic American principles of justice, fairness and equality.   12

To see the urban underclass is to recognize how much remains to be done. It is also worth noting that the violent streets that spawned the radical movements remain violent streets. It was on those streets that Huey Newton's life ended.   13

His death is a reminder that the civil rights movement spawned prophets and protesters. Dr. King pronounced a prophecy that remains a challenge to the conscience of our society. And, although Huey Newton and Dr. King differed on solutions, their deaths are joined as reminders of the nation's unfinished business.   14

Thesis and Organization

1. What tentative thesis does paragraph 1 suggest?
2. Which paragraphs focus on similarities?

3. Which paragraphs focus on differences? On both similarities and differences?

4. Paragraphs 10–14 deal with the time since Martin Luther King, Jr.'s, death. What has changed? What has not changed?

5. Consider your answer to question 1 and the last sentence in paragraph 14. What is the essay's thesis?

Technique and Style

1. In what ways does the title fit the essay?

2. Huey Newton was a controversial figure who many readers may think of negatively. What is Maynard's view of Newton? How does he take negative opinions of Newton into account?

3. Maynard frequently uses parallelism to emphasize his points. Choose one example and rewrite the sentence so that the parallelism disappears or is strengthened. What is gained? Lost?

4. To what extent does Maynard rely on first person? What reasons can you find for his use of it?

5. Alliteration, the use of similar initial sounds, is a technique usually associated with poetry, not prose. What examples can you find in Maynard's essay? What do they add?

Suggestions for Writing

Think about two people who were different yet shared an impact on those about them. You can probably come up with two who influenced you significantly—relatives, teachers, religious people. If you want to write on a less personal subject, think of figures who influenced their fields, those in sports, music, film, medical research, history, politics.

POINTERS FOR USING COMPARISON AND CONTRAST

Exploring the Topic

1. **What are the similarities?** What characteristics do your two subjects share? Are the two so similar that you have little to distinguish them? If so, try another subject; if not, pare down your list of similarities to the most important ones.
2. **What are the differences?** In what ways are your two subjects different? Are they so different that they have little in common? If so, make sure you can handle a humorous tone or try another subject; if not, pare down your list of differences to the most important ones.
3. **Should you emphasize similarities or differences?** Which pattern of organization best fits your material? Block? Point-by-Point? A combination of the two?
4. **What examples will work best?** If your reader isn't familiar with your topic, what examples might be familiar? What examples will make clear what may be unfamiliar?
5. **What other modes are appropriate?** What modes can you draw upon to help support your comparison and the organization of the essay? Do you need to define? Where can you use description? Narration? Example? Do any of your comparisons involve cause and effect?
6. **What is your point? Your purpose?** Do you want to entertain, inform, persuade? Given your point as a tentative thesis, should you spell it out in the essay or imply it? If you are writing to inform, what information do you want to present? If you are writing to persuade, what do you want your reader to do?
7. **What persona do you want to create?** Is it best for you to be a part of the comparison and contrast or to be an observer? Do you have a strongly held conviction about your subject? Do you want it to show? Does your persona fit your audience, purpose, and material?

Drafting the Paper

1. **Know your reader.** Use your first paragraph to set out your major terms and your general focus, and to prepare the reader for the pattern of organization and tone that will follow. Reexamine your list of similarities and differences to see which ones may well be unfamiliar to your reader. Jot down an illustration or brief description by each characteristic that the reader may not be familiar with. If your reader is part of the group you are examining, tread carefully, and if your teacher may have a bias about your topic, try to figure out what that bias is so you can

counter it. Reread your paper from the perspective of the reader who is biased so that you can check your diction as well as your choice of examples and assertions.

2. **Know your purpose.** If you are writing to persuade, keep in mind the reader's possible bias or neutral view and see how you can use your persona as well as logical and emotional appeals to get the reader on your side. Informative papers run the risk of telling the reader something that person already knows, so use description, detail, example, and diction to present your information in a new light. If your paper's main purpose is to entertain, these techniques become all the more crucial. Try adding alliteration, allusions, paradox, and puns to the other techniques you draw upon.

3. **Use other modes to support your comparison.** Description and example are probably the most obvious modes to use, but also consider narration, cause and effect, definition, and analogy. Perhaps a short narrative would add interest to your paper, or perhaps cause and effect enters into your comparisons. Definition may be vital to your thesis, and analogy may help clarify or expand a point.

4. **Check your pattern of organization.** If you are using block comparison,make sure you have introduced your two subjects and that your conclusion brings them back together. In the body of the paper, make sure that what you cover for one, you also cover for the other. In point-by-point comparison, check to see that your points are clearly set out. You may want to use both types of organization, though one will probably predominate.

5. **Make a point.** Perhaps you want to use your comparison to make a comment on the way we live, perhaps to clarify two items that people easily confuse, perhaps to argue that one thing is better than the other. Whatever your point, check it to make sure it is an assertion, not a mere fact. Whether your purpose is to inform or to persuade, take a stand and make sure that your thesis clearly implies or states it.

6

Analogy

*A*nalogies prove nothing, that is quite true, but they can make one feel more at home." So wrote Sigmund Freud in one of his introductory lectures on psychoanalysis, and what he says is particularly true of the use of analogy in essays. To emphasize a point or illuminate an idea, analogy works well. If you are writing about an abstraction, for example, you can make it more familiar by using an analogy to make it concrete and therefore more understandable. An intangible word such as *rumor* becomes more comprehendible if you write of it as cancer. Or if you are explaining a process, analogy can often make the unfamiliar familiar; many a tennis instructor has said, "Hold your racquet as though you are shaking hands with a person."

In exposition, analogy clarifies—because by making *x* analogous to *y*, you bring all the association of *y* to bear on *x*. Analyzing public education by comparing it to an assembly line, for example, quickly gets across the ideas of boredom, repetition, and uniform production, but to use that analogy as primary support for an argument leads to problems: students are not passive, inanimate objects. False analogy is a logical fallacy.

Paying bills may be like having your teeth pulled, but the analogy cannot go much further than conveying the image of pain.

To use analogy well, you have to use it cautiously. Often writers use it quite sparingly, working one into a sentence or paragraph instead of using it as the basic structure for an entire essay. Most of the essays included in this chapter are unusual in that they use analogy extensively, which is all to the good to illustrate how it works. You will see that each author forms an analogy by choosing something dissimilar to the object of comparison. One compares writing to riding a roller coaster; another compares education to cultivating a garden. In finding suitable analogies of your own, think of the analogy as an extended metaphor rather than a simple comparison, and you'll be on the right track.

AUDIENCE AND PURPOSE   When writing a paper that uses analogy, it often helps to list the characteristics of the two subjects you are comparing. That list, together with an analysis of your audience, will help you fill in gaps. For instance, each of the essays that follow uses different comparisons and has a slightly different audience. Lewis Thomas compares the behavior of the Iks—a primitive tribe—to that of nations; to make his analogy work, he must describe the Iks in detail, for his readers probably know little about them. Albert Shanker assumes his audience agrees with the traditional system of schooling, that any weaknesses in it must be the fault of the "teachers or the texts or TV—or the students." Yet from his perspective it is the system that is faulty, for it focuses on "weeding" instead of "cultivating." He argues for change.

Perry James Pitre isn't arguing for anything. Instead, he plays with an analogy for the way he writes, explaining that highly individual process in terms we can easily relate to by comparing it to a roller coaster ride. Richard Selzer, on the other hand, assumes his readers are quite unfamiliar with one element in his analogy—the shaman— and that they may not know enough about the other—the surgeon. Whether his essay is informative or argumentative the reader must decide. In each of the essays, analogy is used to support a purpose, whether it be to express the writer's feelings, to inform, or to persuade.

EXTENDED METAPHOR   All language is metaphoric, substituting a symbol—the word—for reality—the thing—but *metaphor* has a more particular meaning. Through metaphor, a writer equates the primary term with another quite dissimilar term.

Analogy continues metaphor, extending it into multiple, many-layered images. Through Perry James Pitre's description, we feel the anxiety, terror, exhilaration, and relief associated with writing. Essays that employ analogy also are apt to depend on multiple analogies and metaphors, although some center on one fundamental analogy.

OTHER MODES   An analogy can easily get out of hand if it is extended too far; at that point it will lose its effect either by calling more attention to itself than to what it is supposed to highlight or by wearing so thin that it falls apart. The analogy between nation and ship was first expressed by the Greeks and much later in Longfellow's poem as "Sail on, O Ship of State!" but an analysis that sails it for 700 words can make the reader seasick. Most writers limit their use of analogy and supplement it with other modes. Cause and effect undergirds "The Iks," "My Brother Shaman," "The Writer," and "Changing How We 'Grow' Students." All of the essays, of course, use example extensively, and both Selzer and Shanker open their essays with narratives. Because all analogy involves comparisons, these essays can be viewed as a special kind of comparison-and-contrast paper that uses extended or multiple examples to illustrate its assertion.

THESIS AND ORGANIZATION   You might consider using analogy to frame an essay or to dramatize its ending. Or perhaps at some point in your essay an analogy would help make a particular point vivid. Analogies are perhaps best thought of as quick brush strokes, not whole paintings. Yet for short essays—and all of the ones here are short—an analogy can hold together long enough to emphasize the thesis. The essays by Pitre, Shanker, and Selzer employ analogy throughout, and their theses are bound directly to their analogies. Thomas, however, handles analogy differently. He starts with the Iks as symbol and then works toward an analogy, finding a striking similarity between the behavior of the Iks and the behavior of cities and nations. His thesis rises out of his analogies.

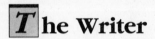he Writer

Perry James Pitre

For some people, the process of writing is similar to cooking or exercising or designing and building furniture, but for Perry James Pitre it's a roller coaster ride. Pitre ought to know. He writes against deadlines for his column in the student newspaper, the Driftwood, *when he's not writing for classes at the University of New Orleans. The essay that follows was written for an English class in 1990.*

1   "Ticket please!"

2   The Writer steps into the roller coaster car and straps himself in as he anticipates the ride to come. Slowly, agonizingly slowly, the car pulls out onto the track, with the huge first hill before it, seemingly an unconquerable mountain. It climbs the hill slowly, almost glacierlike, as The Writer ponders his ideas. Thoughts are discarded, sifted, rearranged, born, die, mutate; but to the observer, all that is apparent is a creeping climb toward the edge of the precipice.

3   As the car nears the pinnacle, The Writer grows excited, scared, triumphant. He clicks on his word processor (which is a real bitch in a roller coaster, but hey, this is a metaphor), and as the car reaches the crest (the program loads) The Writer peers down the incline as the words begin to . . .

4   COME! . . . as the car shrieks down the incline as the words pour out in a torrential flood. Hugging the curves, straining the rails, the car careens down the track, up the next hill, through the 180 degree curve, as the words flow, seemingly directly from his brain onto the screen, in an almost sexual release of stored, tensed thought.

5   Then, it's over. The car slows, as The Writer loads Spell-Chek, observes his handiwork, takes a deep breath, savors a cup of hot chocolate, and lights a cigarette. The car stops, abruptly, as The Writer looks up. . . .

6   "Ticket please!"

Thesis and Organization

1. State the analogy in your own words.
2. What principle lies behind the sequencing of paragraphs 2–5?

3. Spell out the various stages of the analogy and what stands for what.
4. What emotions are associated with those stages?
5. What is the essay's thesis?

Technique and Style

1. In paragraph 3, Pitre destroys the credibility of the roller coaster ride by including a word processor. How does he account for it? How effective is the device he uses?
2. How would you characterize Pitre's diction? Is formal? Informal? What? What effect does he achieve with his choice of diction level?
3. Look up the use of ellipses in your handbook. Does Pitre's use conform to what you found? How or how not?
4. What words, structure, or devices does Pitre use to create a sense of motion?
5. How effective do you find the essay's framework? What meaning do you infer from the final " 'Ticket please' "?

Suggestions for Writing

Think of how you write, defining the process as beginning with your first thought about a subject and ending with your final revision. Are there stages you can identify? Emotions? Generalize upon your experience to write a short essay describing what you find as an appropriate analogy for the way you write.

Changing How We "Grow" Students

Albert Shanker

As president of a teachers' union, the American Federation of Teachers (AFT), Albert Shanker has a special perspective on the future of the public education in this country. Shanker's comments appear every Sunday in the New York Times *in space paid for by the New York State United Teachers and the AFT. This essay, which appeared in 1989, is based on a central analogy and uses cause and effect to develop it.*

1   A few years ago, I had the pleasure of being a member of the Carnegie Forum's Task Force on Teaching as a Profession, which developed *A Nation Prepared: Teachers for the 21st Century*. There were many tough issues the task force wrestled with, but none was more difficult than the question of what impact raising standards for teachers would have on minorities. All of us were committed to a rigorous system of national board certification for teachers. But would that result—as it often has in other professions—in screening minorities out?

2   As we deliberated on our report, Dr. Shirley Malcolm, a task force member who is head of the Office of Opportunities in Science at the American Association for the Advancement of Science and a black, clarified the issue for us. She said that the effect of raising standards would depend on what kind of gardeners we were. There are some who have beautiful gardens by weeding, by removing all the plants that don't seem right or that they don't want and tending those that remain. But others have beautiful gardens through cultivation, by paying attention to plants that don't look so beautiful now and recognizing and developing their potential. The impact of higher standards on minority teachers, Malcolm said, depends on whether we're going to develop the profession largely by weeding or by cultivating. We chose cultivating.

3   I've often thought of Shirley Malcolm's gardening analogy and its applications. During the depression of the 1930s and the period when baby boomers entered the work force, there were plenty of people lined up applying for jobs. Employers needed only to post the qualifications they were looking for and weed out those who didn't ex-

actly meet their standards. But it's different today. "Help Wanted" signs are up all across the country. There may not be anyone lined up who meets the posted qualifications. What do many businesses do? They cultivate. They hire the best available and help to train and develop them, often with creative methods. They sometimes even discover important and unexpected skills and talents in these employees that they weren't originally looking for and that they can use.

Isn't it time our schools learned a similar lesson? Our current   4
school model is the same as the one we had 50 and 100 years ago. We didn't need many high school or college graduates in those days, and there were plenty lined up. The schools were structured in a lockstep fashion, and anyone who didn't fit that lockstep was weeded out: those who could not sit still and keep quiet for five or six hours a day, those who could not learn very well by listening to teachers lecture, those who took a little longer to figure out the answer and those who were not as good as others at manipulating words and numbers. The fact that these youngsters might be good at other things important for their future lives, for our society and the economy, didn't count. The possibility that many of the youngsters who did not appear to be academically able could be if different learning opportunities were presented to them or their strengths were used to overcome their weaknesses wasn't even acknowledged.

The system worked "well." It selected the few who fit into the   5
lockstep and had what it took to go on to more schooling. And it weeded out the rest, who went on to lower tracks in school, watered-down versions of the lockstep, or who dropped out into a job. There were no headlines or editorials when only 25 percent of the students graduated high school in 1940. (Was the word *dropout* even in use then?) The system was producing enough talent to meet the demands of the time.

But we now have a different world and a different ideal. We need   6
and want everybody to have a solid high school education and large numbers to have much more. Instead, we have a much higher percentage of kids graduating high school than ever before—in part because we lowered standards to keep them there and because they don't have jobs to drop into—and huge numbers of them don't have much skill to show for it. And while we also have a large percentage of high school kids who go on to college, according to the National Assessment of Educational Progress only about 5–10 percent of them will really be able to perform real college-level work. What's wrong?

7   The weeding system of schooling doesn't fit our changed world and ideals. We are now shocked that our schools don't work for the many, but the fact is that they were designed to select the few. Yet instead of rethinking or at least questioning the appropriateness of this system, we blame the teachers or the texts or TV—or the students—for our plight.

8   We talk as if we are periodically reforming the school system, but we actually only change our standards from high to low and back again. By now we should realize that having the same high standards for everyone usually doesn't work because not everyone can master the same things in the same way in the same period of time. Lowering standards to keep the slowest on board doesn't work either because everybody suffers. Those at the bottom don't acquire more than the basics and end up with worthless credentials, while those who once did well reduce their efforts because they know that they can get away with it. And so we again raise standards, and the pendulum swings again . . . and again.

9   We need to develop a new system of schooling, a system based on cultivating rather than weeding. We need to recognize that most students don't learn well in the system we designed long ago and still maintain, and that neither we nor they can afford such massive failure. We need to understand that children learn in different ways and at different rates, that they have and our society needs diverse talents that our schools ignore and that many who do not appear able to be academically or vocationally successful could be if we offered them more than only one or two ways of learning. We need to design a system that builds on students' strengths and successes and uses these to overcome their weaknesses. We do *not* need to periodically lower our standards, but instead broaden our ideas and practices about different routes to high standards.

10   Our weeding system of schooling is choking the development of our youth and of our nation. Isn't it time to design a system of cultivation?

Thesis and Organization

1. What are the terms of the analogy spelled out in paragraph 2?
2. Paragraphs 3 and 4 compare the worlds of business and education. What is Shanker's point?

3. Paragraphs 5 and 6 examine the effects of the current educational system. What are they?

4. Paragraphs 7–9 present the problem with present-day schooling and the solution. What are they?

5. Combine the ideas in the last sentence of paragraph 9 with those in paragraph 10 and restate them in a cause-and-effect relationship. The result is the thesis.

Technique and Style

1. What does paragraph 1 contribute to Shanker's persona?

2. At various times in the essay, Shanker uses statistics to back up his points. How effectively does he use them? What would be lost if they were not there?

3. Because of Shanker's position, you might expect his view of education to be biased. Whose "side" would you expect him to be on? Is that the case? How would you characterize his tone?

4. What personal pronouns does Shanker use? What reasons can you think of for his changing his point of view?

5. Shanker concludes his essay with a call to action. Do you find it effective? How or how not?

Suggestions for Writing

Think about your own experience in school, say first through twelfth grade or a particular time that stands out in your memory. What analogy comes to mind to characterize school? Was it heaven or hell? Prison or playground? Assembly line or craft studio? Or think about your curriculum. Was it a gourmet meal or prisoner's rations? Mountain climbing or a leisurely stroll? Scuba diving or water skiing?

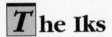he Iks

Lewis Thomas

To the anthropologist who studied them, the Iks seemed an appropriately named tribe. Lewis Thomas, however, reexamines them to see what their culture may say about human nature and society. Thomas has seen a lot of both. As a physician, researcher, and writer, he has dealt extensively with all kinds of people and cultures. This piece was included in his book The Lives of a Cell *(1974), a collection of his essays previously published in the* New England Journal of Medicine.

1   The small tribe of Iks, formerly nomadic hunters and gatherers in the mountain valleys of northern Uganda, have become celebrities, literary symbols for the ultimate fate of disheartened, heartless mankind at large. Two disastrously conclusive things happened to them: the government decided to have a national park, so they were compelled by law to give up hunting in the valleys and become farmers on poor hillside soil, and then they were visited for two years by an anthropologist who detested them and wrote a book about them.

2   The message of the book is that the Iks have transformed themselves into an irreversibly disagreeable collection of unattached, brutish creatures, totally selfish and loveless, in response to the dismantling of their traditional culture. Moreover, this is what the rest of us are like in our inner selves, and we will all turn into Iks when the structure of our society comes all unhinged.

3   The argument rests, of course, on certain assumptions about the core of human beings, and is necessarily speculative. You have to agree in advance that man is fundamentally a bad lot, out for himself alone, displaying such graces as affection and compassion only as learned habits. If you take this view, the story of the Iks can be used to confirm it. These people seem to be living together, clustered in small, dense villages, but they are really solitary, unrelated individuals with no evident use for each other. They talk, but only to make ill-tempered demands and cold refusals. They share nothing. They never sing. They turn the children out to forage as soon as they can walk, and desert the elders to starve whenever they can, and the

146

foraging children snatch food from the mouths of the helpless elders. It is a mean society.

They breed without love or even casual regard. They defecate on 4 each other's doorsteps. They watch their neighbors for signs of misfortune, and only then do they laugh. In the book they do a lot of laughing, having so much bad luck. Several times they even laughed at the anthropologist, who found this especially repellent (one senses, between the lines, that the scholar is not himself the world's luckiest man). Worse, they took him into the family, snatched his food, defecated on his doorstep, and hooted dislike at him. They gave him two bad years.

It is a depressing book. If, as he suggests, there is only Ikness at 5 the center of each of us, our sole hope for hanging on to the name of humanity will be endlessly mending the structure of our society, and it is changing so quickly and completely that we may never find the threads in time. Meanwhile, left to ourselves alone, solitary, we will become the same joyless, zestless, untouching lone animals.

But this may be too narrow a view. For one thing, the Iks are 6 extraordinary. They are absolutely astonishing, in fact. The anthropologist has never seen people like them anywhere, nor have I. You'd think, if they were simply examples of the common essence of mankind, they'd seem more recognizable. Instead, they are bizarre, anomalous. I have known my share of peculiar, difficult, nervous, grabby people, but I've never encountered any genuinely, consistently detestable human beings in all my life. The Iks sound more like abnormalities, maladies.

I cannot accept it. I do not believe that the Iks are representative 7 of isolated, revealed man, unobscured by social habits. I believe their behavior is something extra, something laid on. This unremitting, compulsive repellence is a kind of complicated ritual. They must have learned to act this way; they copied it, somehow.

I have a theory, then. The Iks have gone crazy. 8

The solitary Ik, isolated in the ruins of an exploded culture, has 9 built a new defense for himself. If you live in an unworkable society you can make up one of your own, and this is what the Iks have done. Each Ik has become a group, a one-man tribe on its own, a constituency.

Now everything falls into place. This is why they do seem, after 10 all, vaguely familiar to all of us. We've seen them before. This is precisely the way groups of one size or another, ranging from committees to nations, behave. It is, of course, this aspect of humanity that has lagged behind the rest of evolution, and this is why the Ik seems so primitive. In his absolute selfishness, his incapacity to give anything away, no matter what, he is a successful committee. When he stands at the door of his hut, shouting insults at his neighbors in a loud harangue, he is city addressing another city.

11   Cities have all the Ik characteristics. They defecate on doorsteps, in rivers and lakes, their own or anyone else's. They leave rubbish. They detest all neighboring cities, give nothing away. They even build institutions for deserting elders out of sight.

12   Nations are the most Iklike of all. No wonder the Iks seem familiar. For total greed, rapacity, heartlessness, and irresponsibility there is nothing to match a nation. Nations, by law, are solitary, self-centered, withdrawn into themselves. There is no such thing as affection between nations, and certainly no nation ever loved another. They bawl insults from their doorsteps, defecate into whole oceans, snatch all the food, survive by detestation, take joy in the bad luck of others, celebrate the death of others, live for the death of others.

13   That's it, and I shall stop worrying about the book. It does not signify that man is a sparse, inhuman thing at his center. He's all right. It only says what we've always known and never had enough time to worry about, that we haven't yet learned how to stay human when assembled in masses. The Ik, in his despair, is acting out this failure, and perhaps we should pay closer attention. Nations have themselves become too frightening to think about, but we might learn some things by watching these people.

Thesis and Organization

1. Paragraphs 1 and 2 introduce the essay. What do they establish in terms of the standard journalistic questions?
2. Paragraphs 3–5 focus on the anthropologist's view of the Iks. What assumption does he begin with? How do the Iks confirm that assumption?
3. In paragraphs 6–12, Thomas presents his own view of the Iks. What is his major objection to the anthropologist's view? What theory of defensive response does Thomas present that accounts for the Iks' actions?
4. What analogies does Thomas draw in paragraphs 11–13? What characteristics does Thomas stress in making those analogies?
5. Consider what Thomas believes to be the significance of the Iks. What

does their behavior say about the modern world? What is Thomas's thesis? What sentence or sentences come closest to expressing that thesis? Is Thomas's thesis a conviction he wants to persuade his readers to accept, or is he primarily informing them?

Technique and Style

1. How would you characterize Thomas's tone? Is it strident, meditative, reasonable, speculative, concerned, contentious, ironic, what? How does his tone relate to his purpose?
2. Examine paragraph 3 for sentence variety by counting the number of words in each sentence. Rewrite the paragraph, breaking it into sentences of approximately equal length. What is gained? Lost?
3. Trace the author's point of view. Where in the essay does he use *I? You? We?* What reasons can you find for the changes? How are they related to Thomas's tone? To his purpose?
4. Paragraph 8 consists of two short sentences. What reasons can you perceive behind Thomas's setting them off as a separate paragraph? Given the essay's overall organization, what is the function of paragraph 8? Given the essay's thesis, what does paragraph 8 suggest about cities and nations?
5. Paragraphs 4–7 and 10–13 all begin with sentences of ten words or less that introduce well-developed paragraphs. Analyze the function of each of the first sentences. Which are topic sentences? Parts of topic sentences? What is the overall effect of these sentences on the essay's organization?

Suggestions for Writing

Try looking at a person or group of persons from two perspectives, first as a symbol and then as an analogy. For instance, an outstanding athlete can be seen as a modern-day hero, but from another vantage point, when one considers advertising contracts tied to demeaning commercials and money-raising dinners held in the hustings, the athlete can also be thought of as a suckling pig. Consider the symbolic values and possible analogies for the rock star, the Vietnam veteran, the American farmer, the college graduate.

My Brother Shaman

Richard Selzer

At first glance, the principle of organization behind Selzer's essay may appear to be comparison and contrast, but the gap between ritual magic and surgery seems so wide that the comparison is more metaphysical than literal, closer to metaphor than reality. A practicing surgeon, Selzer has written a number of autobiographical books on the subject. This essay appeared in his book Taking the World in for Repairs *(1986).*

1   In the cult of the Bhagavati, as it has been practiced in southern India, there is a ritual in which two entranced shamans dressed in feathered costumes and massive headgear enter a circle of witnesses. All night long in the courtyard of a temple they lunge and thrust at each other, give shouts of defiance, make challenging gestures. It is all done to the sound of drums, conches and horns. Come daybreak, the goddess Kali "slays" the demon Darika, then plunges her hands into the very bowels of Darika, drinking of and smearing herself with blood. At last Kali withdraws from the field of battle having adorned herself with the intestines of the vanquished.

2   It is a far cry from the bloody trances of shamans to the bloody acts of surgery. Or is it? Take away from Kali and Darika the disciplinary beat of tautened hide and the moaning of flutes, and you have . . . an emergency intestinal resection. The technique is there, the bravado, the zeal. Only lacking in surgery is the ecstasy.

3   In both surgery and shamanism the business is done largely by the hands of the operator. The surgeon holds his scalpel, hemostat, forceps; the shaman, his amulet of bone, wood, metal. For each there is the hieratic honoring of ritual objects. The handling of these objects induces a feeling of tranquillity and power. One's mind is nudged from the path of self-awareness into the pathless glade of the imagination. The nun, too, knows this. She tells her beads, and her heart is enkindled. Surely it is true that the handling of instruments is conducive to the kind of possession or devotion that is the mark of all three—nun, surgeon, shaman. The surgeon and the shaman understand that one must honor, revere and entreat one's tools. Both do their handiwork with a controlled vehemence most

dramatically seen in those offshoots of Buddhism wherein the shaman ties his fingers in "knots," giving them a strange distorted appearance. These priests have an uncanny flexibility of their finger joints, each of which has a special name. During these maneuvers the shaman is possessed by finger spirits. He invokes the good spirits and repels the evil ones. Such hand poses, or mudras, seen in Buddhist iconography, are used in trancelike rituals to call down the gods to possess the shaman. In like manner the surgeon restrains his knife even as he gives it rein. He, too, is the medium between man and God.

The shaman has his drum which is the river of sound through   4 which he can descend to the Kingdom of Shadows to retrieve the soul of his tribesfellow. The surgeon listens to the electronic beep of the cardiac monitor, the regulated respiration of anesthesia, and he is comforted or warned. Even the operating table has somewhat the shape and size of the pagan altars I saw in a tiny sixth-century baptistry in the Provençal village of Vénasque. Upon these slabs beasts and, in certain instances, humans were laid open to appease the gods. Should one of these ancient pagans undergo resurrection and be brought to a modern operating room with its blazing lamps and opulence of linen and gleaming gadgetry, where masked and gowned figures dip their hands in and out of the body of someone who has been plunged into magical sleep, what else would he think but that he had happened upon a ritual sacrifice.

Nor is the toilet of decoration less elaborate for surgeon than for   5 shaman. Take the Washing of the Hands: Behold the surgeon at his ablutions. His lavabo is a deep sink, often of white porcelain, with a central faucet controlled by the knee. The soap he uses is thick and red as iodine. It is held in a nozzled bottle on the wall. The surgeon depresses a pedal on the floor. Once, twice, three times and collects in his cupped palm a puddle of the soap. There it would sit, lifeless, if he did not add a little water from the faucet and begin to brush. Self-containment is part of the nature of soap. Now, all at once, suds break as air and water are incorporated. Here and there in the play of the bristles, bubbles, first one, then another and another, lift from the froth and achieve levitation. For a moment each globule sways in front of the surgeon's dazzled eyes, but only long enough to give him its blessing before winking out. Meanwhile, the stern brush travels back and forth through the slush of forearms, raising wakes of gauze, scratching the skin . . . Oh, not to hurt or abrade, but tenderly, as one scratches the ears of a dog. At last the surgeon thrusts his hands into the stream of water. A dusky foam darkens the porcelain and fades like smoke. A moment later the sink is calm and white. The surgeon too is calm. And purified.

6   The washing of the hands, then, is at once a rational step in the achievement of sterile technique and a ritual act carried out under the glance of God by which one is made ready to behold, to perform. It is not wholly unlike the whirling of dervishes, or the to and fro rocking of the orthodox Jew at his prayers. The mask, cap, gown and gloves that the surgeon puts on prior to surgery echo, do they not, the phylacteries of this same Jew? Prophetic wisdom, if it will come at all, is most likely to come to one so sacredly trussed. By these simple acts of bathing and adorning, both surgeon and shaman are made receptacular.

7   Time was when, in order to become a shaman, one had to undergo an initiatory death and resurrection. The aspirant had to be taken to the sky or the netherworld; often he would be dismembered by spirits, cooked in a pot and eaten by them. Only then could he be born again as a shaman. No such rite of passage goes into the making of a surgeon, it is true, but there is something about the process of surgical training that is reminiscent of the sacred Ur-drama after all. The modern surgical intern must undergo a long and arduous novitiate during which the subjugation of the will and spirit to the craft is virtually complete. After a number of years of abasement and humiliation he or she is led to a room where no one else is permitted. There is the donning of special raiment, the washing of the hands and, at last, the performance of secret rites before the open ark of the body. In this, surgery remains a hieratic pantomime marked by exorcism, propitiation and invocation. God dwells in operating rooms as He does everywhere. More than once I have surmised a presence . . . something hearing and feeling . . .

8   In the selection of students to enter medical school, I wonder whether the present weight given to academic excellence in organic chemistry is justified. At least as valid a selection would be based upon the presence of a bat-shaped mole on the inner aspect of the thigh of the aspirant, or a specific conjunction of the planets on his birthday. Neither seems more prophetic than the other in the matter of intuition, compassion and ingenuity which form the trinity of doctorhood.

9   The shaman's journey through disorder and illness to health has

parallels to the surgeon's journey into the body. Both are like Jason setting out in the *Argos,* weathering many storms to return at last with the Golden Fleece. Or Galahad with the Holy Grail. The extirpated gallbladder, then, becomes the talisman of the surgeon's journey, the symbol of his hard-won manhood. What is different is that the surgeon practices inherited rites, while the shaman is susceptible to visions. Still, they both perform acts bent upon making chaos into cosmos.

Saint John of the Cross alludes to the mystic as a solitary bird who 10
must seek the heights, admit of no companionship even with its own kind, stretch out its beak into the air, and sing sweetly. I think of such a shaman soaring, plummeting, riding ecstatic thermals to the stars, tumbling head over heels, and at last descending among the fog of dreams. If, as it seems, the mark of the shaman was his ability to take flight, soaring to the sky or plummeting to the earth in search of his quarry, only the astronaut or the poet would now qualify.

Ever since Nietzsche delivered his stunning pronouncement— 11
"Dead are all the gods"—man has been forced to assume the burden of heroism without divine assistance. All the connections to the ancestral past have been severed. It is our rashest act. For no good can come to a race that refuses to acknowledge the living spirit of ancient kingdoms. Ritual has receded from the act of surgery. Only the flavor of it is left, giving, if not to the performers, then to the patients and to those forbidden to witness these events, a shiver of mysticism. Few and far between are the surgeons who consider what they do an encounter with the unknown. When all is said and done, I am left with the suspicion that we have gone too far in our arrogant drift from the priestly forebears of surgery. It is pleasing to imagine surgeons bending over their incisions with love, infusing them with the impalpable. Only then would the surgeon, like the shaman, turn himself into a small god and re-create the world.

Thesis and Organization

1. Selzer uses his first two paragraphs to explain an ancient religious ritual and to draw an analogy between it and modern surgery. What general expectations do paragraphs 1 and 2 set up in the reader? What particular ones does the last sentence of paragraph 2 elicit?

2. The body of the essay may be tough reading, but it will be made easier if you analyze each paragraph or paragraph block for subject and meaning. In paragraph 3, for example, Selzer focuses on both shaman and surgeon, and by examining the objects each uses and the method—hands—he finds in both the "hieratic honoring of ritual objects" that signifies the user of those objects is the "medium between man and God." Perform a similar analysis on paragraphs 4, 5 and 6, 7 and 8, and 9. What pattern of cause and effect do you perceive?

3. Selzer concludes his essay with paragraphs 10 and 11. What does paragraph 10 imply—by omission—about the surgeon? What does paragraph 11 imply is missing from most present-day surgery? What should link the surgeon to the shaman? Draw a deep breath, and in one sentence state the thesis of the essay.

4. Your analysis of the body of the essay and its thesis has made clear the elements in the analogy of surgeon as shaman, but Selzer also brings in the nun (3), the whirling of dervishes and the orthodox Jew (6), Jason and Sir Galahad (9), and St. John of the Cross (10). Pick two from this list and explain how those analogies work.

5. Explain what you find to be Selzer's primary purpose in writing the essay. Is he expressing a personal lament? Informing his readers about a relatively esoteric profession? Arguing for reform? Some combination of all three?

Technique and Style

1. If you pay attention to the words Selzer chooses, you'll discover the importance of diction as a characteristic of Selzer's style. How would you describe the level of diction? How does it fit his topic? His thesis?

2. The essay contains a number of allusions, not only the ones singled out above in question 4, but the central one explained in paragraph 1 and also Neitzsche in paragraph 11. What do these allusions imply about Selzer's audience? Does he adequately explain, directly or indirectly, those that his audience might not know?

3. Selzer draws his analogies from a number of different ages and cultures. What times and civilizations does he use? What religions? What effect does he achieve with this variety?

4. Consider your answers to questions 1–3 above and describe the kind of person Selzer appears to be. Would you want him to operate on you? Why or why not?

5. Selzer uses ellipses more than most writers. Examine how he uses them in paragraphs 2, 5, and 7. What functions do they have? Rewrite one of the sentences using different punctuation. What differences do you discern?

Suggestions for Writing

Start with a profession and think about how it may be practiced today. What might be missing? Perhaps waiters or short-order cooks no longer view their professions as skilled ones; perhaps most police officers no longer have a sense of neighborhood precinct; perhaps carpenters are no longer craft workers; perhaps supermarkets treat people strictly as consumers; perhaps voters act on image, not knowledge. No matter what subject you pick, you need only to know what's missing; you do not need to compare and contrast past with present. Next find an analogy for what the profession lacks, one that can serve as your controlling metaphor.

Exploring the Topic

1. **Does your subject have distinctive characteristics?** What are they? Which among them are the most important?
2. **What metaphor does your subject suggest?** Given the metaphor and your subject, what characteristics match? How can the metaphor be extended into an analogy? How can you outline the analogy as an equation, what equals what?
3. **Does the analogy fit?** Are there any weak points in the analogy that need to be recognized and downplayed? What strong points need to be emphasized?
4. **What is your purpose?** Are you using the analogy to explain, persuade, entertain, express your feelings?
5. **How should you use the analogy?** Will it work best as a frame for the essay? Might it be better as a conclusion? Should it run through the essay as a whole?
6. **What other modes are appropriate?** What modes can you draw upon to help support your analogy and the organization of the essay? Do you need to define? Where can you use description? Narration? Example?

Drafting the Paper

1. **Know your reader.** Make up two lists, one column with the heading "What the reader knows," the other with "What the reader doesn't know." Think through your essay, noting what fits in which column. If your reader knows a lot about the topic, consider beginning the essay with something the reader doesn't know; if the reader knows little, consider starting with something familiar or with the most crucial *who, where, what* sort of information. If the reader might have a particular bias, counter it early on by pointing out the disparity involved in your analogy and acknowledging its limitations.
2. **Know your purpose.** Figure out your primary purpose so that you can see what tone and persona might best fit it. If you are using a satiric mask, make sure that the reader will know not only what you are against, but also what you are for. If your purpose is persuasive but you are not using satire, watch your tone to see that it doesn't become righteous or opinionated. Try to build a reasonable case and use authorities and quotations where they might best serve your purpose. If, on the other hand, your purpose is informative, consider a speculative tone. Perhaps you simply want to share an experience or insight with your reader, in

which case a thoughtful, meditative tone may be best. If that is the persona you adopt, beware of sounding sententious or ponderous or overly sentimental. A flash of humor or wit will save you from that pitfall.

3. **Double-check your analogy.** Make sure your analogy is an extended metaphor, not a statement of fact. See what you want to emphasize. If you are using the analogy throughout your essay, see what pattern of organization may work best. Try point-by-point and block patterns, but watch out for stretching your analogy so far that it loses its effectiveness. Keep your focus on your subject and bring in the analogy in bits and pieces. If you find that your analogy can't bear much weight, use one or two others as backups.

4. **Double-check the placement of your analogy.** Make sure that placement is effective by trying out the analogy in different positions. Perhaps it works best as a framing device or standing alone in a sentence or paragraph.

5. **Draw on other modes.** If your analogy runs through the paper as a whole, you will be depending on comparison and contrast to organize your ideas. If you use analogy as a framework or conclusion, you will probably be organizing your paper around example, definition, cause and effect, or description. Narration can also enter in, though usually as an illustrative example or framework. Whatever other modes you use, make sure your analogy has a key role in the essay so that it highlights your major point and makes it more dramatic. Think of analogy as a spotlight, a means of focusing your reader's attention on your assertion.

6. **Make a point.** Like all the other modes, analogy is a means to an end; the end is your major assertion about your topic. Perhaps you are using analogy to satirize a topic or to criticize or correct a popularly held opinion. Perhaps you are using analogy to explore a subject or to create a dominant impression. No matter what your purpose, you should have a thesis.

7

Process

*I*f you have ever been frustrated in your attempts to put together a barbecue grill or hook up a stereo system, you know the value of clear and complete directions. And if you have tried to explain how to get to a particular house or store, you also know that being able to give clear directions is not as easy as it first seems. This practical how-to kind of process analysis is one we deal with every day in recipes, in user's manuals, and in instruction booklets. Basic to this process is dividing the topic into the necessary steps, describing each in sufficient detail, and then sequencing the steps so they are easy to follow. You can also help by anticipating trouble spots. If you are writing a set of directions, for example, you might start by describing the parts that must be put together so that you familiarize the reader with them and also force a quick inventory. And if the plans call for 12 screws but include 15, telling the reader that the package includes 3 extra will stave off the inevitable "I must have done it wrong" that leftover parts usually elicit.

But writing directions is only one kind of process analysis. "How did it happen?" and "How does it work?" are questions that get at other sorts of processes, the scientific and the historical. Lab reports exemplify scientific process analysis, as do the kinds of papers you find published in *Scientific American* or the *New England Journal of Medicine*. Like the practical how-to process paper, the report of an experiment or explanation of a physical process clearly marks the steps in a sequence. The same is true of essays that rely on historical process, though sometimes it's harder to discern the steps. A paper that analyzes how the United States became involved in the Vietnam War, for instance, identifies the major stages of involvement and their chronology, the steps that led up to open warfare. Essays that focus on a historical process often condense time in a way that practical or scientific process analysis does not, but the chronology itself is still important.

Although process analysis is a kind of writing usually associated with specialized subjects—how to do *x,* how *y* works, or how *z* came about—it also finds its way into less formal prose. If you were to write about how you got interested in a hobby, for instance, you would be using process analysis, as you would if you were writing an explanatory research paper on the history of Coca-Cola. Process analysis is also useful as a means of discovery. If you were to analyze the process you go through to revise a draft of one of your papers, you might find out that you overemphasize a particular stage or leave out a step. As a way of thinking and expressing ideas, process analysis tends to be underrated because it is equated with the simpler forms of how-to writing.

AUDIENCE AND PURPOSE   The concept of audience is crucial to process essays, for you must know just how familiar the reader is with the topic in order to know what needs to be explained and how to explain it. Peter Steinhart's "A Nation of Beachwalkers," for instance, assumes the audience is a general one that shares his fascination with the sea but does not know much about the history of our relationship with it; that assumption guides the writer's selection of detail and example. John Berendt writes about tennis shirts, however, and has a different problem, for he is aware that his readers already know what the shirts look like. How they got that way and what they signify are not so readily apparent, so what the readers don't know gives Berendt a good deal to say. Anyone who has ever been a student is familiar with cramming, but how to do it well is not so widely known, and that is the focus of Jill Young Miller's essay.

What you have to say may be surprising, in which case you need to present the information in a believable way. At the same time, you have to be careful to adjust the information to the level of the audience. The process involved in creating lipstick can be explained in terms only a chemist could understand, but Maneka Gandhi is careful to gear her description to the general reader.

On the other hand, if you know not only more but also more specialized information than the reader, you must be careful to adjust the information to the level of the audience. Sometimes a writer explores a process to inform the reader, sometimes to persuade, but always the writer has an assertion in mind and is trying to affect the reader. In her essay "Death by Fasting," for example, Joan Graf depicts the physiology of starvation, outlining the stages the body undergoes. In doing so, she must explain scientific terms so that she doesn't baffle her reader. Berendt's essay on tennis shirts, Peter Steinhart's on beachwalking, and Miller's on cramming may be intended to inform, but all have an assertive edge. That edge becomes more distinct in the essays by Maneka Gandhi and Joan Graf as an informative purpose combines with a persuasive one.

SEQUENCE   Chronology is as crucial to process as it is to narration. In fact, it is inflexible. What provides the stick in lipstick has to precede what makes it look and smell good; the Lacoste shirt had to be popular before it became copied by other manufacturers. The writer must account for all the important steps. If time is crucial to the process, the writer must account for it also, although in a historical process essay, time is apt to be compressed or de-emphasized to underscore a turning point, such as the equating of the Lacoste shirt with the preppy look. And undergirding the concept of sequence, of course, is the pattern of cause and effect: the "alligator" shirt became a mass market item when President Eisenhower was photographed wearing one.

DETAIL AND EXAMPLE   In writing a process analysis, you will draw upon the same skills you use for description, narration, and example papers, for without supporting details and examples to further and describe the process, a process essay can be tedious indeed. "A Nation of Beachwalkers" employs examples from different times, countries, sources, and even disciplines—religion, history, and sociology. Graf intertwines her account of the physiology of fasting with the facts of a particular example, an IRA prisoner's starvation and death. Incorporating references to current events or adding a narrative example or even an amusing aside can make what otherwise might be a list into an interesting paper.

TRANSITIONS To make the stages of the process clear, you will need to rely on logically placed transitions that lead the reader from one stage to the next. Most writers try to avoid depending only on obvious links, such as *first, next, next,* and instead use chronology, shifts in tense, and other indicators of time to indicate sequence. Graf indicates chronology at first with "early in a fast" and "by the third day," and then shifts to "other adjustments," "side effects," and "last stages."

THESIS AND ORGANIZATION The body of a process essay almost organizes itself because it is made up of the steps you have identified, and they must occur in a given sequence. Introductions and conclusions are trickier, as is the thesis, for you must not only set out a process but also make an assertion about it. The author of "Beachwalkers," for instance, concludes the essay with a look at the future and what we need to do; Maneka Gandhi begins her essay by implying her thesis in her first two paragraphs. John Berendt, on the other hand, opts for an implied thesis that evolves out of the historical process he describes. Jill Young Miller and Joan Graf, however, set their process analysis within frameworks. Miller uses a narrative about a particular student to open and close her explanation of the process of cramming for tests. So, too, Graf frames the process of fasting within a particular setting, but she uses the contemporary political situation to add a persuasive edge to her description of a scientific process. In all of these essays, the thesis confronts the reader with a point, implicit or explicit, about the process involved, and in so doing heads off the lethal response, "So what?"

How to Cram

Jill Young Miller

*Cramming, deeply embedded as a way of student life, often turns up
in nightmares as panic over having to take an exam for a course you
never signed up for. Real or imagined, the situations that drive us to
cram are known too well to us all. Appropriately enough, the essay
was published in* Campus Voice *(1987), a magazine distributed free
on many college campuses.*

1   Frances Avila learned the hard way not to expect miracles over-
night. A chronic crammer, the New York University senior did the
usual for her midterm in "Major British Writers" last fall: she pulled
an all-nighter. Fighting off fatigue and anxiety, Avila forced herself
to concentrate on the novels and her notes through dawn, breaking
only to splash cold water on her face. Near noon, she closed her
books to head for the test.

2   The first question—"Expand on the gap between her front
teeth"—was a lulu. Avila didn't recognize the allusion to Chaucer's
Wife of Bath, even though she'd read the section only hours before.
"Not only did I blank out, but I was also frightened," she recalls. "I
didn't expect the test to be that elaborate." The bad situation only
got worse. She fumbled through 14 more stray lines before plunging
into part two, which wasn't any easier. Avila had studied innumer-
able facts for hours, but she knew only one thing for sure: she was
in trouble.

3   "I failed the exam," she explains, "because I had to compare and
contrast two poets from different time periods. In order to do that,
I had to elaborate on all the details within the poetry. But I'd ab-
sorbed just enough information the night before to understand what
I was reading and not enough to catch all the details."

4   Sound familiar? Almost all of us have stood (and sleepwalked) in
Avila's shoes at one time or another. Sometimes push comes to
shove, crunch comes to cram, and before you know it, you have to
read 450 pages in six hours. Pour on the caffeine, you mumble.

5   About 90 percent of all students cram, estimates Don Dansereau,
a psychology professor at Texas Christian University, who defines
cramming as "intense studying the night before or the day of a test."

Quips Ric Schank, a University of Florida senior, "Down here, it's the rule rather than the exception."

Despite its popularity, cramming gets low marks from educators and memory experts, who claim that the last-minute nature of the act kills your chances for payoff at test time. 6

A quick stroll down memory lane explains why. Most experts identify three types of memory: immediate, short-term, and long-term. You use your immediate memory as you read this, remembering each word just long enough to make the transition to the next. 7

Short-term memory is limited, too. For example, you use it when you look up a phone number, close the book, and dial. Short-term memory can supposedly hold a maximum of seven items for only a few seconds. 8

Long-term memory is the big daddy, the one that holds everything you know about the world. It's the memory that last-minute learners need to respect. 9

How well you organize information on its way into your long-term memory determines how quickly you can retrieve it later, or whether you retrieve it at all. Think of a backpack you'd take on a hike, says Laird Cermak, a research psychologist at the Boston Veterans Administration Hospital and the author of *Improving Your Memory* (McGraw-Hill, 1975). "If your backpack is organized and you get bit by a snake, you can go right for the snakebite kit," he explains. 10

The magic lies in spacing your study over days, weeks, or even months. That gives you time to mull over the new stuff, relate it to what you already know, and organize it for exam-time recall. "The reason you forget the information is not because it was learned the night before," Cermak explains. "It's because when you crammed you didn't give yourself good ways to remember it in the future." In other words, last-minute studying limits the number of mental retrieval routes you can create. 11

But it doesn't take a psychologist to explain why cramming often fails. "You throw things into your mind, knowing that you're going to spit them out in a couple of hours and forget them. It's not a good way to learn at all," says NYU journalism senior David Reilly. 12

No quick-and-dirty detours to long-term retention and instant recall exists. But if you're forced into a late-night, last-minute study session, the results don't have to be disastrous. Here's some advice 13 to help make the morning after less anxious than the night before:

14   **Find out what kind of test you're in for.** If you cram, you're likely to fare better on multiple-choice and fill-in-the-blank tests because they jog your memory with cues, Cermak says.

15   **Find a quiet place to study.** When Avila crams, she seeks out a small room at the library that's devoid of distractions. "I'm cornered," she says. "I have no choice but to look at the print."

16   If you like to study with music in the background, go for something without lyrics and keep the volume down low. Classical music such as Bach can have a soothing effect if your nerves are impeding your studies, says Danielle Lapp, a memory researcher at Stanford University and the author of *Don't Forget! Easy Exercises for a Better Memory at Any Age* (McGraw-Hill, 1987).

17   **Compose a scene that you can re-create during the exam.** If you can, study at the desk or in the room where you'll take the test, or do something while you study that you can do again when you take the test. For example, Dansereau suggests that you chew grape gum. "The flavor acts as a cuing device," he explains.

18   **Build your concentration.** Spend ten minutes warming up with a novel or magazine before you tackle a tough chapter. Says Cermak, "It helps you block out whatever else is going on."

19   **Watch what you eat and drink.** Avoid heavy meals and alcohol. Both could make you drowsy, cautions Lapp. If you need a cup of coffee to perk up, fine. But putting too much caffeine in your system can make you jittery and break your concentration.

20   **Mark your book.** Even if you only have time to read the chapter once, it helps to highlight important terms and sections. Identifying the key words and passages requires you to be mentally alert and forces you to be an active rather than a passive reader.

21   **Spend time repeating or discussing facts out loud.** Recitation promotes faster learning because it's more active than reading or listening. (Try it out when you study for your next foreign language vocabulary quiz.) Discussion groups are helpful for this reason.

22   **Take short breaks at least every few hours.** They'll help you beat fatigue, which takes a heavy toll on learning. Two hour-long sittings separated by a 15-minute break are more productive than one two-hour session in which your mind wanders throughout the second half. It doesn't matter what you do during those breaks; just take them.

Experiment with memory techniques. They impose structure   23
on new information, making it easier to remember at test time. The
"house" method is one of the oldest. Let's say you want to remember a list of sequential events for a history exam. Try to imagine the
events taking place in separate but connected rooms of your house.
When the test asks you to recall the events, take a mental amble
through the rooms.

Another simple technique involves acronyms. You may have   24
learned the names of the Great Lakes (Huron, Ontario, Michigan,
Erie, and Superior) with this one: HOMES.

Try some proven learning strategies. Richard Yates, a coun-   25
selor and time management expert at Cleveland State University,
recommends the SQ3R method: survey, question, read, recite, review. Survey the material to formulate a general impression; rephrase titles and headings into questions; read through the material
quickly to find the main points and the answers to your questions;
recite those main ideas, taking brief notes; and review. Even when
you're pressed for time, the strategy can help. "It may take a little
longer," says Yates, "but it's worth the effort."

Get some sleep. UF's Schank quit all-nighters after his freshman   26
year. "I'd go into a final and be so wired from staying up all night that
I'd lose my concentration," he says. "I'd miss questions that I knew
I wouldn't miss if I were in a good frame of mind." Now he crams
until about 3 A.M., sleeps for about four hours, and hits the books
again at 8 A.M.

Psychologists and memory researchers can't specify how much   27
sleep you need—everyone has his or her own threshold—but they
do stress its importance. Says Lapp, "You're better off getting some
sleep so that your mind is rested for the exam than you are cramming the whole night." Just don't forget to set that alarm clock
before you go to bed.

For an early-morning exam, it's best to do heavy-duty studying   28
right before you go to sleep. In other words, unless you've got
back-to-back exams, don't cram and then do something else for a
few hours before a test. Freshly learned material is remembered
much better after a period of sleep than after an equal period of
daytime activity.

Relax. It may sound simplistic, but it's key to good test perfor-   29
mance. "Anxiety is enemy number one of memory," Lapp explains.
She compares a student taking a test to a singer performing onstage.

"There's no way a completely anxious singer can utter a sound," she says.

30   Cramming is like going to the dentist; if you have to do it, you want it to be as painless and as productive as it can be. After all, no one goes to college to take a semester-long class and promptly forget all the new information that's been taught. At least Frances Avila didn't. After her disastrous midterm, she didn't dare risk cramming for her "Major British Writers" final exam. This time, she spaced her studying over a period of weeks, earned an A, and salvaged her grade for the semester.

31   That doesn't mean she's quit cramming for good—in fact, she hasn't even tried to. Instead she's perfected her technique. Ditto for Reilly, who's tried unsuccessfully to break the habit. "Every semester I kick myself a million times and scream that I'm not going to cram next semester," he laments. "But it never seems to work."

Thesis and Organization

1. The steps to follow are given in paragraphs 14–29, which leaves almost half the essay taken up by introduction and conclusion. Examine paragraphs 1–13 and identify the use of narration, example, and definition.
2. Analyze the role of narrative in the introduction and conclusion. What effect does Miller achieve with the story of Avila?
3. How necessary is Miller's definition of cramming? Of types of memory? Explain the relation between the two.
4. What principle do you find behind the sequencing of paragraphs 14–29? How does that principle relate to Miller's informative purpose?
5. Consider what Miller tells you about studying, memory, cramming, and Avila. In your own words, state her thesis.

Technique and Style

1. Miller's paragraphs are shorter than you would usually find in an essay of this length. How can you justify the relative shortness of her paragraphs?
2. What point of view does Miller use in the essay? What reasons can you find for that choice?
3. The imperative can be rude and bossy, as in the command "Shut the door." How would you characterize Miller's use of the imperative? How does she avoid using it rudely?
4. What sources does Miller use in her essay? What purpose do they serve

in relation to Miller's information? Her credibility? Why provide full citations in paragraphs 10 and 16?
5. What kind of person does Miller seem to be? If you were taking a study skills course, would you want her as a teacher? Why or why not?

Suggestions for Writing

Think about the steps in a process you know well and write your own "how-to" essay. Suggestions: worrying creatively, handling stress, coping with obnoxious people; throwing a curve ball, returning a serve, spiking a volleyball; making the perfect burger, frying the perfect egg, baking the perfect brownie.

You Sure You Want to Do This?

Maneka Gandhi

Ever wonder what goes into a simple tube of lipstick? Maneka Gandhi tells us, though she also warns us that we may find out more than we wanted to know. Gandhi writes a regular column in the Illustrated Weekly *of India, although this essay was published in the* Baltimore Sun *(1989).*

1   Are you one of those women who feel that lipstick is one of the essentials of life? That to be seen without it is the equivalent of facial nudity? Then you might like to know what goes into that attractive color tube that you smear on your lips.

2   At the center of the modern lipstick is acid. Nothing else will burn a coloring sufficiently deeply into the lips. The acid starts out orange, then sizzles into the living skin cells and metamorphoses into a deep red. Everything else in the lipstick is there just to get this acid into place.

3   First lipstick has to spread. Softened food shortening, such as hydrogenated vegetable oil, spreads very well, and accordingly is one of the substances found in almost all lipsticks. Soap smears well, too, and so some of that is added as well. Unfortunately, neither soap nor shortening is good at actually taking up the acid that's needed to do the dyeing. Only one smearable substance will do this to any extent: castor oil.

4   Good cheap castor oil, used in varnishes and laxatives, is one of the largest ingredients by bulk in every lipstick. The acid soaks into the castor oil, the castor oil spreads on the lips with the soap and shortening till the acid is carried where it needs to go.

5   If lipstick could be sold in castor oil bottles there would be no need for the next major ingredient. But the mix has to be transformed into a rigid, streamlined stick, and for that nothing is better than heavy petroleum-based wax. It's what provides the "stick" in lipstick.

6   Of course, certain precautions have to be taken in combining all these substances. If the user ever got a sniff of what was in there, there might be problems of consumer acceptance. So a perfume is poured in at the manufacturing stage before all the oils have cooled—when it is still a molten lipstick mass.

At the same time, food preservatives are poured into the mass, because apart from smelling rather strongly the oil in there would go rancid without some protection. (Have you smelled an old lipstick? That dreadful smell is castor oil gone bad.) 7

All that's lacking now is shine. When the preservatives and the perfume are being poured in, something shiny, colorful, almost iridescent—and, happily enough, not even too expensive—is added. That something is fish scales. It's easily available from the leftovers of commercial fish-packing stations. The scales are soaked in ammonia, then bunged in with everything else. 8

Fish scales, by the way, mean that lipstick is not a vegetarian product. Every time you paint your lips you eat fish scales. So lipsticks without them actually are marked "vegetarian lipstick." 9

Is that it then? Shortening, soap, castor oil, petroleum wax, perfume, food preservatives and fish scales? Not entirely. There is still one thing missing: color. 10

The orange acid that burns into the lips only turns red on contact. So that what you see in the tube looks like lip color and not congealed orange juice, another dye has to be added to the lipstick. This masterpiece of chemistry and art will be a soothing and suggestive and kissable red. 11

But it has very little to do with what actually goes on your face. That, as we said, is—but by now you already know more than you wanted to. 12

Thesis and Organization

1. What does paragraph 1 make clear about the essay's audience and subject? What expectations does it set up for the reader?
2. Which paragraphs focus on the ingredients that make lipstick work?
3. Which paragraphs focus on making lipstick attractive?
4. Consider the title of the essay and what Gandhi has to say about what goes into a tube of lipstick. What is her thesis?
5. Given the thesis of the essay, do you find Gandhi's purpose more informative than argumentative or the reverse? Explain.

Technique and Style

1. Considering what you have learned about Gandhi's thesis and purpose, how would you characterize the tone of the essay?

2. What provides the transitions between paragraphs 3 and 4? Between paragraphs 10 and 11? How effective do you find this device?

3. Examine the verbs Gandhi uses in paragraphs 2 and 3. What do they contribute to the essay's tone?

4. Paragraph 9 is more of an aside, a "by the way" comment, than a furthering of the essay's forward motion. What reasons can you think of that make the paragraph appropriate?

5. The last paragraph contains two references that at first may seem vague. What does "it" refer to in paragraph 12's first sentence. What does "That" refer to in the second sentence? Would a summary add to or detract from the conclusion? Explain.

Suggestions for Writing

Think about other items we take for granted and then find out if their ingredients contain a few surprises. You might start with a product (hot dogs, marshmallows, frozen pies, shampoo) first noting the ingredients listed on the package and then consulting an unabridged dictionary.

The Tennis Shirt

John Berendt

*Polo players, foxes, and, in Louisiana, even cockroaches emblazon
the archetypal tennis shirt, but it was a crocodile that started it all.
Who should know best but the editors of* Esquire, *where this essay was
published in 1986.*

1

It's hard to imagine now, but well into the 1920s men played
tennis in full-length trousers and long-sleeved shirts. During
warm-up practice they also wore blazers. Before 1900, they even
wore ties. Tennis was a rather sedate game in its early days, but by
the 1920s a good many players wanted to loosen it up a bit. One
player finally took matters into his own hands—a Frenchman by the
name of René Lacoste.

2

Lacoste was a singles champion in France, Great Britain, and the
United States. His game was fast and so aggressive that the French
called him *Le Crocodile*. Lacoste was the John McEnroe of his era.
He complained that the official uniform interfered with his game,
and when nothing was done about it, he simply showed up on the
court wearing an odd-looking short-sleeved shirt that he had designed himself. It was based on the long-sleeved polo shirt. The
back was longer than the front, and it had a crocodile stitched over
the breast—not an alligator, as many people think; an alligator is a
much slower-moving animal, sluggish, in fact.

3

The distinctive thing about Lacoste's shirt wasn't the crocodile or
the longer back but the fabric, which was a cotton piqué knit that
Lacoste had invented especially for the shirt. It breathed, and it was
resilient. Today the weave is known as "the Lacoste."

4

Lacoste became a professional shirtmaker in 1929, but his tennis
shirt didn't really hit the big time until the early 1950s, when President Eisenhower was photographed playing golf in one. That
launched it.

5

Over the next 20 years, Lacoste shirts developed a certain cachet.
They were cool, comfortable, and neat-looking. At some point, however, things got out of hand. Lacostes came to be seen as part of the
preppy uniform, and as such they came in for a fair amount of

negative PR. It is hard to think of another really good item of clothing, in fact, that has had such scorn heaped upon it.

6   The animus was, and is, directed entirely at the crocodile insignia, not at the shirt. When it comes to the actual shirt itself, there doesn't seem to be any problem. The fabric, the cut, the collar, and the two-button opening have all been slavishly copied by countless imitators. The Lacoste design, moreover, has emerged as the generic tennis shirt. Its imitators, of course, have their own insignias, but none has so far been encumbered by any adverse symbolism. To their credit, the Lacostes steadfastly cling to their crocodiles. Try to take one off and you'll tear holes in the shirt; they are attached with nylon thread in a particularly tenacious stitch.

7   Once René Lacoste had brought the top half of the tennis uniform up to date, it remained for someone else to do the same for the bottom. Bunny Austin was the man who did it. He appeared in shorts at the 1932 Forest Hills championships. But that's another story.

Thesis and Organization

1. Apply the journalistic probes *who, what, when, how,* and *why* to paragraph 1. What answers does this paragraph present? At what point in the essay do you have all the answers? Why might Berendt have held some back in paragraph 1?
2. Trace the time element of the essay. What reasons can you find for the specific mention of a time? For the general statements?
3. Analyze the cause-and-effect pattern in the essay. To what extent does it parallel the time element?
4. Add up all that Berendt tells you about René Lacoste and state it in your own words. Then do the same for the tennis shirt. Put your two statements into one one sentence and you have Berendt's thesis.

Technique and Style

1. A good concluding paragraph can serve many functions. It can, for example, restate the thesis, round out the essay by bringing the reader back to the beginning, summarize the essay, raise a related topic, or appeal to the reader to take a particular stand or action. What function does Berendt's last paragraph serve? How effective is it as a conclusion?
2. In a short essay, it is relatively easy to analyze the writer's transitions and see how the paragraphs are linked together. What transitions does Be-

rendt use to get from one paragraph to another? Is any one type of transition more effective than another? How so?

3. Berendt's essay first appeared in *Esquire*. Take a look at a recent issue and see what you can deduce about the magazine's audience—age, gender, income, occupations. To what extent does Berendt's essay address that audience?

4. Try locating the essay's tone at a point between extremes: heavy or light, formal or informal, condescending or over the reader's heads. What other opposites can you think of? How would you describe Berendt's tone?

Suggestions for Writing

To research a subject similar to Berendt's, think of a public figure associated with a product or institution: Colonel Sanders and Kentucky Fried Chicken, Levi Strauss and Levi's, Henry Ford and the Ford car, L. L. Bean and the store, Sears of Sears, Roebuck. Or if you would prefer a topic closer to your own experience, consider writing on the development of your neighborhood, high school, college or university, church, city, or county.

Death by Fasting

Joan Stephenson Graf

"Death by Fasting" sets a scientific process, how the body reacts to prolonged starvation, within a political context, the hunger strike. Here, the hunger strikers are members of the Irish Republican Army held prisoner by the British. Bobby Sands was the first prisoner to die. Graf's essay appeared more than ten years ago in Science 81, *a publication of the American Association for the Advancement of Science, but the troubles in Ireland live on.*

1   Bad news travels fast in Northern Ireland. Women and children blow whistles and bang dustbin lids on the pavement to telegraph a grim message: Every 11 days, on the average, a convicted member of the Irish Republican Army dies of starvation in the Maze prison near Belfast.

2   The hunger strike, a strategy IRA inmates are using to pressure their British overlords to reclassify them as political prisoners rather than common criminals, has caught the attention of the entire world. IRA leaders advise prisoners when to begin their fasts so that they will have the most political impact. Last winter, for example, the IRA planned 27-year-old Bobby Sands's fast so that he would die on the anniversary of the bloody Easter Rising of 1916 that led to the original partitioning of Ireland.

3   But Sands did not die on Easter. The human body does not conform precisely to timetables calculated for an "average" person, one who can survive fasting for 50 to 70 days, assuming he has water. Sands lasted 66 days.

4   Early in a fast, the body is comparatively profligate in burning its fuels. A normal, nonfasting person's principal source of energy is sugar, or glucose. The brain in particular needs glucose to function, but the body's reserve of it, stored in the liver in the form of a starchy carbohydrate glycogen, is exhausted in less than a day. When that supply runs out, the body makes its own glucose from the next most available source, protein in the muscles. If protein were the only energy supply, however, vital muscles in the heart, kidneys, spleen, and intestines would quickly be destroyed, and death would follow soon thereafter.

So as early as the first day of the fast, certain tissues begin sup-   5
plementing their glucose supply with energy derived from fat, which
comprises 15 to 20 percent of an average person's body weight. By
the third day, when most people lose their hunger pangs, the brain
is getting most of its energy from ketone bodies, which are formed
in the liver from fatty acids.

To protect its vital organs and to conserve energy, the body   6
makes a lot of other adjustments as well. The metabolic rate drops,
pulse slows, blood pressure lowers. A starving person feels chilly.
The body's thermostat cranks down a notch, an energy-saving strategy akin to maintaining a house at 65 degrees during the winter.
According to reports from Belfast, the hunger strikers spend a lot of
time in bed under sheepskin rugs.

Fasting produces a lot of side effects: anemia, dry skin, ulcerated   7
mouth, abnormal heart rhythm, erosion of bone mineral, difficulty
in walking, blindness, loss of hearing, speech impairment, decrease
in sexual drive. Those who visited Bobby Sands in his final days
were shocked at his sunken cheeks, emaciated frame, and rapidly
thinning brown hair.

In the last stages of starvation, when fat is depleted, the body   8
draws exclusively from its protein reserves. At the end of his fast,
when his insulating muscle was consumed, Sands was gently laid on
a waterbed to cushion his frail skeleton.

"The body essentially digests itself," says Arnold E. Andersen, a   9
psychiatrist at Johns Hopkins Medical Institution who treats women
suffering from anorexia nervosa, an affliction of young women who
exist on a semistarvation diet. "There is a point at which the organs
simply stop functioning." Autopsies of the Irish prisoners turn up no
single cause of death.

As hunters and gatherers, our ancestors adapted to survive when   10
harvests were poor. But the body's heroic efforts to save itself while
awaiting better nutritional times simply cannot outlast the determined resolve of the Irish hunger strikers.

Thesis and Organization

1. Process essays emphasize *how* something happens, but other concerns
such as *who, what, when, where,* and *why* are also apt to be important.
Where in this essay does the author first bring out *where? Who? What?
Why?* What device does she use to indicate *when?*

2. At what point does the essay begin to focus on *how?* When does the focus shift again?
3. The mode of cause and effect, like the modes of process and narration, involves sequence. Cause must precede effect. Paragraphs 4, 5, 6, and 7 use cause and effect. Select one of these paragraphs and analyze the cause-and-effect relationship involved.
4. Consider only the scientific process that the author presents. If that alone were the subject of the essay, what would be the author's primary assertion about the subject? Now consider also the political context that the author provides. Given both the process and its context, what is the author's major assertion?
5. What emotions does the author want to elicit from the reader? Is she informing the reader about what some members of the IRA are experiencing or is she persuading the reader to share a particular conviction or take a particular action? What evidence can you cite?

Technique and Style

1. Paragraphs 1–3 set out the overall political context for the essay, but paragraphs 4 and 5 make no mention of it. Where in paragraphs 6–10 is the political context brought back in? How does the author's reintroduction of the context relate to her thesis? Purpose? Why might she have chosen to omit it from paragraphs 4 and 5?
2. The essay deals with two levels of conflict: the IRA versus the British and the body versus itself. How does paragraph 10 bring the two conflicts together? What does the paragraph imply about the nature of the Irish hunger striker's "determined resolve"? How does the implication relate to the essay's thesis?
3. The essay first appeared in *Science 81,* a magazine published by the American Association for the Advancement of Science "to bridge the gap between science and citizen." How does the essay serve the magazine's general purpose?
4. Graf chooses her details with care: "sheepskin rugs" (6); "sunken cheeks, emaciated frame, and rapidly thinning brown hair" (7); "a waterbed to cushion his frail skeleton" (8). What purpose do these details reveal? How is their purpose related to that of the essay?
5. Paragraphs 4–9 contain a great deal of technical information. What examples can you cite to show that the author is *not* writing to a technically sophisticated audience?

Suggestions for Writing

Make your own "death by" arguments, researching the physiological process involved and placing it within a politically sensitive context. Use the

Readers' Guide to Periodical Literature and *The New York Times Index* to find newspaper material to refer to in your argument. Suggestions: death by radiation (the danger of nuclear waste disposal); death by industrial poisoning (hazardous waste); death by diet (the liquid protein fad); death by digging (black lung disease); death by accident (the lawsuits filed over blood transfusions).

A Nation of Beachwalkers

Peter Steinhart

To Peter Steinhart, we are indeed a "nation of beachwalkers," and in this essay he explores the process that has made us so, citing examples based on personal experience and history, and employing analogy, comparison and contrast, and cause and effect. Steinhart is a regular contributor to Audubon, *the magazine of the National Audubon Society. This essay appeared in* Audubon *in 1989.*

1   On the west shore of Hawaii, far from the road, I met a beachcomber. She lived alone under a thatched roof with no immediate neighbors, no electricity, no running water. At night she had the company of stars and the music of surf. She worked when she had to, but preferred to spend her days swimming with sea turtles in the bay, sitting on the beach talking with dogs and fishermen, or just looking out at the sea. She talked engagingly of the island and of people she had met, and then walked down the beach with the grace and dignity of a swaying palm.

2   I envied her. Out of harness, at home in her body, undaunted by summonses and gadgetry, able to look unflinchingly into the light of day and dark of night. The hollow thrump of waves on a winter beach. The soft shredding of sand in summer tides. The cries of gulls like ribbons on the wind. Dolphins winking just beyond the surf.

3   Americans have built exclusive residential resorts like Palm Beach, Hilton Head, Kennebunkport, or Malibu, where we can have the beach and plumbing too. We have beach-culture suburbs like San Diego's Mission Beach or Florida's Fort Lauderdale, where proximity to the sea emphasizes the novelty, vigor, and mystery of youth. We long for islands, the balmy life, the sun on our backs, the sea in our ears, the liquidity of sunlight on wavelet. We are a nation of beachwalkers, summoned by the drumbeat of wave and the sigh of sea foam and the unencumbered whistling of the wind.

4   We hear especially the sea's music. The hiss and plunk of waves on a nightlit beach, the wind-lost shriek of gulls. The eternal surge and ebb, the leap and fall of water. The wave is the elemental chord of nature, the music by which life began. It is imitated in the air by sound and light, but they organize a meaner,

more precise information. The rhythms of wave and tide speak to our hearts and souls.

Of all the elements, the sea still has the capacity to mystify. It is constantly tossing up unfamiliar objects for our edification and awe. A Pacific beach may one day be carpeted with the papery sails of wind-blown velella. Another day the sea may cast up the carcasses of shearwaters. Henry Beston walking Cape Code found old wreck-age, driftwood, and lobster pots. One day he saw "a great strewing of empty sea urchin shells"; another day, "curious wooden pebbles shaped by the sea out of the ancient submerged forest."   5

The sea's mysteries lure us beyond the safety of our conceits. In the shallow waters off a Hawaiian beach, ancient lava flows left undersea tunnels. In places, their roofs have collapsed, making it possible to swim 20 or 30 feet down into these caverns, in search of butterfly fishes or sea monsters or one's own sense of the ghostly. There may be sharks and moray eels in them, but elegant parrot fishes and brilliant wrasses disappear into their narrow entrance-ways. I am drawn as if by sorcery down into the dimly lit grottoes. Furtive shapes dart under overhanging rock ledges. A large unicorn tang swims by on a solemn errand. My lungs weep for air, and I kick from the edge of panic, back through a narrow passage, to the dazzling brightness of the surface. The experience is scary—not just for what may wait in the caverns, but for what sulks inside my own deeper recesses. I dive again and again.   6

We have not always enjoyed this fascination. The sea once rep-resented to us that which nature and thought had not yet fully formed. In the Creation myths of Greek, Christian, Maori, Maya, Yoruba, Athapaskan, and Hopi alike, the primordial world was a chaos of darkness and water, the sea below, the sky above, and nothing in between. Only when land was dribbled down from the heavens were life and purpose possible.   7

The seas were not happy places in the ancient world. The Greeks believed the ocean stretched off into a realm of darkness and obscur-ing fog into chaos, where sea and sky tumbled in a travesty of whirl-pool and wave and howling abyss, into which adventurous ships would plunge. A Phoenician sailor who braved the Atlantic reported that it was windless, fog-shrouded, and filled with sea monsters.   8

Medieval clerics feared the power and immensity of the sea. Adam of Bremen, an eleventh-century scholar, knew of Greenland and Vinland but held that they lay beyond seas "infinite and fearful   9 to behold." Saint Jerome compared the ungodly to a shipwrecked sailor, tumbled in vast emptiness, thrashing in vain for something to cling to. In medieval stories, only God could save a shipwrecked sailor.

10   We have a natural and prudent fear of the sea, of riptides and violent waves and storms that hurl flood-torn trees through our beachfront windows. Perhaps it is only on the warm bays and soft beaches of the tropics that the sea seems hospitable or confiding. Where the waves roar angrily, perhaps trust of water must be learned.

11   Europeans began to learn it only when they ventured onto the high seas in flimsy ships, seeking adventure and empire. As sailing skills grew, we discovered peoples who had a more sensuous relationship with the sea. In the fourteenth century John Mandeville told of natives who "go as well under the water of the sea as they do above the land all dry." Robert Boyle in 1660 quoted reports of pearl divers in the Mediterranean who could stay below for an hour. Sir Francis Drake's *Golden Hind* was attacked by natives in the Pacific who swam from their canoes.

12   The voyages of exploration showed that the seas had comprehensible limits. As Europeans mastered them, they mastered what was best in humanity. Voyaging rewarded unselfish duty, craft, self-sacrifice, imagination, and courage. The sea captain mastered not the mysteries of the ocean but the darkness of human nature. The sea ceased to be primordial confusion and became a source of boldness, vision, and strength. Wrote Tennyson, " 'Tis not too late to seek a newer world . . . to sail beyond the sunset . . . to strive, to seek, to find, and not to yield." To stand at its edge was to breathe gusts of nobility.

13   The sea became part of national identity. "The most advanced nations are always those who navigate the most," Ralph Waldo Emerson declared. "The sea is our approach and our bulwark," Robert Louis Stevenson wrote; "it has been the scene of our greatest triumphs and dangers, and we are accustomed in lyrical strains to claim it as our own."

14   What was good for nations seemed good as well for the individual. By the eighteenth century, authorities were recommending sea bathing as a medical treatment. The first to resort to the French Riviera were British and Swiss tubercular patients. John Anderson, director of the Margate Sea-bathing Infirmary, in 1795 delivered a

scientific defense of sea bathing. He declared that seawater was "nature's richly saturated compound" and that swimming around in it induced a state of supreme harmony called "oceanic feeling."

Sea bathing was criticized on moral grounds for its association 15 with medieval images of the damned and with the decadence of Roman baths. But Margate had resorts at which bathing machines were wheeled out into the ocean, so that bathers entered the sea free from the prying eyes of voyeurs. Laws required men and women to bathe separately, and women to wear full skirts with lead-weighted hems.

It wasn't at all like a modern day at the beach. The bathing 16 machines were platforms with awnings to hide the bathers, who hung by a rope and splashed seawater on themselves, or waded or kneeled in shallow water. Bathers feared great waves, and the ladies hired to supervise female bathers were often described as sea witches, luring women into the sea. Sea bathing was both risqué and dangerous.

But even kings tried it. In 1784 at Weymouth, King George III 17 emerged from a bathing machine while a band of fiddlers played the national anthem. As nobility took up beach life, beach resorts became popular, largely for what went on after the morning plunge. At Brighton the Prince of Wales established his own pavilion with pageants, races, banquets, and balls. In 1785 the *Morning Post* described Brighton as "morning rides, champagne, dissipation, noise, and nonsense."

Seaside resorts sprang up all over England, and at Long Branch, 18 Asbury Park, and Cape May in New Jersey. The dread of the sea passed, and the bathing machines vanished. By the middle of the nineteenth century, people were resorting to the beach for relaxation.

We began to find intense new emotions at the ocean's edge. 19 Charlotte Brontë, on first seeing the sea, was so overpowered that "she could not speak till she had shed some tears." Walt Whitman wrote that the "sea is the brine of life" and addressed himself to the ocean: "I am integral with you. I too am of one phase and of all phases." Vacationers spent hours watching the rise and fall of tides or staring out at the sea.

As our comfort in the water grew, our bathing costumes shrank. 20 Able to converse comfortably with nature, we no longer seemed to need the psychological armor. We now ask of the sea an intimacy unknown 200 years ago. We surf on it or scuba dive in it, mingling its restlessness and its salt with our own. We see it as companionable and healing. "To me the sea is a person," confessed Gertrude Ederle, who was celebrated in 1926 for swimming the English Channel. "It sounds crazy, I know, but when I swim in the sea, I talk to it. I never feel alone when I'm out there."

21 Today we look joyfully into the face of the sea's wildness and mystery. The sea delivers up strange objects, beckons us to far horizons, breathes exotic perfumes into our faces. Standing on a beach you can feel the forces that govern the Earth, see the pull of the moon and sun on Earth, water, blood, tears.

22 To live with such forces, we must have strong character, faith, will, and judgment. The sea once elicited such strength, and exploring both seas and psyches gave us an era of great adventure. Today, poised on the brink of interplanetary travel, we hope space will let us resume the old journey. But it is unlikely we will ever find there either the music or the moral challenges. Space is too silent, and space voyages are too vast, too dependent upon electronic harnesses which wire voyagers to the safety of Earthbound computers and technicians. There will never be sea captains in space, never be fickle winds and storm-tossed seas, or currents carrying the scents of cloves and coconut palms. Space will be a realm of sterile and silent passage.

23 We have come full circle. We have a sense of dread, not of what the sea will do to us, but of what we may do to the sea. It no longer seems vast: We fly across the oceans in a few hours, reading magazines. We have overharvested fish stocks and realize the seas cannot feed a hungry world. Pollution from our factories and households leads to strange plagues among shellfish, seabirds, and perhaps dolphins and whales. Medical trash washes up on our beaches, and plastic garbage strangles sea lions and birds. And now our consumption of fossil fuels is warming the seas, melting the polar ice caps, and raising sea levels. What was once symbolic of our ability to live within the mystery and challenge of nature now suggests our greed and stupidity.

24 When we encounter beachcombers or dive into submarine canyons, we find that the sea is still a place of hope and mystery, discovery and challenge. It is our past and our future. It beckons the finer character we hope lurks within us, though it increasingly floats our vices. And if we can still hear its music, still respond with the

courage, self-discipline, and imagination with which our ancestors braved the sea, there is much we can do.

Thesis and Organization

1. What paragraph or paragraphs serve as the essay's introduction?
2. Paragraphs 4–6 use cause and effect. What effects does the sea have on humans?
3. Paragraphs 7–21 trace the relationship between humans and the sea. What are the steps in that process?
4. Paragraph 22 presents a comparison. What point is Steinhart making?
5. The conclusion is contained in paragraphs 23 and 24. What new ideas does Steinhart raise? Given those ideas, the effect of the sea on humans, and the history of our relationship with it, what is Steinhart's thesis?

Technique and Style

1. How would you characterize Steinhart's level of diction? What does it suggest about his audience?
2. In what ways does Steinhart's use of allusion fit the audience you described above?
3. Choose one of Steinhart's paragraphs that depends heavily on description or narration and discuss what it contributes to the essay as a whole.
4. Given the author's audience and thesis, do you find the essay expressive, informative, argumentative, or some combination of these aims? Explain.
5. Choose one of Steinhart's sentences that uses two sets of parallel words or phrases and rewrite it, adding a third parallel set. What is lost or gained?

Suggestions for Writing

Trace the development of your own fascination with something: a hobby, a sport, a pastime. Or if you wish to write a more exploratory essay, trace our culture's fascination with one of its favorites: football, soap operas, fast food, slasher films, scandal sheets.

Exploring the Topic

1. **What kind of process are you presenting?** Is it a practical, "how-to" one? A historical one? A scientific one? Some mixture of types?
2. **What steps are involved?** Which are crucial? Can some be grouped together? Under what headings can they be grouped?
3. **What is the sequence of the steps?** Are you sure that each step logically follows the one before it?
4. **How familiar is your reader with your subject?** Within each step (or group of steps), what information does the reader need to know? What details can you use to make that information come alive? What examples? What connections can you make to what the reader *does* know?
5. **Is setting or context important?** If so, what details of the setting or context do you want to emphasize?
6. **What is the point you want to make about the process?** Is your point an assertion? Will it interest the reader?

Drafting the Paper

1. **Know your reader.** Using two columns, list what your reader may know about your topic in one column and what your reader may not know in the other. If you are writing about a practical process, figure out what pitfalls your reader may fall into. If you are writing about a historical or scientific process, make sure your diction suits your audience. Be on the lookout for events or actions that need further explanation to be understood by a general audience. If your reader is apt to have a bias against your topic, know what the bias is. If your topic is familiar, shape your first paragraph to enlist the reader's interest; if the topic is unfamiliar, use familiar images to explain it.
2. **Know your purpose.** If you are writing to inform, make sure you are presenting new information and that you are making an assertion about your topic. Don't dwell on information that the reader already knows if you can possibly avoid it. If you are writing to persuade, remember that you do not know whether your audience agrees with you. Use your persona to lend credibility to what you say, and use detail to arouse your reader's sympathies.
3. **Present the steps in their correct sequence.** Make sure that you have accounted for all the important steps or stages in the process and that they are set out in order. If two or more steps occur at the same time, make sure you have made that clear. If time is crucial to your process,

see that you have emphasized that point. If, on the other hand, the exact time at which an event occurred is less important than the event, make sure you have stressed the event and have subordinated the idea of time.

4. **Use details and examples.** Whether you are writing an informative or a persuasive essay, use details and examples that support your purpose. If you are explaining how to make your own ice cream, for example, draw upon what the reader knows about various commercial brands and flavors to bolster your case for making your own. After all, your reader may not want to take the time and trouble for that process and therefore may have to be enticed into trying it. Choose details and examples that combat your reader's attitude if that attitude is apt to be a negative one.

5. **Double-check your transitions.** First mark your stages with obvious transitions or with numbers. After you have turned your notes into a working draft, review the transitions you have used, checking to see that they exist, that they are clear, and that they are not overly repetitious or obvious. Make sure each important stage (or group of stages) is set off by a transition. See if you can indicate shifts by using tense or words and phrases that don't call attention to themselves as transitions.

6. **Make a point.** What you say about a subject is far more interesting than the subject itself, so even if you are writing a practical process essay, make sure you have a point. A paper on a topic such as "how to change a tire" becomes unbearable without a thesis. Given an assertion about changing a tire—"Changing my first flat was as horrible as I had expected it to be"—the paper at least has a chance.

8

Cause and Effect

Cause-and-effect essays investigate why *X* happens and what results from *X*. Though writers examine both cause and effect, most will stress one or the other. Process analysis focuses on *how;* causal analysis emphasizes *why*. Causal analysis looks below the surface of the steps in a process and examines why they occurred; it analyzes their causes and effects. All of the examples mentioned in the introduction to process analysis (page 158) can be turned into illustrations of causal analysis. Let's say you've followed the directions that came with your new stereo system and have finally reached the moment of truth when you are ready to push the switch marked "Power." You push, it clicks, but then nothing happens. The receiver is on, as are the turntable and tape deck, but no sound comes out of the speakers. Probably you first check for the most immediate possible cause of the problem, the hookups. Are all the jacks plugged into the correct sources? Are they secure? Are the speaker wires attached correctly? If everything checks out, you start to search for less immediate causes only to discover that the wrong switch was depressed on the receiver, and it is tuned to a nonexistent compact disc player. You push "Tape," and music fills the room. The problem is solved.

Essays that analyze cause and effect usually focus on one or the other. If you were writing about your hobby, which, let's say, happens to be tropical fish, you could emphasize the causes. You might

have wanted a pet but were allergic to fur; you might have been
fascinated with the aquarium in your doctor's office, and your aunt
gave you two goldfish and a bowl. Reasons such as these are causes
that you would then have to sort out in terms of their importance.
But if you wished to focus on effect, you might be writing on how
your interest in tropical fish led to your majoring in marine biology.

You can quickly see how causal analysis can get confusing in that
a cause leads to an effect which can then become another cause.
This kind of causal chain undergirds Benjamin Franklin's point that
"a little neglect may breed great mischief . . . for want of a nail the
shoe was lost; for want of a shoe the horse was lost; and for want of
a horse the rider was lost."

You can avoid the traps set by causal analysis if you apply some
of the skills you use in division and classification and in process
analysis:

1. Divide your subject into two categories, causes and effects.
2. Use process analysis to identify the steps or stages that are
   involved and list them under the appropriate heading, causes
   or effects.
3. Sort out each list by dividing the items into primary or secondary causes and effects, that is, those that are relatively
   important and those that are relatively unimportant.

When you reach this final point, you may discover that an item
you have listed is only related to your subject by time, in which case
you should cross it out.

If you were writing a paper on cheating in college, for instance,
your notes might resemble these:

Cause	*Importance*
Academic pressure	Primary
Need an A	
Peer pressure	Primary
Everybody does it	
System	Secondary
Teachers tolerate it	
No real penalty	
Moral climate	Secondary

Income taxes
Insurance claims
Infidelity
Breakup of family unit

Effect	Importance
Academic	Primary
Grades meaningless	
Peers	Primary
Degree meaningless	
System	Secondary
Erodes	
Moral climate	Secondary
Weakens	

The train of thought behind these notes chugs along nicely. Looking at them, you can see how thinking about the moral climate might lead to speculation about the cheating that goes uncaught on tax and insurance forms, and for that matter the cheating that occurs in a different context, that of marriage. The idea of infidelity then sets off a causal chain: infidelity causes divorce which causes the breakup of families. Pause there. If recent statistics show that a majority of students have cheated and if recent statistics also reveal a large number of single-parent households, it isn't safe to conclude that one caused the other. The relationship is one of time, not cause. Mistaking a temporal relationship for a causal one is a logical fallacy called *post hoc* reasoning.

It is also easy to mistake a primary cause or effect for a secondary one. If the notes above are for an essay that uses a narrative framework, and if the essay begins by relating an example of a student who was worried about having high enough grades to get into law school, the principle behind how the items are listed according to importance makes sense. To bring up his average, the student cheats on a math exam, justifying the action by thinking, "Everybody does it." The essay might then go on to speculate about the less apparent reasons behind the action, the system, and moral climate. For the student who cheated, the grade and peer pressure are the more immediate or primary causes; the system and climate are the more remote or secondary causes.

AUDIENCE AND PURPOSE   What you know or can fairly safely assume about the intended audience determines both what to say and how to say it. Writing about the beginnings of the magazine *Sassy,* Elizabeth Larsen, for instance, assumes her readers will be unaware of the causes behind the major shift in the magazine's editorial philosophy. But when George Felton writes about the cause-and-effect relationships involved in the current trend in advertising, he knows he is writing to readers bombarded by advertisements and commercials. He can drop brand names and know they will be recognized. Most readers are equally aware of Shelley Moore's topic of teenage pregnancy, but the scope of the problem and the efforts being made on behalf of the fathers involved are news. Also new to many readers is what a person feels like when taken for a criminal. In "Black Men and Public Space," Brent Staples details those emotions in such a way that his audience feels the full irony of the situations he describes. And while his readers may take up whistling Vivaldi or look twice before scuttling to the other side of the street, they will not be offended by Staples's essay. Indeed all of the writers must be careful not to step on their readers' toes. When Constance L. Hays writes about the student demonstrations of the 1960s, she writes to a variety of readers. Some may have occupied an administration building, some may have sympathized with the police, some may not have been born yet. She has to walk a careful line, explaining and reporting coolly.

FALSE CAUSAL RELATIONSHIPS   As the introduction to this chapter points out, it is easy to mistake a temporal relationship for a causal relationship and to assign significance to something relatively unimportant. But if you carefully analyze the essays included in this chapter, you will see how their writers solved these problems. Elizabeth Larsen, writing in "Censoring Sex Information: The Story of *Sassy,*" is careful to point out that the advertisers' objections to the magazine's content were based not on morals but on money, thus identifying the true cause for the loss of advertising accounts.

Multiple examples form the base of Brent Staples's "Black Men and Public Space," but Staples's essay is more expressive than argumentative. He explores not only the effect he—a black man—has on others as he walks the darkened city streets but also the feelings those effects elicit in him. He mentions, for instance, that "women are particularly vulnerable to street violence, and young black males are drastically overrepresented among the perpetrators of that violence." The next sentence shows how that fact is irrelevant to him: "Yet these truths are no solace against the kind of alienation that comes of being ever the suspect, a fearsome entity with whom pedestrians avoid making eye contact."

VALID CAUSAL RELATIONSHIPS   Evidence and logical reasoning are essential to cause-and-effect essays. At the time of the student demonstrations cited in Constance L. Hays's essay, campuses were also torn by anti-Vietnam marches and violent actions based on political agendas that were seemingly far afield from curricular matters. Hays, therefore, must be careful to cite only those demonstrations closely tied to university policies and practices. This she does by using multiple examples. Shelley Moore's sequence of causal relationships is much more complex, so Moore relies heavily on statistics and interviews to explain the nature of the problem—teenage pregnancy—and its solution. All of the writers included in this chapter draw upon many sources for their evidence. Whether statistics, interviews, popular culture, folklore, scientific studies, quotations, or personal experience, varied sources can provide you with a wide variety of examples to use as supporting evidence.

THESIS AND ORGANIZATION   Although a cause can lead to an effect that then becomes a cause leading to another effect and so on, most essays are organized around either cause or effect: why today's students participate as fully as they do in university governance, why teenage pregnancy plagues the black community, what happens if a magazine's editorial staff decides to provide information about sex, what "Healthism" really means, what effects being a black male and walking the streets at night have not only on city dwellers but on the walker.

Censoring Sex Information: The Story of *Sassy*

Elizabeth Larsen

As much as American teenagers need information about sex, the editors of Sassy *discovered it's sex, not sex education, that sells. Elizabeth Larsen was on Sassy's editorial staff when that lesson became clear. She now works for the* Utne Reader, *where this essay was published in 1990.*

At the first editorial meeting of *Sassy* magazine, in 1987, the staff sat around the editor in chief's office discussing how to make our new magazine different from other teenage publications. The unanimous first priority was to provide sex education: since we had read the competition during our own adolescence, we knew the sex information published by teen magazines was scarce and usually couched in judgmental terms. 1

We had a good reason to put this issue high on our agenda. The United States has the highest teen pregnancy rate of any similarly industrialized Western nation, and we felt this was not an issue that would go away by just telling teens to say no. The rock stars and athletes speaking out against drugs and drunk driving on TV weren't making any pitches for virginity. The situation had become even more confusing for teenagers because of the attention that abstinence was getting as the only sure way to prevent AIDS. Our readers were left with a lot of unanswered questions that we felt were important to address. 2

Sassy's initial advertisers did not feel as strongly as its editors about leading the sex education of America's youth. Many were concerned about an article in the prototype issue entitled "Sex for Absolute Beginners," which had previously run in *Dolly*, *Sassy*'s Australian counterpart. The article answered questions ranging from "Can I get pregnant?" and "What is an orgasm?" to "Am I homosexual?" and "Is masturbation wrong?" A few advertisers were offended by the thought of their own teenage daughters reading the information and decided not to advertise, while others reluctantly signed contracts, fearing that if the magazine were a huge success, they 3

191

couldn't afford to be left out. It became clear to me later that their concerns were business rather than moral ones when I realized that many of the same companies who objected to "Sex for Absolute Beginners" in *Sassy* nevertheless advertised without complaint in *Dolly*—the most widely read teenage magazine in the world in terms of circulation per capita. For what the advertisers understood long before the editors did is that sex may sell billions of dollars of U.S. products every year, but responsible, direct information about sex directed toward U.S. teenagers would not.

4   In the first issue, *Sassy* printed an article entitled "Losing Your Virginity." We ran this because we felt that at least one reason so many teens were having sex was that the media had successfully convinced them that losing their virginity was going to be the biggest moment of their lives. Our strategy was to provide our readers with more realistic accounts to debunk the celluloid stereotype. After setting up some alternative scenarios, we left the moral decisions to the reader while providing detailed information about birth control and sexually transmitted diseases and answers to frequently asked questions such as, "Will it hurt?" "Can he tell I'm a virgin?" "What if I change my mind?" and "How long will it take?"

5   The reader response to this article was phenomenal. *Sassy* and the article's author received hundreds of letters saying that finally someone had spoken to them in a way with which they felt comfortable. Mail started pouring in to the "Help" column, which I wrote, making apparent that we had only scratched the surface of a teenager's reality. What was most disconcerting to us was the tone of fear and shame these letters portrayed. Many young women were desperate for answers—we even received phone calls requesting advice. The next few articles we ran on sex were in response to these frantic letters asking about pregnancy, abortion, incest, suicide, and homosexuality.

6   "The Truth About Boys' Bodies," "Getting Turned On," "And They're Gay," "My Girlfriend Got Pregnant," and "Real Stories About Incest" were articles written to let girls know that whatever choices they made about their sexuality weren't shameful as long as they were responsible about safe sex, birth control, and emotional self-care.

7   Much of our reader response was positive. Mothers and even grandmothers called to say that they had read our articles with their daughters and granddaughters and as a result felt closer to each

other. There was also relief among some parents that we had explained something important they were uncomfortable communicating. On the other hand, there was also a fair share of irate screaming directed our way. Most of these callers felt the information we printed was "pornographic" and reeled off the old saw that information just encourages young women to have sex. Perhaps the most alarming phone call came from a father who screamed, "Anything my daughter learns about sex, she'll learn from me!" before he slammed down the receiver. These people canceled their subscriptions—a routine response to a publication one disagrees with and something we had counted on.

What we hadn't counted on was the mass reader/advertiser boycott led by a woman whose kids didn't even read *Sassy*. As a member of a group called Women Aglow was to show us, it is possible in this country for a vocal minority to bring about what amounts to censorship. Through the Jerry Falwell-supported publication *Focus on the Family,* Women Aglow organized a letter-writing campaign aimed at our major advertisers in which they threatened to boycott their products if those companies continued to advertise in *Sassy*. Within a matter of months *Sassy* had lost nearly every ad account, and we were publishing what we jokingly called *The Sassy Pamphlet*. We were told that to stay in business we must remove the "controversial" content from the magazine. That was reluctantly done, and today *Sassy* has regained its advertisers but not its detailed information on sex education. 8

Sadly, what was to a few young editors just a sobering lesson about the power of advertising was a great loss to young women, who need the information *Sassy* once provided. 9

Thesis and Organization

1. How does paragraph 1 answer the questions *who, where, when, why, how?*
2. What reasons does paragraph 2 state as what caused the editorial staff to focus on sex information?
3. How did that focus affect the advertisers? What primary cause lay behind that response?
4. Paragraphs 4–8 detail the readers' and advertisers' responses. What were they?
5. Reread paragraphs 3, 8, and 9. What do you conclude is the essay's thesis?

Technique and Style

1. How would you characterize the author's tone? Angry? Disappointed? Demoralized? What? On the whole, is it objective or subjective?
2. Given that tone, how would you describe the author's persona? Do you find it credible? Why or why not?
3. How would you define the author's purpose? Expressive, argumentative, informative, or some mixture? Explain.
4. What does the author gain by her use of the first-person plural, *we?*
5. What does the use of quotations add to the essay? What might be lost without them?

Suggestions for Writing

Think about times when you have met censorship head-on. Perhaps there were films you weren't allowed to see, books you couldn't read, topics you couldn't discuss, or places you couldn't go. Or perhaps censorship has been an issue in your family, church, or community. No matter what subject you choose, you might start by looking up *censorship* in an unabridged dictionary.

Black Men and Public Space

Brent Staples

*Any woman who has lived in a city knows the fear Brent Staples
speaks of, but not many of us realize how that reaction affects the
innocent. Staples's essay was first published in* Harper's *in 1986. He's
still whistling.*

My first victim was a woman—white, well-dressed, probably in   1
her early twenties. I came upon her late one evening on a deserted
street in Hyde Park, a relatively affluent neighborhood in an otherwise mean, impoverished section of Chicago. As I swung onto the
avenue behind her, there seemed to be a discreet, uninflammatory
distance between us. Not so. She cast back a worried glance. To her,
the youngish black man—a broad 6 feet 2 inches with a beard and
billowing hair, both hands shoved into the pockets of a bulky military jacket—seemed menacingly close. After a few more quick
glimpses, she picked up her pace and was soon running in earnest.
Within seconds she disappeared into a cross street.

That was more than a decade ago. I was 22 years old, a grad-   2
uate student newly arrived at the University of Chicago. It was in
the echo of that terrified woman's footfalls that I first began to
know the unwieldy inheritance I'd come into—the ability to alter
public space in ugly ways. It was clear that she thought herself the
quarry of a mugger, a rapist, or worse. Suffering a bout of insom-
nia, however, I was stalking sleep, not defenseless wayfarers. As a
softy who is scarcely able to take a knife to a raw chicken—let
alone hold one to a person's throat—I was surprised, embar-
rassed, and dismayed all at once. Her flight made me feel like an
accomplice in tyranny. It also made it clear that I was indistin-
guishable from the muggers who occasionally seeped into the area
from the surrounding ghetto. That first encounter, and those that
followed, signified that a vast, unnerving gulf lay between nighttime pedestrians—particularly women—and me. And I soon gathered that being perceived as dangerous is a hazard in itself. I only
needed to turn a corner into a dicey situation, or crowd some
frightened, armed person in a foyer somewhere, or make an errant
move after being pulled over by a policeman. Where fear and

weapons meet—and they often do in urban America—there is always the possibility of death.

3   In that first year, my first away from my hometown, I was to become thoroughly familiar with the language of fear. At dark, shadowy intersections, I could cross in front of a car stopped at a traffic light and elicit the *thunk, thunk, thunk, thunk* of the driver—black, white, male, or female—hammering down the door locks. On less traveled streets after dark, I grew accustomed to but never comfortable with people crossing to the other side of the street rather than pass me. Then there were the standard unpleasantries with policemen, doormen, bouncers, cabdrivers, and others whose business it is to screen out troublesome individuals *before* there is any nastiness.

4   I moved to New York nearly two years ago and I have remained an avid night walker. In central Manhattan, the near-constant crowd cover minimizes tense one-on-one street encounters. Elsewhere—in SoHo, for example, where sidewalks are narrow and tightly spaced buildings shut out the sky—things can get very taut indeed.

5   After dark, on the warrenlike streets of Brooklyn where I live, I often see women who fear the worst from me. They seem to have set their faces on neutral, and with their purse straps strung across their chests bandolier-style, they forge ahead as though bracing themselves against being tackled. I understand, of course, that the danger they perceive is not a hallucination. Women are particularly vulnerable to street violence, and young black males are drastically overrepresented among the perpetrators of that violence. Yet these truths are no solace against the kind of alienation that comes of being ever the suspect, a fearsome entity with whom pedestrians avoid making eye contact.

6   It is not altogether clear to me how I reached the ripe old age of 22 without being conscious of the lethality nighttime pedestrians attributed to me. Perhaps it was because in Chester, Pennsylvania, the small, angry industrial town where I came of age in the 1960s, I was scarcely noticeable against a backdrop of gang warfare, street knifings, and murders. I grew up one of the good boys, had perhaps a half-dozen fistfights. In retrospect, my shyness of combat has clear sources.

7   As a boy, I saw countless tough guys locked away; I have since buried several, too. They were babies, really—a teenage cousin, a

brother of 22, a childhood friend in his mid-twenties—all gone down in episodes of bravado played out in the streets. I came to doubt the virtues of intimidation early on. I chose, perhaps unconsciously, to remain a shadow—timid, but a survivor.

The fearsomeness mistakenly attributed to me in public places   8
often has a perilous flavor. The most frightening of these confusions occurred in the late 1970s and early 1980s, when I worked as a journalist in Chicago. One day, rushing into the office of a magazine I was writing for with a deadline story in hand, I was mistaken for a burglar. The office manager called security and, with an ad hoc posse, pursued me through the labyrinthine halls, nearly to my editor's door. I had no way of proving who I was. I could only move briskly toward the company of someone who knew me.

Another time I was on assignment for a local paper and killing   9
time before an interview. I entered a jewelry store on the city's affluent Near North Side. The proprietor excused herself and re-turned with an enormous red Doberman pinscher straining at the end of a leash. She stood, the dog extended toward me, silent to my questions, her eyes bulging nearly out of her head. I took a cursory look around, nodded, and bade her good night.

Relatively speaking, however, I never fared as badly as another   10
black male journalist. He went to nearby Waukegan, Illinois, a cou-ple of summers ago to work on a story about a murderer who was born there. Mistaking the reporter for the killer, police officers hauled him from his car at gunpoint and but for his press credentials would probably have tried to book him. Such episodes are not uncommon. Black men trade tales like this all the time.

Over the years, I learned to smother the rage I felt at so often   11
being taken for a criminal. Not to do so would surely have led to madness. I now take precautions to make myself less threatening. I move about with care, particularly late in the evening. I give a wide berth to nervous people on subway platforms during the wee hours, particularly when I have exchanged business clothes for jeans. If I happen to be entering a building behind some people who appear skittish, I may walk by, letting them clear the lobby before I return, so as not to seem to be following them. I have been calm and extremely congenial on those rare occasions when I've been pulled over by the police.

And on late-evening constitutionals I employ what has proved to   12 be an excellent tension-reducing measure: I whistle melodies from Beethoven and Vivaldi and the more popular classical composers. Even steely New Yorkers hunching toward nighttime destinations seem to relax, and occasionally they even join in the tune. Virtually everybody seems to sense that a mugger wouldn't be warbling bright, sunny selections from Vivaldi's *Four Seasons*. It is my equivalent of the cowbell that hikers wear when they know they are in bear country.

Thesis and Organization

1. Reread paragraph 1. What expectations does it evoke in the reader? For paragraph 2, state in your own words what Staples means by "unwieldy inheritance." What effects does that inheritance have?
2. The body of the essay breaks into three paragraph blocks. In paragraphs 3–5, what effects does the author's walking at night have on others? On himself?
3. In paragraphs 6 and 7, Staples refers to his childhood. Why had he been unaware of his effect on others? What effect did the streets he grew up on have on him?
4. Staples uses examples in paragraphs 8–10. What do all three have in common? What generalization does Staples draw from them?
5. Summarize the causes and effects Staples brings out in paragraphs 11 and 12, and in one sentence, makes a general statement about them. What does that statement imply about being a black male? About urban life? About American culture? Consider your answers to those questions and in one sentence state the thesis of the essay.

Technique and Style

1. A large part of the essay's impact lies in the ironic contrast between appearance and reality. What details does Staples bring out about himself that contrast with the stereotype of the mugger?
2. In paragraph 1, Staples illustrates the two uses of the dash. What function do they perform? Rewrite either of the two sentences so that you avoid the dash. Which sentence is better and why?
3. Trace Staples's use of time. Why does he start where he does? Try placing the time period mentioned in paragraphs 6 and 7 elsewhere in the essay. What advantages does their present placement have? What is the effect of ending the essay in the present?
4. Examine Staples's choice of verbs in the second sentence of paragraph 5. Rewrite the sentence using as many forms of the verb *to be* as possible. What differences do you note?

5. Staples concludes the essay with an analogy. In what ways is it ironic? How does the irony tie into the essay's thesis?

Suggestions for Writing

Think about a situation you have been in where a stereotype determined your effect on others. Age, race, gender, physique, clothing are only a few of the physical characteristics that can spawn a stereotype.

Pain, Not Pleasure, Now the Big Sell

George Felton

Today, according to Felton, the "sweat/pain motif" is being used to sell products, and "Healthism" is the latest craze. Felton, who teaches writing and copywriting at the Columbus College of Art and Design, explores why this is so in an essay that appropriately enough appeared in the "Living Today" section of the Miami Herald *(1989).*

1   Advertising is a funny thing. We tell it our dreams, we tell it what to say, but after a while it learns the message so well, it starts telling us.

2   What are we being told now? Simply this: not only can we extend our life, we are required to. Nike, assuming responsibility for our physical and, by implication, our spiritual health, has raised the pitch of its admonitions, the newest campaign being "Just Do It." Bold type and bold people look up from the page or from their workouts and scold us for being our usual, sloppy selves. "Just Do It," we are warned, and as one of the players adds, "And it wouldn't hurt to stop eating like a pig, either." Ouch. Yes, ma'am.

3   We've asked for this, of course. Ever since the first jogger spurted out the back door, we've been headed on a course past simple health and toward self-denial, asceticism, pain as pleasure. "Let's live forever," we say with no particular joy, and advertising couldn't agree more.

4   In this Era of Healthism, any marketer with his finger in the wind knows that Nike need not be alone in selling the virtue of self-denial. "No Pain, No Gain" can now sell much more than workout gear.

5   Take food, for instance. Advertising has taught us that eating isn't fun anymore, not if we do it right. Breakfast has become the day's first moral test—will we or won't we do the right thing?

6   Quaker Oats' new pretty boy is not the smiling Quaker of the package but the noticeably unsmiling Wilford Brimley of *Our House* and *Cocoon,* who admonishes us to eat oatmeal, not because it tastes good, but because "it's the right thing to do." Casting a baleful

eye upon us, he says, "First thing tomorrow morning, do something that brings down your cholesterol." We have our marching orders. Breakfast has been redefined as work: out of bed and on the job.

The cereal aisle at the grocery store now presents us with one   7
trail mix after another designed for the long march through our large intestines, each another grainy way to combat cancer, cholesterol, our own weak desire for pleasure. I now walk down the aisle trying, not to satisfy my hunger, but to represent my colon. What would *it* like? What does *it* need? Even Cheerios has come to see its own name as deeply ironic, no longer a smiling matter. The current ad's headline straightens the minds of those inclined to play with their food: "The O stands for oat bran."

Everywhere, Healthism's central advertising strategy is to rede-   8
fine the product away from fun and toward functionalism. Take shoes for instance. Forget stylish, sexy, chic—forget all that. A cur-rent Rockport campaign headlines itself: "Shoes that help you live longer," and the copy explains that shoes are really well-engineered things we stick on our feet for fitness walking. Similarly, we see watches sold, not as jewelry nor as fashion, but as ways to time our workout. Listerine mouth rinse, which could promise to make us more kissable, opts for health maintenance instead; a recent ad asks us to "Pick one: 'Gingivitis or Listerine.' "

Even gum chewing need not be idle amusement. Trident tells us   9
it's really a fighter in the war for healthy teeth: "An ounce of pre-vention" one ad claims. "Toothpaste should come in as many fla-vors," says another. In the war against sloth and decay, no product is unarmed, no movement without its purpose.

And our purpose, more and more ads tell us, is to sweat. Cher   10
and Heather Locklear sell the sexiness of sweating at Scandinavian Health Spas. In harness in their machines, they fuse pain with plea-sure until we the viewers/voyeurs see sex and sweat as indistin-guishable.

Advertising also extends this glorification of sweat to other con-   11
texts. Hewlett Packard, for instance, in its celebrated "What if . . . ?" campaign, has equated sweating with thinking: its compulsive, driven types are out sculling on the river or doing laps in a pool, sweating inside and out, when the brilliant ideas strike hard enough to drive them to the phone with their inspiration, "What if . . . ?" We admire them and trust them: good ideas and good people *are* sweaty, we say.

12   Cars are sweaty, too—recent Chevrolet advertising has featured cars driving past sweat-drenched runners and bikers, equating the glory of the car with the glory of their pain. More than a means to an end, sweat is becoming an end unto itself, a psychological destination.

13   This sweat/pain motif in recent advertising may signal new national restraint, a cultural move away from self-gratification and toward control, the awareness of limits, the virtue of a Just Say No trek to self-actualization. However, it might simply be good old-fashioned hedonism's greatest idea: through denial we can live forever and thus have everything.

14   There is, after all, nothing stronger than the Healthism promise. It's better than sex, it's better than money, it's even better than love, not least because it makes all these more possible with the extra time we'll have. In an era so health conscious that we apologize for not knowing our cholesterol count, what can be stronger than the me-too-ism of longer life? Much of this advertising is aimed at the late 30s-to-early-40s crowd, the Boomers, who overdid things in the sixties and may be overdoing them again. Self-indulgence could be masquerading as asceticism. The temper of our times, healthism first, is really an inverted hippie principle via William Blake: "The road of excess leads to the palace of wisdom." And the endorphin gobblers, straining in their Gore-Tex, couldn't agree more.

Thesis and Organization

1. Summarize what paragraphs 1–3 say about advertising. What tentative thesis do you deduce for the essay that will follow?
2. Paragraphs 4–9 use example to trace cause-and-effect relationships. What are they?
3. Paragraphs 10–12 discuss the "glorification of sweat." What is the author's point?
4. The conclusion, paragraphs 13 and 14, analyzes the meaning of "Healthism." State that meaning in terms of cause and effect.
5. Reread paragraphs 1–3, 13, and 14. What is the thesis of the essay?

Technique and Style

1. Is Felton trying to persuade or inform the reader? Or is he merely telling the reader how he feels about "Healthism"? Explain your response.

2. The essay has a humorous tone, but how would you characterize the humor? Is it snide, sarcastic, exaggerated, understated, what?
3. Look over the essay, scanning it for Felton's use of capitals. What conclusions can you draw about his use of this device?
4. The author uses many brand names throughout the essay. What is lost or gained by this choice?
5. What examples can you find of formal diction? Slang? What reasons can you find for the author's wide range of diction?

Suggestions for Writing

Leaf through a magazine to see what advertisements fall into what categories; cars, cosmetics, clothes, educational products, and liquor are apt to be only a few. Pick one and consider the pitch behind the ads. What, in addition to the product, is being sold? What cause-and-effect relationships are involved?

*H*ow an Era Empowered Students

Constance L. Hays

Constance Hays focuses on college campuses to see how the issues and demonstrations of the 1960s affected university life. Then, student power was a slogan; now it's a reality. The essay was published in the October 1989 issue of the New York Times *in its special section on education that appears quarterly.*

1   Where once decisions about college life were made by administrators and faculty, the sixties changed all that. Today student representatives sit on panels and committees alongside faculty and officials. Where once students were seen and heard only in the classroom context, the sixties empowered them. Now their counsel is institutionalized, in an effort to avoid potential conflicts.

2   "I wasn't part of the administration then, but my sense was that the administration had for years been moving along without any particular sense that it had to be responsive to a student constituency," said the associate dean of Columbia College, Michael Rosenthal, referring to the 1968 demonstrations that closed the school down. "Since those days, I don't think any university has felt that immunity."

3   At the University of California at Berkeley, much student power now taken for granted was achieved only after marches and sometimes-bloody confrontations with the authorities. Most student roles in administration, as well as the independence of the campus newspaper, evolved during this tumultuous decade.

4   In 1964, the protest known as the Free Speech Movement brought to campus a political activism that was previously denied by rules set by the university system's board of regents. Its key incident, in which nearly 800 students were arrested during a sit-in at Sproul Hall, the administration building, was a nonviolent event "which attracted much more attention than later demonstrations that became violent," says Ray Colvig, whose career as a university spokesman spans 25 years. Shortly afterward, the faculty voted to support the student demands, and in early 1965 the board of regents ruled

that it could not restrict the actual content of political activity on the state campuses.

Thereafter, Berkeley students participated in university commit-   5
tees, including those on education policy and university administration, areas previously closed to them. "Twenty-five years ago,
student government was referred to as a sandbox," Mr. Colvig said.
"Today the students are on committees. They run enterprises. They
operate a lobby in Sacramento, which has been quite successful. It's
very, very different."

Within a year after the F.S.M., however, violent demonstrations   6
replaced peaceful ones, and by the summer of 1968 street battles
between students and police had become commonplace. One of the
most protracted and bloody episodes occurred with the People's
Park riots of 1969.

In April of that year, about 500 students, faculty members and   7
hippies began planting flowers and vegetables on a vacant lot that
the university had planned eventually to use for student housing.
They added swings, benches and pieces of sculpture. One idea for
the park also aired at the time was to have the university establish
on the site a separate "Third World College" for Asians, African and
Hispanic studies.

Early on May 15, in response to a directive from the university's   8
president, Roger W. Heyns, hundreds of policemen removed a
group of people from the park and began putting up a fence to keep
them out. The students rallied at the university later in the day and
marched on the park to take it over again. In the ensuing confrontation the students threw rocks and Alameda County sheriff's deputies used tear gas. When the protesters would not disperse, the
deputies then fired into the crowd with birdshot-loaded riot guns,
wounding about 70 rioters and bystanders, one of whom later died.

Ronald Reagan, then governor of California, ordered the National   9
Guard into Berkeley and imposed a curfew on the city. But protests
continued, some by Berkeley faculty members who held vigils to
condemn the violence. During a march by 500 students and others
on the home of President Heyns, on the Berkeley campus, a National Guard helicopter sprayed tear gas powder over the crowds.
The demonstrations continued until May 24, when most of the guard
troops were removed from the city.

The university subsequently introduced a third-world focus into   10
its curriculum, albeit in compromise form. An academic entity was

established outside the arts and sciences department, but with faculty control. It included divisions for Afro-American, Native American, Chicano and Asian-American Studies. The Afro-American division eventually became a formal department; the others award degrees through the Department of Ethnic Studies.

11   At Cornell University, student demands for altering the curriculum's focus on European thought and culture was met with a plan for an African Studies and Research Center by the spring of 1969. But shortly after the plan was approved, a still-unidentified group burned a cross, Ku Klux Klan-style, on the lawn outside a black woman's dormitory. In a protest that the director of the center, Robert L. Harris, Jr., described as "the culmination of a great deal of frustration," a group of black students took over Willard Straight Hall, the university's student union.

12   While that incident is remembered as one in which students were armed with guns, Professor Harris said this was not true. "What happened was that the students were not armed at the time they took over Straight," he said. "Members of a white fraternity came and tried to recapture the building. A fight broke out. The white students said, "We'll be back, and you better be ready."

13   "At that point, the black students secured guns," Professor Harris said. "It wasn't their intention to go in armed."

14   The black students' protest lasted several days. At one point, white students formed a ring around the building, Professor Harris said, to head off possible violence by preventing other groups from trying to retake it.

15   Today the African Studies and Research Center has about a dozen people enrolled in its degree program. About 900 students enroll in courses offered by the department. "It is now much more fully integrated into the affairs of the university," said Cornell's provost, Robert Barker. Though plans for the center had been made at the time of the takeover, the protest accelerated its funding and the center's opening.

16   Part of the center's academic success over the last 19 years, according to Mr. Barker, stems from the increase in black faculty members in the university. Similar centers, less well known, have been formed at Cornell for Native American students, and for Asian-American and Hispanic-American Studies.

17   At Columbia, students took over five university buildings in 1968.

The takeover was the culmination of a protest against military research at the university and a plan to build a university gym in Morningside Park. About 700 people were arrested and scores were injured.

The takeover and its bloody aftermath led to the formation of a   18
university senate the next year, Dean Rosenthal said. Today the senate includes students, faculty members, administrators and staff who may bring resolutions before the floor, and an executive committee. "That has occupied a substantial amount of political energy that, prior to 1968, had no place particular to go," Dean Rosenthal said.

Also in 1968, students at predominantly black Howard University   19
who were chafing at a conservative curriculum that failed to place adequate emphasis on black literature and culture took over the college's administration building. That protest marked a convergence of the student power and Black Power movements operating independently elsewhere around the country. At least 1000 students staged a sit-in at the building, forcing the closing of dormitories and classroom buildings. A list of student demands, including a call for the university's president to resign, was submitted to negotiators.

The sit-in ended peacefully, and subsequently a permanent judi-   20
ciary system was established that guaranteed students a hearing before a student-dominated board. The unrest also produced a faculty-student committee to study existing programs and come up with changes in academic and extracurricular life.

Today Howard offers an Afro-American Studies Resource Center,   21
part of the College of Liberal Arts. There is also an African Studies and Research Program for graduate students. In addition, many courses include discussions on events from a black perspective, but with a less rhetorical, more scholarly attitude, according to university officials.

Most historians agree that the sixties helped institutionalize stu-   22
dent participation in the affairs of their colleges and universities by establishing channels for dialogue—sometimes using civil disobedience. "Do we respond to pressure?" asked Mr. Barker, Cornell's provost. "I would say yes. We don't always see students' needs as they do, and we reserve the right to make our own determinations. But we do try very hard to have student input. We don't wait until they're marching in the streets to discover what is of concern."

Thesis and Organization

1. Paragraphs 1 and 2 introduce the essay. What does the introduction lead you to expect in what is to follow?
2. The University of California, Berkeley, is the subject of paragraphs 3–10. What cause-and-effect relationships do these paragraphs make clear?
3. Paragraphs 11–16 focus on Cornell University. What are the cause-and-effect relationships in these paragraphs?
4. How do the cause-and-effect relationships in the examples from Columbia and Howard universities differ from those mentioned earlier?
5. Consider the introduction, the examples, and paragraph 22. What thesis do they suggest for the essay?

Technique and Style

1. Given your answer to question 5 above, how would you characterize Hays's tone?
2. What does Hays gain by her use of examples? How would the essay be weakened if she had used fewer?
3. Why might Hays have brought in the question of the students being armed at Cornell? Why does she go into the question as closely as she does?
4. What effect does Hays achieve by her extensive use of quotation?
5. Reread Hays's description of the violent demonstrations at Berkeley, paragraphs 6–9. How does she link the paragraphs together?

Suggestions for Writing

Demonstrations can take on any form, ranging from a child's temper tantrum to a nation's revolt. Think about the various kinds of protests and protest movements: picketing, marches, sit-ins, letter-writing campaigns—all for particular reasons and aimed at specific effects. Or on a more individual level, consider the causes and effects involved in nonconformist dress, hairstyle, or behavior.

*F*ather and Child

Shelley Moore

Teenage pregnancy is a widely recognized social problem, but the programs and social services that deal with the problem usually focus on the mothers. Shelley Moore, however, takes a look at the problem from the perspective of the fathers. Moore's essay appeared in The Crisis, *a journal founded by W. E. B. DuBois and published by the NAACP. The time of publication was 1987, but the problem remains today.*

James was in a bind. He was behind in his child support pay- 1
ments, and the Department of Social Services was on his back.

James was 19 years old, making $80 a week. Sheila, the mother 2
of his baby, was under 18, so Social Services had been sending
benefits to her father instead of to her. James did not trust that
arrangement. That is why he started giving his money directly to
Sheila instead of to Social Services. And that is why Social Services
was on his back. James did not know what to do about it.

Fortunately, James found out about the Fatherhood Project, a 3
counseling and training program at the local Albany (New York)
area Urban League for young men who are parents. Today, James
no longer has any hassle with Social Services. He is employed in a
full-time job *and* a part-time job, and he and his young family have
an apartment. Sheila has gone back to high school. After she graduates this year, James will return to school, too. But for now, he is
working hard enough, taking care of business and a baby, too.

The Fatherhood Project is part of a growing movement of 4
community-based initiatives around the country addressing teen
parenthood from the male side of the issue, for a change. And a lot
of young fathers care more about their young families than they are
given credit for.

"We get a lot of bad press," says one young father named Robert. 5

Traditionally, responsibilities for parenthood and parenthood 6
prevention have fallen most heavily on those most likely to get
pregnant—women and girls. And for a teenage girl without an income or a high school diploma, parenthood usually forecasts a
bleak future for both mother and child.

7   Yet, it happens all the time. In 1982, more than one-half million girls under the age of 20 in the United States became mothers. Over 145,000 of those young mothers were black, and 87 percent of black teen mothers were unmarried at the time their babies were born. According to a research study by Child Trends, 22 percent of black girls, married and unmarried, became mothers by age 18. By the time they turn 20, the motherhood rate zooms to 41 percent.

8   One might assume that teenage pregnancies are fathered by teenage boys. That is not always the case. Many of the fathers are young men in their early twenties. Some are older than that. The data is sketchy, however, since fatherhood patterns are difficult to research, and research results are not extremely reliable.

9   But it appears that being a teenager, being black and being male is a likely recipe for becoming a father in this country. Consider some of the findings of a 1986 Planned Parenthood poll of teenagers about sex and contraception: Sexual activity starts younger among teenagers of the lowest socioeconomic backgrounds. Among black teens who had sex before age 18, 71 percent were sexually active by the time they turned 14. Forty percent of sexually active black teenagers never use any form of contraception. Thirty-five percent of black teenagers feel contraceptives are too expensive.

10   Black teenagers are less knowledgeable about conception and contraception than white teenagers are, and boys are less knowledgeable than girls. Black teenagers are less likely than white teenagers, and boys are less likely than girls to have taken sex education courses in school. Fifty-two percent of black teenagers have had no sex education courses at all. And boys are less likely than girls to talk about sex, conception and contraception with their parents.

11   Teenage parenting is not just a "black" problem, but it is now considered one of the major stumbling blocks to economic progress in the black community. Babies come along before their parents have an opportunity to finish school, start careers, or stash any money away.

12   In a recent study of young men just beyond their teens, researchers for the Children's Defense Fund found that the average inflation-adjusted earnings of men aged 20 to 24 fell by nearly 30 percent between 1973 and 1984. For black men in that age group, earnings fell a staggering 50 percent. This decline resulted largely from the nation's employment shift from high-paying manufacturing jobs to low-paying service jobs during that decade. The percentage of

young men earning enough to lift a family of three out of poverty fell from 60 percent to 42 percent, and the percentage of such men who were married fell from 40 percent to 20 percent.

The study concluded that as the earnings of young men declined, 13 so did their marriage prospects. As a result, the rate of babies born out of wedlock has skyrocketed.

If times are hard for black fathers in their early twenties, the plight 14 of black fathers in their early teens can be only worse.

That is why organizations like Alpha Phi Alpha Fraternity, the 15 Council of Black Churchmen and the National Urban League are addressing teen fatherhood issues more aggressively than they have in the past.

Three years ago, the National Urban League launched an award- 16 winning public service advertising campaign to reach young black men with the messages: "Don't Make A Baby If You Can't Be A Father" and "Think Before You Do." Produced by Mingo-Jones Advertising on the Urban League's behalf, the campaign consists of radio commercials, posters, and a television spot.

"We want to encourage boys to do their part in preventing preg- 17 nancy," said Ed Pitt of the National Urban League. "And if they do become parents, we want to help them become more responsible parents." As a result of the national advertising, at least 21 local Urban Leagues across the country have launched programs to serve teen fathers.

Other grass roots projects are cropping up, too—like the Teen 18 Fathers program at the Youth and Family Centers in Lawndale, California, just outside of Los Angeles; the Black Fathers Collective in Brooklyn, New York; the March of Dimes' Male Involvement Project in Washington, D.C., and the Teen Fathers Program at the Medical College of Pennsylvania Hospital. Typically, the programs help fathers find jobs, train for careers, get back in school or negotiate social service systems. Counseling and support groups are also important components of the programs. Teen fathers bear a lot of pressures in the face of sudden adult responsibility.

In a recent interview in *People* magazine, Ron Johnson, director 19 of the program in Lawndale, stated: "Most teenage fathers want to be with their children, but they can't support the child, and it's hard to feel good about yourself as a man if you earn only $4 to $5 an hour."

"My sister has money she can lend me," says Raymond, a father 20 of two young boys, "but she won't let me have it. She wants me to learn a lesson."

21   "It's not easy," says Robert, who recently married his baby daughter's mother. "Sometimes I have to borrow money from my folks." He adds proudly: "I always pay it back."

22   Most young fathers feel public funds should not have to support their children. They also feel there is no other alternative. Some community-based programs teach fathers the basics of caretaking, like diapering, feeding and rocking babies to sleep. In the process, fathers not only learn practical skills; they also form close, personal bonds with their children and strengthen their sense of commitment.

23   "They look so much like me," says Raymond of his boys. "I love it when they call me Daddy. I still have a good relationship with my girlfriend, too. We may get married, but I want to go slow. I want to find a steady job first."

24   "I don't feel like I'm stuck," says Robert. "I got the girl I wanted, and I don't feel a need to see other girls. I also stay away from old friends who I know would be a bad influence on me, although I'd like them to see how well I'm doing."

25   Robert is grateful for the moral support he and his wife have received from both sets of parents. Families can make or break successful teen fathering. It is not unusual for the baby's maternal grandparents to shut the father out. He is seen as the problem, not the solution. Good-bye and good riddance.

26   "I want to get it together before too many people start coming between us," says Raymond. "I don't want a lot of family and friends telling us what to do."

27   "Her mother takes control and tries to do everything for her daughter. She just excludes me completely," complains another young father named Kevin. "Why should she be angry with me? Having children is natural."

28   For Michael, his emotional bonds to his children cause him a lot of pain. He is one of thousands of teen parents who have given up their rights to their children. Today, his 2-year-old son lives in a foster home in another state. "I haven't seen him in 10 months," he says, biting his lip. "I try not to think about him, because it hurts so bad—especially around Christmas and his birthday."

29   Local teen fatherhood programs, most of which are less than three years old, have been highly successful. "Seventy-five percent

of the young men that have come to us have been successful in getting their lives back on track," reports Harold Robinson of Albany's Fatherhood Project. "We surprised everybody with those results. We even surprised ourselves."

In Baltimore this past January, the Urban League paid tribute to   30
a number of local fathers at a celebration in honor of Martin Luther King, Jr.'s birthday. Men and boys alike were recognized for their exemplary commitments to parenting.

Good fathering is not an issue for teenage boys who avoid mak-   31
ing babies in the first place. That is why many pregnancy prevention efforts are now targeting boys as well as girls. Planned Parenthood and other family planning clinics that were once considered "female" facilities are now reaching out more strongly to males. The most common advice given to boys is, in a word, condoms—the most effective preventative measure they can use, next to abstinence. Communities have also put pressure on school systems to balance their sex education curricula, which tend to focus on the female side of the issues. Boys are therefore less likely to sign up for the courses. But knowing the details about making babies is not enough. Boys as well as girls need to clearly understand that becoming parents too soon is not in their best interest.

The Planned Parenthood study observed that: "Contraceptives   32
are more likely to be used by those teenagers who objectively have a lot at stake and who stand to lose a lot by being involved in an unintended pregnancy." Teenagers with strong, realistic plans for college and careers are least likely to become parents. Too many low-income teenagers—and black teenage boys in particular—do not have such bright hopes for their futures.

Believing in one's self is perhaps the best contraceptive of all.   33

Thesis and Organization

1. The essay opens with a brief narrative example (1–3). What are the causes of James's problem? The effects? What are the effects of his participating in the Fatherhood Project? Summarize what this introduction establishes about the essay's subject, pattern of organization, and purpose.

2. The general problem of black teenage pregnancy is addressed in paragraphs 4–15. List the causes. What topics do paragraphs 14 and 15 set up? How do those topics relate to the rest of the essay?

3. Analyze the cause-and-effect pattern in paragraphs 16–30 by examining

the specific means that are used to help teen fathers. What effects do they have? What works against solving the problem? What results?
4. Moore concludes the essay by examining the group that is *not* a problem. What reasons do paragraphs 31 and 32 provide for teenagers who avoid the problem of pregnancy?
5. The amount of information Moore includes suggests that the essay has an informative goal, yet it is also apparent that the author finds both the problem and the ways it can be avoided or resolved compelling. Does Moore lean more to persuasion or to informing the reader? How can you support your view? What is the thesis of the essay?

Technique and Style

1. The essay originally appeared in *The Crisis,* a journal founded by W. E. B. DuBois and published by the NAACP. What evidence can you find to show that the essay is or is not aimed at a predominantly black audience?
2. Throughout the essay, Moore intersperses examples drawn from the lives of particular people. What effect does this technique achieve?
3. Moore weaves various statistics into the essay. What would be lost if those numbers were not included?
4. A one-sentence paragraph is often used like a quick left jab; it surprises and carries a lot of punch. Consider the last paragraph and analyze its implications and the effect it has on the reader.
5. Moore's essay appeals not only to reason but to emotion. What examples can you find of an emotional appeal? What emotions does Moore want you to feel toward the young fathers? How does the emotional appeal tie into the essay's purpose?

Suggestions for Writing

Consider other problems and the agencies designed to deal with them: career choice and your institution's counseling service; crime and neighborhood watch groups; dieting and Weight Watchers; problem children and Tough Love; the homeless and the Salvation Army; alcoholism and Alcoholics Anonymous. The odds are that any research you have to do will be easy; these groups and others like them usually publish material that will provide you with the necessary facts and information.

Exploring the Topic

1. **Have you stated the topic as a question that asks why *X* happened?** What are the possible causes? The probable causes? Rank the causes in order of their priority.

2. **Have you stated the topic as a question that asks what results from *X*?** What are the possible effects? The probable effects? Rank the effects in order of their priority.

3. **Is a temporal relationship involved?** Review your lists of causes and effects and rule out any that only have a temporal relationship to your subject.

4. **Which do you want to emphasize, cause or effect?** Check to make sure your focus is clear.

5. **What is your point?** Are you trying to show that something is so or to explore your topic?

6. **What evidence can you use to support your point?** Do you need to cite authorities or quote statistics? If you depend on personal experience, are you sure your experience is valid, that is, representative of general experience?

7. **What does your reader think?** Does your audience have any preconceived ideas about your topic for which you need to account? What are they? How can you deal with them?

8. **What role do you want to play in the essay?** Are you an observer or a participant? Is your major intention to inform, to persuade, or to entertain? What point of view best serves your purpose?

Drafting the Paper

1. **Know your reader.** Figure out what attitudes your reader may have about your topic. If the cause-and-effect relationship you are discussing is unusual, you might want to shape your initial attitude so that it is as skeptical as your reader's. On the other hand, you may want to start with a short narrative that immediately puts the reader on your side. Consider how much your reader is apt to know about your topic. If you are the expert, make sure you explain everything that needs to be explained but without doing so condescendingly.

2. **Know your purpose.** Adjust your tone and persona to suit your purpose. If you are writing a persuasive paper, make sure your persona is credible and that you focus your ideas so that they may change the mind of a reader who initially does not agree with you—or short of that, that

your ideas make the reader rethink his or her position. If you are writing an informative paper, choose a persona and tone that will interest the reader. Tone and persona are even more crucial to essays written to entertain, where the tone can range from the ironic to the lighthearted.

3. **Emphasize a cause or effect.** Essays that focus on cause more than likely will cover a variety of probable reasons that explain the result. Though there may be only one effect or result, you may want to predict other possible effects in your last paragraph. For instance, an essay that explores the causes of violence examines a number of reasons or causes for the result or effect—violence—but may conclude by speculating on the possible effects of the rising crime rate. On the other hand, essays that focus on effect more than likely will cover a number of possible effects that are produced by a single cause, though again you may want to speculate on other causes. If you are writing about the effects of smoking, at some point in the essay you may want to include other harmful substances in the air such as coal dust, hydrocarbons, and carbon monoxide.

4. **Check for validity.** Don't hesitate to include quotations, allusions, statistics, and studies that will support your point. Choose your examples carefully to buttress the relationship you are trying to establish, and be sure you don't mistake a temporal relationship for a causal one.

5. **Make a point.** The cause-and-effect relationship you examine should lead to or stem from an assertion: video games not only entertain, they also stimulate the mind and improve coordination; video games are not only habit-forming, they are also addictive.

Definition

When I use a word," said Humpty Dumpty, "it means just what I choose it to mean—neither more nor less." To that Alice replied, "The question is whether you can make words mean so many different things." Humpty Dumpty then pronounced, "The question is which is to be the master—that's all." Writers are the masters of their words, although not to the extent Humpty Dumpty would like, and often a discussion or argument boils down to the meaning of a crucial word. *Liberty, justice, civil rights, freedom,* and other similar concepts, for example, are all abstractions until they are defined.

If you had to write a paper on what *freedom* means to you, you might be tempted first off to look up the word in a dictionary, but you will discover more to say if you put aside the dictionary and first think about some basic questions, such as "whose freedom?" If it's your freedom that you are writing about, who or what sets limits on your freedom? The law? The church? Parents? Family responsibilities? After you mull over questions such as these, you are in a better position to make use of a dictionary definition. The dictionary is the most obvious place to find what the word means, but what you find there is only explicit meaning, the word's *denotation*. Look up *freedom* in a collegiate dictionary and you'll see the different ways in which the word can be used and also its etymology, but that won't convey the rich layers of meaning that the word has accumulated through the years. The dictionary will not reveal the word's associative or emotional meanings, its *connotation*. One way to discover connotation is to ask yourself questions about the word, questions similar to those above that get at how the concept of freedom touches your life. The more specific your examples, the more concrete your definition can be, and the less the danger of slipping into clichés. Unless the word you are defining is quite unusual, most readers will be familiar with its dictionary definition; your own definition and your speculations on the word's connotation are of much greater interest.

A paper that defines a familiar word can hold just as much interest as one that examines an unfamiliar one or one that is particularly powerful. "What does *boredom* mean?" "Why is *synergism* a useful concept?" "What does it mean to be called *handicapped?*" Questions such as these can call upon almost any mode of thinking and writing, as the following list demonstrates.

Description
What details best describe it? What senses can you appeal to?

Narration
What story might best illustrate it? What kind of conflict might the word involve?

Example
What sorts of examples illustrate it? What different times and sources can you use to find examples?

Comparison and contrast
What is it similar to? What is it different from?

Analogy
What metaphor would make it vivid? What might the reader be familiar with that you can draw an analogy to?

Division and classification
How can it be divided? What categories can it be placed in?

Process
What steps or stages are involved in it? Which are the crucial ones?

Cause and effect
What are the conditions that cause it? What effect does it have?

When questions such as these are tailored to the particular word or concept under scrutiny, they will help you explore your subject.

AUDIENCE AND PURPOSE   For the most part, you can assume that your audience has a general understanding of the word or phrase that is to be defined. The nature of that general understanding, however, differs. For instance, answering machines provoke reactions that range from irritation to relief, from dismay to amusement—all emotions the readers know. In his essay "Let It Beep," however, Craig Stoltz analyzes why his readers feel the way they do and reveals meanings they may not have thought about. He explores his subject. But in "Discrimination Is a Virtue," Robert Keith Miller wants to change his reader's understanding, to make his reader aware of how the changed meaning of *discrimination* is, in turn, reflected in our society. He argues for a redefinition of the word.

Redefinition is also the point of Kurt Andersen's essay, "Not the Best of Times, Not the Worst," where he argues that ambivalence is an appropriate response to the times we live in. Garrison Keillor, in "O the Porch," calls not for redefinition but reexamination. He assumes that his audience is generally familiar with the old-fashioned porch, but he takes that familiarity and particularizes it, showing why the classic porch makes a house a home. William Raspberry also calls for reexamination, but his purpose is twofold—as is his audience. In "The Handicap of Definition," he seeks to inform his white readers and persuade his black audience. While blacks must instill a more positive image in their children, whites need to know just how limiting the present image is.

EXAMPLE   To flesh out the definition of a term, you can draw upon a number of sources. William Raspberry's initial examples come from the world around us, the world of the Boston Celtics' Larry Bird and of popular performers Tom Jones and Teena Marie, worlds where the adjective *black* is a compliment. Moving on to examples from education and business, Raspberry explores what black children mean when they call something "white." He then examines examples of "positive ethnic traditions," the Jews and

Chinese, to argue that the black ethnic tradition is limiting, if not self-defeating.

OTHER MODES   Definition, perhaps more than any other rhetorical pattern, depends on other modes to serve its purpose. While example is the most obvious, all the others also come into play. Process, cause and effect, and comparison and contrast enter into Kurt Andersen's "Not the Best of Times, Not the Worst," while narration introduces the essays by Craig Stoltz and Robert Keith Miller. Miller also briefly uses process to trace the historical meaning of *discrimination,* turning from process to cause and effect to point out why the meaning shifted to the negative and the effects of that shift on our culture. Cause and effect provides impact in William Raspberry's "The Handicap of Definition," for he first shows the reader the harmful effects of a limited definition of *black* in order to argue for change.

THESIS AND ORGANIZATION   Although a definition can play a key role in an essay, it is not the essay's thesis. The thesis rises from the author's assertion about the definition. Most frequently, the reader can derive the essay's thesis by combining two or more of the author's statements, which is the case in the essays by Garrison Keillor, Kurt Andersen, and William Raspberry. Sometimes the barebones thesis is contained in one statement—in Miller's essay, the title. This kind of thesis is easy to identify. More elusive is the implied thesis, illustrated here by Craig Stoltz's "Let It Beep."

An essay's organization can also be straightforward or somewhat complex. Robert Keith Miller uses a roughly chronological pattern of organization, starting with his childhood and an ancient tale similar to that of *King Lear,* moving through the seventeenth century into the nineteenth and finally the twentieth, where most of the essay is focused. Structuring an essay so that it moves from the least to the most important point is another obvious pattern, and it is the one used by Kurt Andersen and William Raspberry. Perhaps the hardest to handle successfully is the organization that goes from the particular to the general, as illustrated by Craig Stoltz's "Let It Beep" and Garrison Keillor's "O the Porch."

O the Porch

Garrison Keillor

Anyone who has heard "Prairie Home Companion" is familiar with Garrison Keillor, whose radio show made rural living downright attractive. It's no wonder we should pity the poor city dweller with no porch and therefore no company, no friends, no comfort, no grace. This essay by Keillor appeared in his 1989 collection We Are Still Married.

Of porches there are two sorts: the decorative and the useful, the porch that is only a platform and the porch you can lie around on in your pajamas and read the Sunday paper.   1

The decorative porch has a slight function, similar to that of the White House portico: it's where you greet prime ministers, premiers, and foreign potentates. The cannons boom, the band plays, the press writes it all down, and they go indoors.   2

The true porch, or useful porch, incorporates some of that grandeur, but it is screened and protects you from prying eyes. It strikes a perfect balance between indoor and outdoor life.   3

Indoors is comfortable but decorous, as Huck Finn found out at the Widow's. It is even stifling if the company isn't right. A good porch gets you out of the parlor, lets you smoke, talk loud, eat with your fingers—without apology and without having to run away from home. No wonder that people with porches have hundreds of friends.   4

Of useful porches there are many sorts, including the veranda, the breezeway, the back porch, front porch, stoop, and now the sun deck, though the veranda is grander than a porch need be and the sun deck is useful only if you happen to like sun. A useful porch may be large or not, but ordinarily it is defended by screens or large shrubbery. You should be able to walk naked onto a porch and feel only a slight thrill of adventure. It is comfortable, furnished with old stuff. You should be able to spill your coffee anywhere without a trace of remorse.   5

Our family owned a porch like that once, attached to a house overlooking the St. Croix River east of St. Paul, Minnesota, that we rented from the Wilcoxes from May to September. When company   6 came, they didn't stop in the living room but went straight through to the porch.

7   You could sit on the old porch swing that hung from the ceiling or in one of the big wicker chairs or the chaise lounge, or find a spot on the couch, which could seat four or accommodate a tall man taking a nap. There was a table for four, two kerosene lanterns, and some plants in pots. The porch faced east, was cool and shady from midday on, and got a nice breeze off the river. A lush forest of tall ferns surrounded this porch so the occupants didn't have to look at unmowed lawn or a weedy garden and feel too guilty to sit. A brook ran close by.

8   In the home-building industry today, a porch such as that one is considered an expensive frill, which is too bad for the home buyer. To sign up for a lifetime of debt at a vicious rate of interest and wind up with a porchless home, a home minus the homiest room—it's like visiting Minnesota and not seeing the prairie. You cheat yourself. Home, after all, doesn't belong to the bank, it's yours. You're supposed to have fun there, be graceful and comfortable and enjoy music and good conversation and the company of pals, otherwise home is only a furniture showroom and you may as well bunk at the YMCA and get in on their recreation programs.

9   The porch promotes grace and comfort. It promotes good conversation simply by virtue of the fact that on a porch there is no need for it. Look at the sorry bunch in the living room standing in little clumps and holding drinks, and see how hard they work to keep up a steady dribble of talk. There, silence indicates boredom and unhappiness, and hosts are quick to detect silence and rush over to subdue it into speech. Now look at our little bunch on this porch. Me and the missus float back and forth on the swing, Mark and Rhonda are collapsed at opposite ends of the couch, Malene peruses her paperback novel in which an astounding event is about to occur, young Jeb sits at the table gluing the struts on his Curtiss biplane. The cats lie on the floor listening to birdies, and I say, "It's a heck of a deal, ain't it, a *heck* of a deal." A golden creamy silence suffuses this happy scene, and only on a porch is it possible.

10   When passersby come into view, we say hello to them, but they don't take this as an invitation to barge in. There is something slightly *forbidding* about the sight of people on a porch, its grace is almost royal. You don't rush right up to the Queen and start telling her the story of your life, and you don't do that to porch sitters

either. We are Somebody up here even if our screens are torn and the sofa is busted and we're drinking orange pop from cans. You down there are passersby in a parade we've seen come and go for years. We have a porch.

It is our reviewing platform and observation deck, our rostrum and dais, the parapet of our stockade, the bridge of our ship. We can sit on it in silence or walk out naked spilling coffee. Whatever we do, we feel richer than Rockefeller and luckier than the President. 11

Years ago, my family moved from that luxurious porch to a porch-less apartment in the city. Our friends quit visiting us. We felt as if we had moved to Denver. Then we moved to a big old house with two porches, then to another with a long veranda in front and a small sleeping porch in back. Now we have arrived in Manhattan, at an apartment with a terrace. A porch on the twelfth floor with a view of rooftops, chimney pots, treetops, and the street below. A canvas canopy, a potted hydrangea, and two deck chairs. Once again, we're ready for company. 12

Thesis and Organization

1. Keillor introduces his essay in paragraphs 1–3. How does he use comparison and contrast? Cause and effect? What working thesis does the introduction establish?
2. In the body of the essay (4–11), how does Keillor use cause and effect? Comparison and contrast? Description? Example? Classification? What does each pattern of organization contribute to his definition?
3. In paragraphs 6 and 7, Keillor refers to where he has lived, a subject that comes up again in his conclusion (12). What do those references add to his definition?
4. Add up all the positive qualities Keillor attributes to the "true porch." What is his definition? Think about the cause-and-effect relationships in the essay and that definition. What is Keillor's thesis?

Technique and Style

1. Garrison Keillor is probably best known for his radio show "The Prairie Home Companion." If you are familiar with that show, describe the personality Keillor reveals there and compare it to the one in this essay. If you don't know that program, examine Keillor's use of diction, point of view, simile, and sentence structure and describe the personality he creates for himself.

2. In general, writers choose one point of view and stick with it, but here, Keillor keeps shifting his point of view from *you* to *we*. Analyze his point of view by figuring out exactly to whom the pronouns refer. For example, does the second person in paragraph 1 refer to the same person as the second person in paragraph 10? What justification can you find for the switching of point of view?

3. Examine the allusions Keillor makes: Huck Finn and the Widow Douglas (4), the Minnesota prairie (8), the Curtiss biplane (9), and Rockefeller and the president (11). What generalizations can you make about these allusions? What do they add to Keillor's tone?

4. In an earlier version of this essay, Keillor used three similes in paragraph 8: ". . . it's like ordering Eggs Benedict and saying 'Hold the hollandaise'; it's like buying a Porsche with a Maytag motor; it's like flying first-class and being seated next to a man who bores the eyeballs right out of you." He replaced those three with ". . . it's like visiting Minnesota and not seeing the prairie." What might account for Keillor's decision to rewrite this passage using just one simile? What function does this simile serve? Create one of your own that would fit with or substitute for the one Keillor uses.

5. Keillor relies heavily on description to make his point in paragraph 9. What do the descriptive details add to his tone? How are they framed?

Suggestions for Writing

Write your own "O the" essay, finding a topic among the everyday objects around you: easy chair, sofa, television set; hamburger, ice cream cone, pizza; tie, purse, cap, jogging shoes; backyard, barbecue grill, garage.

*L*et It Beep

Craig Stoltz

The answering machine is now so commonplace that we don't think about the connotations of the term, but what the answering machine really means is the subject of Craig Stoltz's essay. When it was first published in Philip Morris Magazine *in 1988, it had a subtitle: "How America Has Come to Learn to Love the Telephone Answering Machine. And If You Don't Love It Now, You Soon Will.*

It was not that long ago when those first god-awful phone calls took place. You probably remember the night: You had only called up your sister to see whether she was coming over on Sunday, and what you encountered on the phone was not your sister at all, but a tape recording of her sounding strangely excited and a bit trembly around the larynx. You began to fear that some amateur terrorist had broken into her house, held a Smith & Wesson to her head, and forced her to read a statement ordering all callers to leave their name, number, date and time of call, and a brief message. Then suddenly the order came to begin speaking, followed by that dingbat beep. Self-conscious and annoyed, you simply hung up.

But that was then, as the saying goes, and this is now. And the telephone answering machine has gained, if not exactly respectability, then at least acceptance. When the devices first hit the American home in the early 1970s, people hated when a machine answered the phone. But now, strangely, they hate it when one *doesn't*. Apparently the indignity of talking to a spool of tape has somehow become preferable to the indignity of not talking at all. I called up the people who are responsible to see if they could explain. Happily, a machine did not answer.

"When answering machines first appeared for home use, there was a certain, well, *negative* perception about them," reports Allan Schlosser, vice president for communications for the Electronic Industries Association, a trade group that represents the makers of all sorts of electronic gadgetry. "But now, there seems to have been a 180 degree attitudinal switch. People are much more accepting of the technology." In 1982, the year the group began tracking answering machine sales, around 850,000 units reached the American market. The number more than doubled the following year, and then doubled again by mid-1985. This year, EIA estimates, nearly 6 million machines will enter American homes. By now 17 percent of American homes are armed with the machines, and industry officials estimate that one of three households will have an answering machine five years from now.

4   There are, of course, good reasons why so many decent people have invited these robo-secretaries into their homes. One is pretty simple: Big extended families tend not to live under the same roof these days, and smaller households where two people work are closer to the norm. As a result, nobody's around to get the phone anymore. And the price has dropped during the past 15 years so that more people can afford answering machines. Ten years ago, the most basic model fetched more than $300; nowadays, a hundred bucks will get you a machine that has a built-in telephone, a single cassette tape the size of your thumb, and a selection of perplexing features with exotic-sounding names like voice activation, ring delay, and remote message retrieval.

5   Shop aggressively, and you can wind up with a bonus speakerphone feature that will let you take calls without lifting the handset, but makes you sound, at least to the person on the other end, as if you've set up shop in the bottom of an empty dumpster.

6   One of the happiest consequences of the spread of the answering machine in America is the retreat of those insufferably cute messages designed to keep callers from hanging up. You probably encountered one of these a few weeks after your sister got her machine. First came the tinny, somewhat distant sounds of Dolly Parton singing "Nine to Five," followed by a new version of your sister's old message, this time gussied up with an overrehearsed apology about being *so* sorry to be away at work. The performance ended with an up-volume chorus of Dolly, and, of course, that dingbat beep. The first time it was cute. The second time it was trying. You never called to hear it a third time.

7   And suddenly, it seemed, every night was amateur night. Fred's place was wired with the opening salvos of Beethoven's Fifth accompanied by Fred talking through his teeth and sounding, at least for Fred, pretty genteel. Jim Bob was doing a spirited Rodney Dangerfield ("I get no respect, but I get lots of phone calls . . .), and everywhere you turned, a jowly Richard Nixon was back in office (". . . and I promise not to erase the tapes . . ."). Mini-dramas were

staged on cassette tape all across the land: one guy I know yelled a message that he was out swimming with a pod of whales; in the background were some strange bovine moans and the sound of water sloshing around the bathtub.

The good news is that as people have gotten used to mechanical 8 greetings, this awkward period of technological adjustment seems to have ended. Succinct messages seem to be the order of the day. My favorite comes from my pal David: "Hi. You know how this thing works." And, of course, that darn beep.

Yes, answering machines are practical and affordable, but I sus- 9 pect there's another reason why they're so popular these days. It turns out that one of the most popular features buyers request is something known as "call screening," a capability that lets you hear the message while it comes in, and then—if you are so moved— pick up the phone and take the call.

And by doing this, the answering machine has finally made it 10 possible to regain some sense of control. Normally when the phone rings it's the caller who holds all the cards: he knows who you are, and he knows who he is and what he wants. It's the fellow who picks up the phone who has absolutely no idea what game he's about to play. An automatic secretary turns that relationship on its head. Suddenly you're in charge, and the caller is forced to explain his intentions for your approval. If it happens to be your long-lost cousin Cal calling to hit you up for another handout, you can simply let him talk to the machine. If, on the other hand, the caller is that fabulous blonde from work you've been dying to meet, you take the call. If answering machines eventually become as common as toast- ers in American homes, as some people in the industry predict, it will be because they restore the freedom of choice that a simple telephone takes away.

There are no limits on how far this can go, of course. Word is 11 out that researchers at MIT have developed something called Phone Slave, an answering machine that grills callers, records re- sponses to several questions, and eventually will be able to talk right back based on what is said to it. This means that at some date in the near future, some poor soul will return home, hit the "play message" button on his device, and listen to a recording of two machines having a conversation. When that happens, it may finally be time to hang it up—the phone *and* the answering machine—for good.

Thesis and Organization

1. The essay opens with a narrative. What point is the author making?
2. Paragraphs 3 and 4 trace the popularity of answering machines. What reasons does the author give?
3. Paragraphs 6–8 present the good news and the bad. What is it?
4. Another reason for the popularity of the machines comes out in paragraph 9. What other paragraphs tie in directly to this one?
5. How does the machine "turn the tables"? What does the answering machine mean? What is the essay's thesis?

Technique and Style

1. How would you characterize the author's humorous tone? Does he make fun of answering machines? Admire them? Misunderstand them? What?
2. Explain what you identify as the essay's purpose: expressive, explanatory, argumentative, or some combination.
3. What examples can you find of repetition? What effect does it achieve?
4. What pronouns does Stoltz use? What justification can you find for his switching his point of view?
5. How satisfactory do you find the essay's conclusion? To what extent is the pun out of place or appropriate?

Suggestions for Writing

Consider an object that we may take for granted yet one that has far more meaning than a simple dictionary definition might suggest. The car, for instance, is usually much more than a vehicle mounted on wheels. Other suggestions: the remote-control device, the microwave oven, the disposable razor, the liquid diet, the exercycle, the word processor.

Not the Best of Times, Not the Worst

Kurt Andersen

Writing for the Rolling Stone *in 1989, Kurt Andersen sees his gener-ation of today's adults as "comfortably adrift, bobbing on a sea of ambivalence." We live, he says, in complicated times, and ambiva-lence is an appropriate response to them, thus his choice of title, which comes from the first line of Charles Dickens's* Tale of Two Cities. *How we got that way and just what that ambivalence means is the subject of his essay.*

Nowadays, there are two sides to every answer. We don't face facts and, hell, simply *decide*. No. That would be too instinctual, too easy, too blithe, too unlike us. 1

Instead, we consider every alternative and feel complete enthu-siasm for none of them. We postpone. We fret. We second-guess. Whether it's a matter of deciding what to have for lunch (a sand-wich? a salad?) or how to spend the rest of our lives (duplicitous corporate scumbag in New York? bad lyric poet in Seattle?), nei-ther a wholehearted yes nor an unequivocal no comes naturally. We say maybe. We try to act on both impulses, to be unsenti-mental romantics, to work uptown but live downtown or vice versa, to have it all, foreclosing no option. As individuals, and even as a nation, we grow faint at the prospect of absolute com-mitment, whether it's marriage, or military intervention in the Third World, or 30-year fixed-rate mortgages. We find it hard to feel unalloyed pleasure (Would you say you love Bette Midler's Disney movies?) or unmitigated disapproval (Would you say you hate George Bush?). To most of us, every city, every book, prac-tically every way of life is an interesting place to visit, but we wouldn't want to live there. Would we? Ours is a generation com-fortably adrift, bobbing on a sea of ambivalence. 2

But that's not all bad. Probably. 3

Today's ambivalence is a post-Vietnam syndrome, civilian shell shock. The war was a mess of second thoughts from beginning to end. Presidents Kennedy and Johnson were ambivalent about sending U.S. troops. The war was waged ambivalently by infan- 4 trymen ordered to kill and protect the same people by generals ambivalent about strategy and tactics. From 1968 on, the American public was composed not mainly of hawks or doves but of confused, anxious citizens. Even to those who demanded withdrawal, the final spectacle—GIs bashing would-be refugees on the helipad, North Vietnamese tanks rolling through Saigon—was not exactly gladdening. The memorial to Vietnam veterans in Washington, D.C., is a grand, heartbreaking dead end, ambivalence in black granite.

5   By the time the war ended, a certain "Hey, who cares?" fecklessness had already set in among the young, a rejection of both hippie abandon and conventional sobriety. It was cocaine-and-hot-tub swingerism; the order of the day was still self-indulgence, now without any pretext of forging a new order. A generation was gradually giving up, along with its adolescence, its late-sixties habit of certitude. But the need to believe had not disappeared. In the seventies, thanks to est and its ilk, you could believe in yourself, only yourself—and even that faith lasted only long enough to make Werner Erhard and Michael Korda rich. By the time of Reagan, thoroughgoing ambivalence was back.

6   The rebellion of the sixties sought to discredit orthodoxies in nearly all realms—religion, music, sex, race, work, politics, foreign policy. But it succeeded most thoroughly at displacing the idea of orthodoxy itself, of easy moral consensus and clarity. Americans now come equipped with a snickery skepticism that runs as deep as the hopeful stoicism of the forties. After the sixties, nobody took heroes seriously. After the seventies, nobody even took antiheroes very seriously. After Vietnam, Americans didn't become pacifists, but they could no longer imagine any plausible circumstances that would justify large-scale U.S. military involvement. After Watergate, they didn't become anarchists, but they stopped investing much hope in politicians and national politics. And after Paul McCartney formed Wings, they never listened to music again.

7   It's not that thinking people don't want to believe in leaders and ideas wholeheartedly. In fact, as pundits grope for a handle on the nineties, they look wishfully to the sixties, imagining that the spirit of social activism really does run in fixed 30-year cycles. To some would-be believers, environmentalism looks like a perfect way out of the trough of ambivalence. Come the nineties, they figure, as

worries about pesticide-coated apples and the Brazilian rain forests turn to anger, we will become once again the concerned, committed people we used to be, or like to imagine we used to be.

Maybe. Ambivalence can be paralyzing. It can make us ineffectual, unwilling to engage. It does not necessarily make for a gusto-grabbing life. But ambivalence may also be the natural emotional and intellectual state of grown-ups—childhood is sweet, adulthood bittersweet. Who isn't ambivalent? Madmen, children, ideologues. Ambivalence is not weak-mindedness. It is a function of habitual self-criticism, of seeing both sides, of an eclectic unwillingness to cast one's lot with the avant-garde or MOR, with tidiness or funk, with West or East, with one zealotry or its opposite. Until the world turns uncomplicated, ambivalence only makes sense.   8

Thesis and Organization

1. Paragraphs 1–3 set out the situation and the central term. What do you deduce as a working thesis?
2. Paragraphs 4–6 employ process, example, and cause and effect to explain how the present situation came into being. Summarize the process as a time line. What examples support what cause-and-effect relationships?
3. What does paragraph 7 contribute to the development of the essay?
4. Paragraph 8 presents the negative and positive aspects of ambivalence. Which does Andersen favor?
5. Write out a full definition of *ambivalence*. What is Andersen's assertion about it?

Technique and Style

1. Including the title, what allusions can you identify in the essay? What does Andersen achieve by using them?
2. What examples can you find of made-up words? What purpose do they serve?
3. How would you characterize Andersen's level of diction? What examples can you cite to make your point?
4. Andersen seems very certain of his views. How does his "This is the way it is" tone affect you? How does he qualify his opinions?
5. Examine paragraph 2 for sentence variety. What range do you find? What does Andersen achieve by employing such variety?

Suggestions for Writing

In the United States, the 1950s were called the time of the silent generation; the sixties, the age of the flower children; the seventies, the me generation. Think of words that summarize your generation, or if you prefer, think of terms that might summarize the 1980s or the past year. As you consider possible topics, try to draw upon political events and popular culture as examples you can use.

Discrimination Is a Virtue

Robert Keith Miller

By examining the connotations and denotations of the word discrimination, *Robert Keith Miller shows us not only that we misuse it, but that it misuse points to a flaw in our "public policies." Miller's essay appeared in the "My Turn" column in* Newsweek *in 1980. His argument still holds.*

When I was a child, my grandmother used to tell me a story about 1
a king who had three daughters and decided to test their love. He asked each of them "How much do you love me?" The first replied that she loved him as much as all the diamonds and pearls in the world. The second said that she loved him more than life itself. The third replied "I love you as fresh meat loves salt."

This answer enraged the king; he was convinced that his young- 2
est daughter was making fun of him. So he banished her from his realm and left all of his property to her elder sisters.

As the story unfolded it became clear, even to a 6-year-old, that 3
the king had made a terrible mistake. The two older girls were hypocrites, and as soon as they had profited from their father's generosity, they began to treat him very badly. A wiser man would have realized that the youngest daughter was the truest. Without attempting to flatter, she said, in effect, "We go together naturally; we are a perfect team."

Years later, when I came to read Shakespeare, I realized that my 4
grandmother's story was loosely based upon the story of King Lear, who put his daughters to a similar test and did not know how to judge the results. Attempting to save the king from the consequences of his foolishness, a loyal friend pleads, "Come sir, arise, away! I'll teach you differences." Unfortunately, the lesson comes too late. Because Lear could not tell the difference between true love and false, he loses his kingdom and eventually his life.

We have a word in English which means "the ability to tell dif- 5
ferences." That word is *discrimination*. But within the last 30 years, this word has been so frequently misused that an entire generation has grown up believing that "discrimination" means "racism." People are always proclaiming that "discrimination" is something that

should be done away with. Should that ever happen, it would prove to be our undoing.

6 Discrimination means discernment; it means the ability to perceive the truth, to use good judgment and to profit accordingly. The *Oxford English Dictionary* traces this understanding of the word back to 1648 and demonstrates that for the next 300 years, "discrimination" was a virtue, not a vice. Thus, when a character in a nineteenth-century novel makes a happy marriage, Dickens has another character remark, "It does credit to your discrimination that you should have found such a very excellent young woman."

7 Of course, "the ability to tell differences" assumes that differences exist, and this is unsettling for a culture obsessed with the notion of equality. The contemporary belief that discrimination is a vice stems from the compound *discriminate against.* What we need to remember, however, is that some things deserve to be judged harshly: we should not leave our kingdoms to the selfish and the wicked.

8 Discrimination is wrong only when someone or something is discriminated against because of prejudice. But to use the word in this sense, as so many people do, is to destroy its true meaning. If you discriminate against something because of general preconceptions rather than particular insights, then you are not discriminating—bias has clouded the clarity of vision which discrimination demands.

9 One of the great ironies of American life is that we manage to discriminate in the practical decisions of daily life, but usually fail to discriminate when we make public policies. Most people are very discriminating when it comes to buying a car, for example, because they realize that cars have differences. Similarly, an increasing number of people have learned to discriminate in what they eat. Some foods are better than others—and indiscriminate eating can undermine one's health.

10 Yet in public affairs, good judgment is depressingly rare. In many areas which involve the common good, we see a failure to tell differences.

11 Consider, for example, some of the thinking behind modern education. On the one hand, there is a refreshing realization that there are differences among children, and some children—be they gifted or handicapped—require special education. On the other hand, we are politically unable to accept the consequences of this perception.

The trend in recent years has been to group together students of radically different ability. We call this process "mainstreaming," and it strikes me as a characteristically American response to the discovery of differences: we try to pretend that differences do not matter.

Similarly, we try to pretend that there is little difference between the sane and the insane. A fashionable line of argument has it that "everybody is a little mad" and that few mental patients deserve long-term hospitalization. As a consequence of such reasoning, thousands of seriously ill men and women have been evicted from their hospital beds and returned to what is euphemistically called "the community"—which often means being left to sleep on city streets, where confused and helpless people now live out of paper bags as the direct result of our refusal to discriminate.   12

Or to choose a final example from a different area: how many recent elections reflect thoughtful consideration of the genuine differences among candidates? Benumbed by television commercials that market aspiring officeholders as if they were a new brand of toothpaste or hair spray, too many Americans vote with only a fuzzy understanding of the issues in question. Like Lear, we seem too eager to leave the responsibility of government to others and too ready to trust those who tell us whatever we want to hear.   13

So as we look around us, we should recognize that "discrimination" is a virtue which we desperately need. We must try to avoid making unfair and arbitrary distinctions, but we must not go to the other extreme and pretend that there are no distinctions to be made. The ability to make intelligent judgments is essential both for the success of one's personal life and for the functioning of society as a whole. Let us be open-minded by all means, but not so open-minded that our brains fall out.   14

Thesis and Organization

1. Paragraphs 1–4 use narration. What is the "lesson" of the narrative? Why might Miller have chosen a narrative to introduce the essay?
2. Paragraph 5 deals with the popular connotations of *discrimination*. What are they? What other paragraph or paragraphs bring out the misuse of the word?
3. Paragraph 6 presents the denotative meaning of the word. What other paragraph or paragraphs emphasize that meaning?
4. Where does Miller maintain that the idea of differences runs counter to our notion of equality? How is that idea related to paragraphs 9–13?

5. Paragraph 14 concludes the essay. Consider the essay's title and the last paragraph. What is a full statement of Miller's thesis? Is the essay primarily expressive, informative, or persuasive?

Technique and Style

1. Consult a handbook of grammar and usage for discussion of the rhetorical question. Where in the essay do you find examples of this device? To what extent do the examples fit the handbook's definition?
2. What modes does Miller use to define his central terms? Which does he use most frequently?
3. Note all the times Miller uses quotation marks. What different functions do the quotation marks serve?
4. What sort of a person does Miller seem to be? In what ways does his persona fit his tone? How would you characterize his tone?
5. What sources does Miller draw his examples from? Group them according to the generalizations they support. In what ways are they appropriate or inappropriate to the generalizations? What do the examples add to Miller's persona?

Suggestions for Writing

Think of a word that is commonly misused or has outworn its meaning and make a case for its linguistic correction or restoration. Commonly misused words can be found in a handbook of grammar and usage, usually in the glossary of usage. You might come up with *virtually, disinterested, flaunt, irritate,* or words formed with the suffice *pre-,* as in *preheat, prewrite, pre-owned.* As for outworn words, they are all around us, particularly in advertisements: *fabulous, lovely, elegant.* Or you might consider how words once considered inappropriate to everyday conversation have now become more or less accepted. No matter what the topic, bring out its significance so that you use definition to make a larger point.

The Handicap of Definition

William Raspberry

The terms black *and* white *have connotations that we don't often think about. William Raspberry shows us that if we stop to think about* black, *we'll see that it has so narrow a definition that it is "one of the heaviest burdens black Americans—and black children in particular—have to bear." Not much has changed since 1982, when this essay first appeared in William Raspberry's syndicated column.*

I know all about bad schools, mean politicians, economic deprivation and racism. Still, it occurs to me that one of the heaviest burdens black Americans—and black children in particular—have to bear is the handicap of definition: the question of what it means to be black.

Let me explain quickly what I mean. If a basketball fan says that the Boston Celtics' Larry Bird plays "black," the fan intends it—and Bird probably accepts it—as a compliment. Tell pop singer Tom Jones he moves "black" and he might grin in appreciation. Say to Teena Marie or The Average White Band that they sound "black" and they'll thank you.

But name one pursuit, aside from athletics, entertainment or sexual performance in which a white practitioner will feel complimented to be told he does it "black." Tell a white broadcaster he talks "black," and he'll sign up for diction lessons. Tell a white reporter he writes "black" and he'll take a writing course. Tell a white lawyer he reasons "black" and he might sue you for slander.

What we have here is a tragically limited definition of blackness, and it isn't only white people who buy it.

Think of all the ways black children can put one another down with charges of "whiteness." For many of these children, hard study and hard work are "white." Trying to please a teacher might be criticized as acting "white." Speaking correct English is "white." Scrimping today in the interest of tomorrow's goals is "white." Educational toys and games are "white."

An incredible array of habits and attitudes that are conducive to success in business, in academia, in the nonentertainment professions are likely to be thought of as somehow "white." Even economic success, unless it involves such "black" undertakings as numbers banking, is defined as "white."

7   And the results are devastating. I wouldn't deny that blacks often are better entertainers and athletes. My point is the harm that comes from too narrow a definition of what is black.

8   One reason black youngsters tend to do better at basketball, for instance, is that they assume they can learn to do it well, and so they practice constantly to prove themselves right.

9   Wouldn't it be wonderful if we could infect black children with the notion that excellence in math is "black" rather than white, or possibly Chinese? Wouldn't it be of enormous value if we could create the myth that morality, strong families, determination, courage and love of learning are traits brought by slaves from Mother Africa and therefore quintessentially black?

10   There is no doubt in my mind that most black youngsters could develop their mathematical reasoning, their elocution and their attitudes the way they develop their jump shots and their dance steps: by the combination of sustained, enthusiastic practice and the unquestioned belief that they can do it.

11   In one sense, what I am talking about is the importance of developing positive ethnic traditions. Maybe Jews have an innate talent for communication; maybe the Chinese are born with a gift for mathematical reasoning; maybe blacks are naturally blessed with athletic grace. I doubt it. What is at work, I suspect, is assumption, inculcated early in their lives, that this is a thing our people do well.

12   Unfortunately, many of the things about which blacks make this assumption are things that do not contribute to their career success—except for that handful of the truly gifted who can make it as entertainers and athletes. And many of the things we concede to whites are the things that are essential to economic security.

13   So it is with a number of assumptions black youngsters make about what it is to be a "man": physical aggressiveness, sexual prowess, the refusal to submit to authority. The prisons are full of people who, by this perverted definition, are unmistakably men.

14   But the real problem is not so much that the things defined as "black" are negative. The problem is that the definition is much too narrow.

15   Somehow, we have to make our children understand that they are intelligent, competent people, capable of doing whatever they

put their minds to and making it in the American mainstream, not just in a black subculture.

What we seem to be doing, instead, is raising up yet another generation of young blacks who will be failures—by definition. 16

Thesis and Organization

1. Examine paragraphs 1–4 as a unit. What sentence functions as the major assertion for this group of paragraphs? What examples support that assertion? What conclusion does Raspberry draw from the examples? How is that conclusion related to the paragraphs that follow?

2. Take paragraphs 5–7 as a unit and analyze it also, looking for the controlling assertion, the examples, and the conclusion.

3. Paragraphs 8–11 also form a paragraph block. What is its controlling assertion? What examples support it? What conclusion does Raspberry draw?

4. Examine paragraphs 12–16 as a concluding paragraph block. What is the relationship between paragraph 12 and the paragraphs that precede it? In what way is the point raised in paragraph 13 an analogy? Is the analogy apt or false? What is the function of paragraph 14? Paragraphs 15 and 16 look to the future and assess the present. What cause-and-effect relationship do they point out?

5. Consider the controlling ideas that guide the paragraph blocks and the conclusions Raspberry draws from the examples that support those assertions. Stated fully, what is Raspberry's thesis? Do you agree or disagree with this thesis? Why or why not?

Technique and Style

1. This essay was one of Raspberry's syndicated columns; as a result, it appeared in a large number of newspapers with equally large readerships, mostly white. What evidence can you find that Raspberry is trying to inform his white audience and persuade his black readers?

2. How and where does Raspberry establish his credibility as a writer on this subject? What grammatical point of view does he use? What is the effect of that point of view?

3. Where in the essay does he qualify or modulate his statements? What is the effect of that technique?

4. Many techniques can be used to give a paragraph coherence, but an often neglected one is syntax. Examine paragraphs 2, 3, 5, and 9 to discover the similar sentence structure at work. What do you find?

5. Paragraphs 3, 7, 13, and 14 all begin with a conjunction. What effect does this technique achieve? Consult a handbook of grammar and usage for a discussion of this device. To what extent does Raspberry's usage conform to the handbook's advice?

6. Paragraph 16 is an example of a rhetorical paragraph, a one-sentence paragraph that gives dramatic emphasis to a point. If you eliminate the dash or substitute a comma for it, what happens to the dramatic effect? What does the pun add?

7. A militant who read this essay would argue that Raspberry is trying to make blacks "better" by making them white. Is there any evidence to support this view? Explain.

8. A feminist who read the essay would argue that it is sexist. Is there any evidence to support this view? Explain.

Suggestions for Writing

Find a word that has accumulated broad connotations and then see what definitions have evolved and their effect. Like Raspberry, you may want to consider two terms but emphasize only one. Possibilities: *man, hero, student, woman, worker, love, politician.*

Exploring the Topic

1. **What are the denotations of your term?** You should consult an unabridged dictionary and perhaps a more complete or specialized one, such as the *Oxford English Dictionary* or a dictionary of slang.
2. **What are the connotations of your term?** What emotional reactions or associations does it elicit from people? What situations evoke what responses and why?
3. **What other words can be used for your term?** Which are similar?
4. **What are the characteristics, qualities, or components of your term?** Which are most important? Are some not worth mentioning?
5. **What other modes are appropriate?** What modes can you draw upon to help support your definition and the organization of the essay? Where can you use description? Narration? What examples can you use to illustrate your term?
6. **Has your word been used or misused in the past?** If so, might that misuse be turned into an introductory narrative? A closing one?

Drafting the Paper

1. **Know your reader.** Review your lists of denotations and connotations together with the characteristics related to your term to see how familiar they are to your reader. Check to see if your reader may have particular associations that you need to redirect or change. Or, if your reader is directly related to your topic, make sure your definition does not offend.
2. **Know your purpose.** Unless your term is unusual, one of your biggest problems is to tell the reader something new about it. Work on your first paragraph so that it will engage the reader from the start. From that point on, keep your primary purpose in mind. If you are writing a paper that is basically self-expressive or persuasive, make sure you have an audience other than yourself. If your aim is informative, consider narration, example, cause and effect, and analogy as possible ways of presenting familiar material in a fresh light.
3. **Use examples.** Provide examples to illustrate what your key term means. Also consider using negative examples and setting out distinctions between the meaning of your word and others similar to it.
4. **Draw upon a variety of sources.** Define your term from several perspectives. Perhaps a brief history of the word would be helpful or maybe some statistical information is in order. See if a brief narrative might provide additional meaning for the term.

5. **Make a point.** Don't mistake your definition for your thesis. The two are certainly related, but one is an assertion, the other is not. Perhaps your definition is a jumping-off place for a larger point you wish to make or a key part of that point. Or perhaps your term evokes a single dominant impression you want to convey. Whatever purpose your definition serves, it supports your thesis.

Argument

*I*n everyday speech, *argument* is so closely associated with *quarrel* or *fight* that it has a negative connotation, but that connotation does not apply to the word as it is used in the writing of essays. If you were to analyze an essay by examining its argument, you would be looking at the writer's major assertion and the weight of the evidence on which it rests. That evidence must be compelling, for the aim of all argumentative writing is to move the reader to adopt the writer's view. In writing argumentative papers, sometimes you might want to go further than that and call for a particular action, but most of the time you'll probably work at convincing your reader to share your position on the issue. Often, however, it's possible to get so involved in a subject you feel strongly about that you end up writing only to readers who already share your views.

One way to avoid that trap is to start work on your topic by brainstorming on the subject, not your position on it. Phrase the subject as a question and then list the pros and cons. If you are writing on gambling, for instance, you would ask, "Should gambling be legalized?" Then you would define your terms: Who would be legalizing it—the federal government, the state, the county, the city? What kind of gambling—betting, gaming, playing a lottery? Answer those kinds of questions and you can draw up your pros and cons more easily because your focus will be more specific. Once you've listed the arguments that can be used, you can then sort through them, noting the evidence you can cite and where to find it. Having done all that, you then are in a position to choose which side you wish to take, and you know the arguments that can be used against you.

The next step is to think about the ways in which you can appeal to your readers. Citing facts and precedents will appeal to their reason; exploring moral issues will appeal to their emotions; and presenting yourself as a credible person will appeal to their sense of fairness. *Reason* is the primary appeal in most argumentative writing, and to use it successfully, you may need to do some research on your subject. Once your argument begins to take shape, however, you will find that dealing with one or two of the opposing views will not only strengthen your own case but also earn you some points for fairness.

Argumentative writing ranges from the personal to the abstract and draws upon the various modes that can be used to structure an essay. For instance, waiting tables in a restaurant may have convinced you that tips should be automatically included in the bill. To make the case that the present system is unfair to those in a service trade, you might draw primarily on your own experience and that of others, though to avoid a hasty generalization you need to make sure that your experience is representative. A quick check among others similarly employed or a look at government reports on employment statistics should suffice and should also help you generalize logically from the particular.

Hasty generalization is one of many logical fallacies in argument. If you were to argue that the reader should only consider the present system of tipping or the one you propose, you will be guilty of either-or reasoning, which is false because it permits no middle ground. Quote William "The Refrigerator" Perry on the subject and you will be citing false authority; he knows football but not the restaurant industry. And obviously if you call a 5-percent tipper a cheap idiot, you will be accused quite rightly of name-calling, the *ad hominem* fallacy.

Post hoc reasoning is harder to spot in that it is tied to the claim that a temporal relationship is really a causal one. Say you noticed that as closing time loomed, your tips got smaller. Is that because people who dine late tip minimally or because your customers felt rushed? Assume the former and you fall into the *post hoc* trap.

You will find that if you are assigned an argumentative topic, it is often best to shape it so that you have a direct connection to it. Because you already know something about the subject, you have done some thinking about it instead of having to start from scratch or to use secondhand opinions. Even abstract topics such as euthanasia can be made concrete and will probably be the better for it. Though you may have never been confronted directly by the issue of mercy killing, you probably have had a member of your family who was terminally ill. Would euthanasia be an appropriate alternative? Should it be? In addition to using your own experience, consider using your local newspaper. Newspaper accounts and editorials can also help give form and focus to the abstract, and in addition to the book and periodical sources you consult, they will help you delineate your topic more clearly.

AUDIENCE AND PURPOSE Audience plays a greater role in argument than in any other type of writing, and therein lies a problem: you must adapt both form and content to fit your audience, yet at the same time maintain your integrity. If a writer shapes an argumentative position according to its probable acceptance by the audience rather than its belief by the writer, the result is propaganda, not argument. Knowingly playing false with an audience by omitting evidence or shaping it to fit an assertion, by resorting to logical fallacies, or by stacking the deck are all dishonest tricks.

Within honest bounds, however, you have much to draw upon, and a sense of what the audience may or may not know and of what the audience believes about a topic can guide you. In their essays, Suzan Shown Harjo, the *New York Times,* and Ellen Goodman all rely heavily on example to familiarize the audience with their topics. Charles B. Rangel, Daniel Lazare, Pete Shields, and J. Warren Cassidy, however, deal with well-worn subjects, Rangel and Lazare on the legalization of drugs, Shields and Cassidy on handgun control. Rangel and Lazare respond to the crisis in drug use but find very different solutions. Shields and Cassidy, however, share some examples, but that's all. They cite different sources to prove opposing views on similar subjects.

Whether the writers start with their audience's beliefs or lack of information, or with reviewing current situations, all aim at convincing the audience to adopt their convictions, perhaps even to act on them. Not all readers will be convinced, of course, but if they at least respond, "Hmm, I hadn't thought of that" or "Well, I may have to rethink my position," the essay has presented an effective argument.

APPEAL TO REASON   Logical thinking must undergird all argumentative essays, even those that stress an emotional appeal. Pete Shields, for instance, ardently supports handgun control and brings out the personal nature of his involvement; at the same time, however, he cites credible authority and pertinent examples to prove his point. So, too, J. Warren Cassidy cites an example guaranteed to make you feel the irony of a community's banning of handguns, but he also uses facts and figures to make his case. Cause and effect, definition, analogy, and various other patterns of development can all aid the writer in appealing to reason.

APPEAL TO EMOTION   Example, description, and narration are the basic tools of the emotional appeal. In what amounts to a short narrative summary of her life, Patricia Raybon opens her essay by citing herself as an example that emphasizes the difference between the media's portrayal of black Americans and the reality. Later in the essay she makes the same point by describing first the kinds of neighborhoods millions of black Americans live in and then her own inner-city neighborhood, comparing what the media claims goes on there to what she sees. By comparing the false impression created by the media to what she knows to be true, Raybon conveys her own anger and enlists the reader's appreciation for all of the "beautiful, healthy, funny, smart black Americans I have known and loved over the years."

APPEAL OF PERSONA   The appeal of persona, known in classical rhetoric as *ethos* (which translates somewhat ambiguously as "the ethical appeal"), is more subtle than the others; the writer is not appealing directly to the reader's emotions or intellect but instead is using his or her persona to lend credence to the essay's major assertion. The point gets tricky. A fair and honest writer is one who is fair and honest with the reader. Such a writer takes on a persona, not like donning a mask to hide behind but like selecting a picture to show those elements in the personality that represent the writer at his or her best. The personal tragedy that led to Pete Shields's fight

for handgun control must have evoked a number of emotions—
anger, hostility, frustration, anxiety, fear, confusion, and perplexity
among them. His essay, however, focuses on preventing similar
tragedies. His rational presentation of the cause-and-effect relationships involved in handgun control forms the basis of the essay's
appeal to reason. His persona shows him to have strong feelings,
but more to the point, it reveals his concern for the law-abiding and
responsible gun owner and for all past, present, and potential victims of handguns, those who are the victims not just of crimes but
of accidents as well.

LOGICAL FALLACIES   Logical fallacies abuse the various appeals.
Slips in the use of cause and effect, example, analogy, and so on can
result in logical fallacies. Ellen Goodman, for instance, accuses Justices Burger and Stewart of several errors in logic in their ruling on
the rights of children versus the rights of parents. In arguing that
Prohibition serves as a historical precedent for the federal war on
drugs, Daniel Lazare is careful not to fall into the trap of false analogy. He skirts the trap by qualifying his claims carefully. So, too,
Patricia Raybon avoids the pitfall of hasty generalization by switching quickly from personal experience to more generalized examples.

   Logical fallacies are, as the term implies, flaws in the appeal to
reason, and they are usually classified according to type, such as
begging the question, misuse of authority, false analogy, non sequitur, shifting definition, straw man, either-or oversimplification, and
post hoc, propter hoc. Argument *ad hominem* or *ad populem,* Latin
terms for name-calling, are errors in reason as well as an abuse of
the appeal to emotions. (See the Glossary of Terms for a fuller
discussion of these fallacies.)

THESIS AND ORGANIZATION   The thesis of an argumentative
essay should be readily identifiable: it is the conviction that you
want an audience to adopt. J. Warren Cassidy, for instance, wants
his reader to agree with his conviction that "controlling handguns
will not deter people bent on crime from committing their heinous
acts, nor will it reduce the availability of guns to the criminal population." To support his assertion, he organizes his ideas according
to the principle of deduction, leading the reader from his thesis to
his explanation and evidence for it. Steven Zak's "Courts Still Lax on

Animal Abuse," Suzan Shown Harjo's "Last Rites for Indian Dead," Anthony D'Amato's "Toward a Representative Judiciary," Patricia Raybon's "A Case of 'Severe Bias,'" Charles B. Rangel's "Legalize Drugs? Not on Your Life," and Pete Shields's essay in favor of handgun control follow the same principle. Induction, on the other hand, leads the reader from evidence and explanation to the thesis, as in the case of the essays by Thomas B. Stoddard, Sara Paretsky, Ronald Takaki, Ellen Goodman, the *New York Times*'s editorial writer, Brad Wackerlin, and Daniel Lazare.

Courts Still Lax on Animal Abuse

Steve Zak

Laws against animal abuse have been on the books in America since 1641, but Steve Zak points to the discrepancy between law and enforcement. The article appeared on the editorial page of the Rocky Mountain News, *July 12, 1990.*

One day last month police in North Hollywood noticed that a man   1
was walking down the street wearing a hummingbird necklace. The
man had tied the live bird by its legs to a string around his neck. The
arrest report said the bird's tail feathers had been removed and its
right wing broken.

The bird died in an animal shelter that evening. When asked by   2
police why he was wearing the fluttering necklace, the man report-
edly laughed and bounced the bird in his hands.

Americans have long believed that animals should be protected   3
from abuse. Massachusetts Puritans in 1641 forbade "Tirranny or
Crueltie towards any bruite Creature." States have passed laws ranging from weak to stringent in an effort to thwart abuse. Enforcement,
though, appears to be another matter.

Since there is no central reporting on animal abuse cases, reliable   4
statistics on instances and prosecutions are nonexistent. Dr. Randall
Lockwood of the Humane Society of the United States estimates that
a typical major city records 5000 animal abuse complaints a year out
of which 10 to 20 result in prosecutions. Of those, less than 10
percent result in jail terms.

In a nation with a growing interest in animal rights, many animal   5
rights advocates argue that there remains a wide gap between what
the law defines as a crime and the kinds of animal abuse cases that
go to court. Prosecutors and judges, they say, often show little interest in enforcing animal abuse laws to the full.

"We're in business to protect people, not animals," explains one   6
veteran Los Angeles district attorney.

Humane Society investigators report that judges, by and large,   7
now take animal abuse cases more seriously than they did five or ten

years ago, when such cases were "treated as a joke." But the prevailing view on the bench is that animal abuse is a low priority because "we have enough cases involving people," as one judge noted.

8   In the hummingbird case, the district attorney could have prosecuted the offender for felony abuse, with a maximum penalty of three years in state prison and a $20,000 fine. Instead, he sent the case to a lower court as a misdemeanor. The man pleaded guilty and, through a plea bargain, was sentenced to six months in the county jail.

9   Earlier this year, the same DA prosecuted two other animal abuse cases as felonies, winning one. Both involved the shooting of dogs. The difference in approach, animal rights advocates maintain, stems from the fact that the dogs belonged to people, who could demand justice.

10   Decisions about how to handle cases of animal abuse tend to reflect priorities that have more to do with human interests than those of the animal, their advocates say. The rare cases prosecuted as felonies usually involve harm to other people's animals and thus can be seen as crimes against property.

11   Animal rights advocates argue for stiffer enforcement of abuse laws on several grounds. They cite studies that show that animal abusers often harm people as well. One 1983 study found that in 88 percent of homes in which children were physically abused, animals were also abused by at least one family member. A 1986 study of prison inmates found that "aggressive" ones were more than four times as likely as "nonaggressive" ones to have engaged in animal abuse.

12   Organized animal abuse, such as dogfighting or cockfighting, also has been associated with other crimes, including gambling, drug pushing, illegal possession of guns and knives, and rape, according to law enforcement officials.

13   But animal rights advocates also argue that animal abuse ought to be taken seriously on its own terms because of the often savage nature of the suffering inflicted. Token punishment for vicious attacks trivializes viciousness and the lives it affects, they maintain.

Thesis and Organization

1. Zak begins his essay with a narrative, paragraphs 1 and 2. What is the nature of the conflict? What is the effect of the narrative?

2. What connection is there between paragraphs 1 and 2 and paragraph 3?
3. Paragraphs 4–10 present the present-day status of animal abuse cases. Describe it.
4. Paragraphs 11–13 present the animal rights advocates' arguments. Summarize them.
5. Considering the title, the examples Zak uses, and your summary above, what is the thesis of the essay?

Technique and Style

1. The example Zak uses to introduce his essay is an emotional one. How does Zak keep his description from being overly emotional?
2. What paragraphs can you cite as examples of logical appeal?
3. What effects does Zak achieve by using quotations?
4. Zak avoids first person and depends instead on a distanced point of view. He is not a part of the action he describes, and instead of presenting evidence directly, he depends on the arguments of animal rights advocates. Does this choice weaken or strengthen the essay? Explain.
5. How would you characterize the audience for this essay? What attitudes or beliefs does Zak appear to believe that audience holds?

Suggestions for Writing

While the murderer, thief, and robber commit acts that often make headlines, there's a category of people whose acts usually go unreported—the drunken drivers, shoplifters, underage drinkers, reckless drivers. Choose one type of lawbreaker and argue for the kind of punishment that would best suit the crime.

L ast Rites for Indian Dead

Suzan Shown Harjo

Writing as a Cheyenne, Suzan Shown Harjo points to a problem that affects Native Americans and, she argues, it raises an ethical issue for the rest of us. Her essay appeared on the editorial page of the Los Angeles Times *in September 1989.*

1   What if museums, universities, and government agencies could put your dead relatives on display or keep them in boxes to be cut up and otherwise studied? What if you believed that the spirits of the dead could not rest until their human remains were placed in a sacred area?

2   The ordinary American would say there ought to be a law—and there is, for ordinary Americans. The problem for American Indians is that there are too many laws of the kind that make us the archaeological property of the United States and too few of the kind that protect us from such insults.

3   Some of my own Cheyenne relatives' skulls are in the Smithsonian Institution today, along with those of at least 4500 other Indian people who were violated in the 1800s by the U.S. Army for an "Indian Cranial Study." It wasn't enough that these unarmed Cheyenne people were mowed down by the cavalry at the infamous Sand Creek massacre; many were decapitated and their heads shipped to Washington as freight. (The Army Medical Museum's collection is now in the Smithsonian.) Some had been exhumed only hours after being buried. Imagine their grieving families' reaction on finding their loved ones disinterred and headless.

4   Some targets of the Army's study were killed in noncombat situations and beheaded immediately. The officer's account of the decapitation of the Apache chief Mangas Coloradas in 1863 shows the pseudoscientific nature of the exercise. "I weighed the brain and measured the skull," the good doctor wrote, "and found that while the skull was smaller, the brain was larger than that of Daniel Webster."

5   These journal accounts exist in excruciating detail, yet missing are any records of overall comparisons, conclusions or final reports

of the Army study. Since it is unlike the Army not to leave a paper trail, one must wonder about the motive for its collection.

The total Indian body count in the Smithsonian collection is more   6
than 19,000, and it is not the largest in the country. It is not inconceivable that the 1.5 million of us living today are outnumbered by our dead stored in museums, educational institutions, federal agencies, state historical societies and private collections. The Indian people are further dehumanized by being exhibited alongside the mastodons and dinosaurs and other extinct creatures.

Where we have buried our dead in peace, more often than not   7
the sites have been desecrated. For more than 200 years, relic hunting has been a popular pursuit. Lately, the market in Indian artifacts has brought this abhorrent activity to a fever pitch in some areas. And when scavengers come upon Indian burial sites, everything found becomes fair game, including sacred burial offerings, teeth and skeletal remains.

One unusually well-publicized example of Indian grave desecration   8
tion occurred two years ago in a western Kentucky field known as Slack Farm, the site of an Indian village five centuries ago. Ten men—one with a business card stating "Have Shovel, Will Travel"— paid the landowner $10,000 to lease digging rights between planting seasons. They dug extensively on the 40-acre farm, rummaging through an estimated 650 graves, collecting burial goods, tools and ceremonial items. Skeletons were strewn about like litter.

What motivates people to do something like this? Financial gain   9
is the first answer. Indian relic-collecting has become a multimillion-dollar industry. The price tag on a bead necklace can easily top $1000; rare pieces fetch tens of thousands.

And it is not just collectors of the macabre who pay for skeletal   10
remains. Scientists say that these deceased Indians are needed for research that someday could benefit the health and welfare of living Indians. But just how many dead Indians must they examine? Nineteen thousand?

There is doubt as to whether permanent curation of our dead   11
really benefits Indians. Dr. Emery A. Johnson, former assistant surgeon general, recently observed, "I am not aware of any current medical diagnostic or treatment procedure that has been derived from research on such skeletal remains. Nor am I aware of any during the 34 years that I have been involved in American Indian . . . health care."

12   Indian remains are still being collected for racial biological studies. While the intentions may be honorable, the ethics of using human remains this way without the full consent of relatives must be questioned.

13   Some relief for Indian people has come on the state level. Almost half of the states, including California, have passed laws protecting Indian burial sites and restricting the sale of Indian bones, burial offerings and other sacred items. Representative Charles E. Bennett (D-Fla.) and Sen. John McCain (R-Ariz.) have introduced bills that are a good start in invoking the federal government's protection. However, no legislation has attacked the problem head-on by imposing stiff penalties at the marketplace, or by changing laws that make dead Indians the nation's property.

14   Some universities—notably Stanford, Nebraska, Minnesota and Seattle—have returned, or agreed to return, Indian human remains; it is fitting that institutions of higher education should lead the way.

15   Congress is now deciding what to do with the government's extensive collection of Indian human remains and associated funerary objects. The secretary of the Smithsonian, Robert McC. Adams, has been valiantly attempting to apply modern ethics to yesterday's excesses. This week, he announced that the Smithsonian would conduct an inventory and return all Indian skeletal remains that could be identified with specific tribes or living kin.

16   But there remains a reluctance generally among collectors of Indian remains to take action of a scope that would have a quantitative impact and a healing quality. If they will not act on their own—and it is highly unlikely that they will—then Congress must act.

17   The country must recognize that the bodies of dead American Indian people are not artifacts to be bought and sold as collectors's items. It is not appropriate to store tens of thousands of our ancestors for possible future research. They are our family. They deserve to be returned to their sacred burial grounds and given a chance to rest.

18   The plunder of our people's graves has gone on too long. Let us rebury our dead and remove this shameful past from America's future.

Thesis and Organization

1. Paragraphs 1 and 2 introduce the essay by presenting a "What if?" situation. Why might Harjo have chosen this kind of opening?

2. Harjo presents examples in paragraphs 3–8. Summarize them.

3. Paragraphs 9–12 explain why people dig up Indian burial sites. What reasons does Harjo give?

4. Harjo explains what is being done, and what needs to be done, about the situation in paragraphs 13–18. What solution does she call for?

5. Considering the situation Harjo describes, the steps that are being taken to address that situation, and what remains to be done, what is the thesis of the essay?

Technique and Style

1. Describe the audience the essay is aimed at as precisely as you can. What evidence do you base your description upon?

2. How would you characterize the diction Harjo uses in connection with her examples? Choose one or two examples and substitute more, or less, loaded words. What is gained? Lost?

3. Considering the way the essay is written, what kind of person does Harjo appear to be? How would you describe her?

4. To what extent does the essay rest its appeal on Harjo's persona? On emotion? On logic? Which appeal predominates?

5. The essay concludes with a call for action. Evaluate the effectiveness of that call.

Suggestions for Writing

Think of an action that in the past was considered acceptable but today is either questionable or unacceptable. Years ago, for instance, no one thought much about the hazards of smoking, or of cholesterol levels, or of needing to inspect meat. Segregation was acceptable, as were other forms of racism. Choose a subject and think about the ethics involved and how present knowledge has changed how we live.

Gay Marriages: Make Them Legal

Thomas B. Stoddard

What is traditional is not always what is right, so Thomas B. Stoddard argues in the essay that follows. He calls for a redefinition of marriage that accommodates the legal status of matrimony to the present times. Stoddard is an attorney and executive director of the Lambda Legal Defense and Education Fund, a gay rights organization.

1   "In sickness and in health, 'til death do us part." With those familiar words, millions of people each year are married, a public affirmation of a private bond that both society and the newlyweds hope will endure. Yet for nearly four years, Karen Thompson was denied the company of the one person to whom she had pledged lifelong devotion. Her partner is a woman, Sharon Kowalski, and their home state of Minnesota, like every other jurisdiction in the United States, refuses to permit two individuals of the same sex to marry.

2   Karen Thompson and Sharon Kowalski are spouses in every respect except the legal. They exchanged vows and rings; they lived together until November 13, 1983—when Ms. Kowalski was severely injured when her car was struck by a drunk driver. She lost the capacity to walk or to speak more than several words at a time, and needed constant care.

3   Ms. Thompson sought a court ruling granting her guardianship over her partner, but Ms. Kowalski's parents opposed the petition and obtained sole guardianship. They moved Ms. Kowalski to a nursing home 300 miles away from Ms. Thompson and forbade all visits between the two women. Last month, as part of a reevaluation of Ms. Kowalski's mental competency, Ms. Thompson was permitted to visit her partner again. But the prolonged injustice and anguish inflicted on both women hold a moral for everyone.

4   Marriage, the Supreme Court declared in 1967, is "one of the basic civil rights of man" (and, presumably, of woman as well). The freedom to marry, said the Court, is "essential to the orderly pursuit of happiness."

Marriage is not just a symbolic state. It can be the key to survival, emotional and financial. Marriage triggers a universe of rights, privileges and presumptions. A married person can share in a spouse's estate even when there is no will. She is typically entitled to the group insurance and pension programs offered by the spouse's employer, and she enjoys tax advantages. She cannot be compelled to testify against her spouse in legal proceedings.

The decision whether or not to marry belongs properly to individuals—not the government. Yet at present, all 50 states deny that choice to millions of gay and lesbian Americans. While marriage has historically required a male partner and a female partner, history alone cannot sanctify injustice. If tradition were the only measure, most states would still limit matrimony to partners of the same race.

As recently as 1967, before the Supreme Court declared miscegenation statutes unconstitutional, 16 states still prohibited marriages between a white person and a black person. When all the excuses were stripped away, it was clear that the only purpose of those laws was, in the words of the Supreme Court, "to maintain white supremacy."

Those who argue against reforming the marriage statutes because they believe that same-sex marriage would be "antifamily" overlook the obvious: marriage creates families and promotes social stability. In an increasingly loveless world, those who wish to commit themselves to a relationship founded upon devotion should be encouraged, not scorned. Government has no legitimate interest in how that love is expressed.

And it can no longer be argued—if it ever could—that marriage is fundamentally a procreative unit. Otherwise, states would forbid marriage between those who, by reason of age or infertility, cannot have children, as well as those who elect not to.

As the case of Sharon Kowalski and Karen Thompson demonstrates, sanctimonious illusions lead directly to the suffering of others. Denied the right to marry, these two women are left subject to the whims and prejudices of others, and of the law.

Depriving millions of gay American adults the marriages of their choice, and the rights that flow from marriage, denies equal protection of the law. They, their families and friends, together with fair-minded people everywhere, should demand an end to this monstrous injustice.

Thesis and Organization

1. Paragraphs 1–3 present an example that holds a "moral for everyone." What is it?
2. Paragraphs 4 and 5 define marriage. What point does Stoddard make about marriage?
3. Paragraphs 6–9 are aimed at countering arguments that can be used against Stoddard's view. Summarize them.
4. What is the effect of paragraph 10? What other paragraphs does it connect with?
5. The essay concludes with a statement of thesis and a call to action. Who should demand what and how?

Technique and Style

1. What paragraph or paragraphs appeal to the reader's emotions?
2. What paragraph or paragraphs appeal to the reader's reason?
3. Where in the essay can you identify an ethical appeal, an appeal based on the author's persona?
4. Stoddard cites the arguments that can be used against his. Does he cite obvious ones? Is his treatment of them fair? How so?
5. Stoddard's subject is a sensitive one and his views may not be shared by many readers. Where in the essay can you find evidence that he is aware of his readers and their potential sensitivity to the issue he writes about?

Suggestions for Writing

Think of an issue that ought to be covered by a law or one that is governed by law and should not be. For example, you may think some laws unjust—the 55 mph speed limit, the legal age, zoning or IRS regulations. Or you may think of something that should be required by law—car insurance, automobile safety seats for infants, helmets for motorcycle riders, neutering of pets.

Soft Spot for Serial Murder

Sara Paretsky

At the time Sara Paretsky wrote this essay, April 1991, the United States had just come out of the Gulf War and violence was very much a part of popular culture. As a writer of mysteries, Sara Paretsky depends on violent death for her plot lines, but she has trouble understanding why American women buy books about criminals who abuse and murder women. Paretsky's essay appeared in the Op Ed section of the New York Times.

The record jacket, showing a girl who looks as if she'd just been raped, carried the caption "Guns and Roses were here." Last year, thousands of teenaged girls paid good money to bring this heavy metal album into their homes. 1

Millions of women go to movies to watch themselves assaulted on screen. When I told a (woman) reporter I didn't want to see *Presumed Innocent* because I didn't think I could take another deranged, nymphomaniac career woman, she replied, "You have to be able to overlook the treatment of women and just enjoy the movie." 2

So why should I be surprised that women are paying to read about a man flaying women alive and stripping off their skins? Or a man releasing starving rats inside a woman's vagina? That's what we're doing. And we're doing it enough to make *The Silence of the Lambs* and *American Psycho* best-sellers. 3

The FBI says about 30 of the 7000 murders committed every year are the work of serial killers. But books and movies about serial killers are a national obsession. With one or two exceptions, serial killers are always men. Their victims are always women, children or homosexual men. 4

Why do women as well as men want to read about these exploits in vivid detail that seeks to re-create the pain and humiliation of the attack? 5

Women are conditioned to believe they are victims. We are also taught from childhood that victims of rape and violence were "asking for it." Good girls who don't dress provocatively, get speeding tickets or go to late-night beach parties at the homes of U.S. senators won't be assaulted. We are led to believe, too, that those who object 6 to the perpetual sexual humiliation of women in print, film and music are strident, man-hating feminists. And who wants to be one of those?

7   According to a Senate Judiciary Committee study on violence against women released last month, rape rose faster than any other reported violent crime in America. Though 100,000 rapes are reported every year, the report estimates that the actual number is really between 1.3 and 2 million. Our rape rate is the world's highest.

8   We tolerate a staggering amount of sexual assault on our daughters. Some social psychologists think that as many as 40 percent of our little girls are assaulted by their fathers or other men in their lives. No one puts the number at less than 25 percent.

9   With that much violence toward girls, we silence our daughters before they have even begun to speak. That kind of violation makes it hard for a little girl to establish the boundaries that allow her to see herself as distinct from the world around her. A recent survey commissioned by the American Association of University Women concluded that girls emerge from adolescence with a much lower sense of self-esteem than boys.

10   Sexual assault, or the fear of it, controls vast parts of women's lives. It's no wonder that we see ourselves as inevitable, acceptable targets for violation. And when these violations occur, we're trained to blame ourselves. In *Female Perversions: The Temptations of Emma Bovary,* the psychoanalyst Louise J. Kaplan documents the self-torture women inflict on themselves in response to the violations that have been inflicted on them. We turn our rage inward against ourselves. We don't have any acceptable means to turn it outward.

11   According to the FBI, serial killers share a history of violent childhood abuse. As adults, the only way they can maintain emotional equilibrium is to torment a weaker person as they themselves were tormented.

12   In reading about their exploits, women can share in that torment. If we feel shame for being weak enough to be abused, we may find a perverse release in reading about someone else's torment. Just as hostages may imitate their kidnappers, or concentration camp inmates their captors, so we women loathe ourselves so much for our weakness that we start identifying with those who torment us. If you can't beat them, join them.

That feeling makes us quick to join in condemning those really   13
bad girls, the strident feminists who question the degradation of
women. When Sisters in Crime, an organization for women interested in crime fiction, proposed a study of violence against women
in mysteries, many members were alarmed. If we start studying and
labeling, we'll be called censors, they cried. And who can blame
them for resisting? *Vanity Fair*'s recent article on *American Psycho*
had in its subtitle the phrase: "Feminists Against the First Amendment."

We thought it was pretty horrible that Iraqis were raping Kuwaiti   14
women, and we pledged our lives and fortunes to make them stop.
Meanwhile, here at home we women fund an industry of torment
against ourselves. Can't we put our money to better use?

Thesis and Organization

1. What paragraph or paragraphs provide an introduction to the essay?
   What does Paretsky present as her subject? A working thesis?
2. Paragraph 5 poses a question. Outline the answers given in paragraphs
   6 and 9–12.
3. Why include paragraphs 7 and 8? What do they add?
4. Why include paragraph 13? What does it contribute to the essay?
5. Considering the question Paretsky poses, her answers, and paragraph
   14, what is the thesis of the essay?

Technique and Style

1. Look up rhetorical questions in your handbook. Does Paretsky's use
   conform to the handbook's description? What effect do the rhetorical
   questions in the essay achieve?
2. To what extent does Paretsky's use of examples seem sensational? What
   effect do they have?
3. Where in the essay can you find allusions to then current events? To
   what extent do these allusions date the essay?
4. What point of view does Paretsky use? What reasons can you find for her
   choice?
5. How would you characterize Paretsky's argumentative appeal? Is it primarily emotional? Logical? Ethical? Some combination?

Suggestions for Writing

To what extent is violence a part of popular culture? Think about record
lyrics and labels, videos, movies, television shows, television news cover-

age, newspaper coverage of crimes, pulp magazines, best-selling novels, and art exhibits. No matter how much or how little violence is a part of these subjects, you can think of many different arguments: the violence is or is not justified; does or does not have an adverse effect on the audience; is or is not racist or sexist; should or should not be tolerated. The last, of course, raises the issue of censorship.

*M*ulticulturalism and the Curriculum

Ronald Takaki

Today, the term literacy *has many meanings. Students are not only print literate but computer literate as well, and Ronald Takaki argues that they also need to be culturally literate. Living as we do in a nation made up of many cultures, Takaki argues, we must be culturally literate to understand and live with people of different cultural backgrounds. Takaki's essay appeared in the* Chronicle of Higher Education *in March 1989. As the article reveals, Takaki teaches at the University of California, Berkeley, where he is professor of ethnic studies.*

In Palolo Valley, Hawaii, where I lived as a child, my neighbors were Japanese, Chinese, Portuguese, Filipino, and Hawaiian. I heard voices with different accents and I heard different languages. I played with children of different colors. Why, I wondered, were families representing such an array of nationalities living together in one little valley? My teachers and textbooks did not explain our diversity.

After graduation from high school, I attended a college on the mainland where students and even professors would ask me how long I had been in America and where I had learned to speak English. "In this country," I would reply. "I was born in America, and my family has been here for three generations."

Today, some 20 years later, Asian and also Afro-Americans, Chicano/Latino, and Native American students continue to find themselves perceived as strangers on college campuses. Moreover, they are encountering a new campus racism. The targets of ugly racial slurs and violence, they have begun to ask critical questions about why knowledge of their histories and communities is excluded from the curriculum. White students are also realizing the need to understand the cultural diversity of American society.

In response, colleges and universities across the country, from Brown to Berkeley, are currently considering requiring students to take courses designed to help them understand diverse cultures. The debate is taking place within a general context framed by academic pundits like Allan Bloom and E. D. Hirsch. Both of them are asking: What is an educated, a culturally literate person?

6   I think Bloom is right when he says: "There are some things one must know about if one is to be educated. . . . The university should try to have a vision of what an educated person is." I also agree with Hirsch when he insists that there is a body of cultural information that "every American needs to know."

7   But the question is: What should be the content of education and what does cultural literacy mean? The traditional curriculum reflects what Howard Swearer, former president of Brown University, has described as a "certain provincialism," an overly Eurocentric perspective. Concerned about this problem, a Brown University visiting committee recommended that the faculty consider requiring students to take an ethnic-studies course before they graduate. "The contemporary definition of an educated person," the committee said, "must include at least minimal awareness of multicultural reality."

8   This view now is widely shared. Says Donna Shalala, chancellor of the University of Wisconsin at Madison: "Every student needs to know much more about the origins and history of the particular cultures which, as Americans, we will encounter during our lives."

9   This need is especially felt in California, where racial minorities will constitute a majority of the population by 2000, and where a faculty committee at the University of California at Berkeley has proposed an "American-cultures requirement" to give students a deeper understanding of our nation's racial and cultural diversity. Faculty opposition is based mainly on a disdain for all requirements on principle, an unwillingness to add another requirement, an insistence on the centrality of Western civilization, and a fear that the history of European immigrant groups would be left out of the proposed course.

10   In fact, however, there are requirements everywhere in the curriculum (for reading and composition, the major, a foreign language, breadth of knowledge, etc.). The American-cultures requirement would not be an additional course, for students would be permitted to use the course to satisfy one of their social-sciences or humanities requirements. Western civilization will continue to dominate the curriculum, and the proposed requirement would place the experiences of racial minorities within the broad context

of American society. Faculty support for some kind of mandatory course is considerable, and a vote on the issue is scheduled this spring.

But the question often asked is: What would be the focus and content of such multicultural courses? Actually there is a wide range of possibilities. For many years I have been teaching a course on "Racial Inequality in America: A Comparative Historical Perspective." Who we are in this society and how we are perceived and treated have been conditioned by America's racial and ethnic diversity. My approach is captured in the phrase "from different shores." By "shores," I intend a double meaning. One is the shores that immigrants left to go to America—those in Europe, Africa, Latin America, and Asia. The second is the different and often conflicting shores or perspectives from which scholars have viewed the experiences of racial and ethnic groups.

In my course, students read Thomas Sowell's *Ethnic America: A History* along with my *Iron Cages: Race and Culture in 19th-Century America*. Readings also include Winthrop Jordan on the colonial origins of racism, John Higham on nativism, Mario Barrera on Chicanos, and William J. Wilson on the black underclass. By critically examining the different "shores," students are able to address complex comparative questions: How have the experiences of racial minorities such as blacks and Asians been similar to, and different from, one another? Is "race" the same as "ethnicity?" How have race relations been shaped by economic developments, as well as by culture? What impact have these forces had on moral values about how people should think and behave, beliefs about human nature and society, and images of the past as well as the future?

Other courses could examine racial diversity in relation to gender, immigration, urbanization, technology, or the labor market. Courses could also study specific topics such as Hollywood's racial images, ethnic music and art, novels by writers of color, the civil rights movement, or the Pacific Rim. Regardless of theme or topic, all of the courses should address the major theoretical issues concerning race and should focus on Afro-Americans, Asians, Chicanos/Latinos, and Native Americans.

Who would teach these courses? Responsibility could be located solely in ethnic-studies programs. But this would reduce them to service-course programs and also render even more remote the possibility of diversifying the traditional curriculum. The sheer logistics of meeting the demand generated by an institution-wide requirement would be overwhelming for any single department.

15   Clearly, faculty members in the social sciences and humanities will have to be involved. There also are dangers in this approach, however. The diffusion of ethnic studies throughout the traditional disciplines could undermine the coherence and identity of ethnic studies as a field of teaching and scholarship. It could also lead to area-studies courses on Africa or Asia disguised as ethnic studies, to revised but essentially intact Western civilization courses with a few "non-Western" readings tacked on, or to amorphous and bland "American studies" courses taught by instructors with little or no training in multicultural studies. Such courses, though well intentioned, could result in the unwitting perpetuation of certain racial stereotypes and even to the transformation of texts by writers and scholars of color into "mistexts." This would only reproduce multicultural illiteracy.

16   But broad faculty participation in such a requirement can work if there is a sharply written statement of purpose, as well as clear criteria for courses on the racial and cultural diversity of American society. We also need interdisciplinary institutes to offer intellectual settings where faculty members from different fields can collaborate on new courses and where ethnic-studies scholars can share their expertise. More importantly, we need to develop and strengthen ethnic-studies programs and departments as academic foundations for this new multicultural curriculum. Such bases should bring together a critical mass of faculty members committed to, and trained in, ethnic studies, and should help to preserve the alternative perspectives provided by this scholarly field.

17   In addition, research must generate knowledge for the new courses, and new faculty members must be trained for ethnic-studies teaching and scholarship. Berkeley already has a doctoral program in ethnic studies, but other graduate schools must also help prepare the next generation of faculty members. Universities will experience a tremendous turnover in teachers due to retirements, and this is a particularly urgent time to educate future scholars, especially from minority groups, for a multicultural curriculum.

18   The need to open the American mind to greater cultural diversity will not go away. We can resist it by ignoring the changing ethnic composition of our student bodies and the larger society, or we can

realize how it offers colleges and universities a timely and exciting opportunity to revitalize the social sciences and humanities, giving both a new sense of purpose and a more inclusive definition of knowledge.

If concerted efforts are made, some day students of different 19 racial backgrounds will be able to learn about one another in an informed and systematic way and will not graduate from our institutions of higher learning ignorant about how places like Palolo Valley fit into American society.

Thesis and Organization

1. Paragraphs 1–3 serve as the essay's introduction. What does it suggest about the essay's subject? Thesis? Audience? The writer's persona?
2. What is the "debate" that paragraphs 4–10 focus on?
3. Summarize the solutions presented in paragraphs 11–17.
4. Paragraphs 18 and 19 conclude the essay. How does Takaki make his proposal positive?
5. Originally the essay was preceded by a headline that gave a bare-bones statement of the thesis: "An Educated and Culturally Literate Person Must Study America's Multicultural Reality." Restate that bare-bones idea to include Takaki's major arguments.

Technique and Style

1. Where in the essay do you find evidence that some readers already agree with Takaki?
2. Where in the essay do you find evidence that some readers disagree?
3. How would you characterize the diction level of the essay? Given the diction and the place where the essay was originally published, how would you describe the audience?
4. How would you describe the Takaki you find in this essay? What role does his persona play in the essay's argumentative appeals?
5. Takaki begins and ends with mention of Palolo Valley. How effective do you find this framing device? How does it tie into the body of the essay?

Suggestions for Writing

Rethink the curriculum you had in high school or the one at your college. To what extent did it prepare you for a multicultural society? Are you "culturally literate"? Depending on your answer, you might argue for curricular change or for other schools to adopt a curriculum similar to yours.

Toward a Representative Judiciary

Anthony D'Amato

This essay appeared in Northwestern Perspective (*1989*), *the alumni magazine of Northwestern University, where Anthony D'Amato is a professor of law. A specialist in international law and legal education, D'Amato argues that gender influences judicial decisions.*

1   Why shouldn't approximately 50 percent of our judges be women? My first answer may strike you as simple and my second one as, perhaps, interesting. The simplistic answer is that the low number of female judges reflects discrimination against women that ought to be eliminated.

2   Although sexism in the United States has diminished significantly over the last 20 years, a look at the highest ranks of government and industry reveals an obvious and overwhelming male prevalence. As of November 1, 1988, there were 17 female circuit court judges out of 160, 49 female district court judges out of 549, and 1 female Supreme Court justice out of 9. Granted, the low percentage of females in high-level positions relates to the relatively recent influx of women into middle management and the professions. But if it were not for past discrimination, women would have climbed higher on their respective career ladders much sooner.

3   My second answer relates to my first. Because of sexism and discrimination, women and men perceive the world differently. Thus, the low percentage of female judges greatly skews decisions handed down from our courts. Let me explain. Our brains teach us to cope in a difficult and dangerous world not by memorizing a billion solutions to a billion possible problems but by the more efficient process of learning a few thousand ways of dealing with factual patterns. Researchers in artificial intelligence call the pathways "K-lines."

4   Most of the gender-influenced K-lines form in our brains during childhood. By high school we are already fairly set in our ways,

although we are still on a learning curve. By college, we simply become absorbers of more facts that we file away in our minds and later recall according to preexisting K-lines. By the time of law school, the mind of a would-be judge is practically closed. He or she will learn a great many legal rules that do not solve cases but are expected to be displayed in written opinions. These legal rules will simply be plugged into preexisting mental pathways. Thus, far more significant than the abstract content of "law" are the K-lines in the future judge's mind. According to the legal realists of the 1930s, all law is a rationalization for a judge's interpretation of the facts.

Take, for instance, a bitterly contested divorce in which the wife   5
claims the husband brutalized the 4-year-old daughter. The husband denies it and wants custody. He claims the desperate nature of the wife's argument affirms that she is an unfit mother. The "law" of divorce, including every legal precedent, cannot tell us who should be awarded custody in this case. A male and female judge may arrive at certain versions of the truth based on gender-influenced interpretations of the case. A male judge might be insensitive to the importance of strong relations within the family, such as bonding between mother and daughter. A female judge might be insensitive to a husband's claim for equality under the marriage contract irrespective of behavior during the marriage.

Plato's solution to a judiciary that is subject to the vagaries of   6
individuals' minds was to choose judges at birth and isolate them from the rest of society. He recommended that their minds be filled with legal theories and at the proper time they be plucked from their sheltered community to begin preordained judicial careers. Plato thought this would ensure consistency and predictability among judges.

The trouble with that approach is that with no experience in the   7
real world the judges' superior knowledge of "law" would be useless in dispensing real justice. Rejecting the platonic model, the best we can do to achieve an egalitarian judiciary is to maintain a bench that mirrors societal compositions. Therein lies my argument for a bench that is 50 percent female. That is not to say that the argument applies to each of the multitude of groups discriminated against in society. If Presbyterians are not discriminated against vis-à-vis Episcopalians, for instance, then that lack of socially engendered difference

means that the bench should not reflect the numbers of one religious group compared to the other. In short, we need representative minds on the bench. If society makes some minds different from others—due to the way society treats persons based on characteristics such as race or gender—then the bench should reflect those different perspectives.

8   Once society eliminates discrimination against women—if that time ever arrives—my argument would no longer be valid. Then we should no longer actively try to attain equal numbers of women and men in the judiciary. We could wind up with 90 percent women or 90 percent men. It would make no difference to our real-world model of judging since gender would no longer be a socially determined factor in mental difference. By that time, however, we may possibly be dealing with other less blatant (but nonetheless real) discriminations that we are only vaguely aware of today.

Thesis and Organization

1. In what ways does paragraph 1 prepare you for the rest of the essay?
2. D'Amato presents a "simple" answer and an "interesting" one. Which does paragraph 2 support?
3. Paragraphs 3 and 4 explain K-lines. What role does this explanation play in D'Amato's argument?
4. How does D'Amato's argument relate to Plato? What is the relationship between "societal compositions" (7) and experience in the "real world"?
5. Take D'Amato's statement that 50 percent of our judiciary should be women and add why. What is the resulting thesis?

Technique and Style

1. To what extent does D'Amato use cause and effect to make his case?
2. What sort of sentence variety do you note in paragraph 3? What effect does it have?
3. How would you characterize D'Amato's diction level? Is it casual? Learned? Informal? Stuffy? What?
4. What devices does D'Amato use to get from one paragraph to another? Identify his techniques.
5. D'Amato concludes his essay by looking to the future. How effective do you find his conclusion? Why?

Suggestions for Writing

Often the case for affirmative action or quotas is made by arguing that we must make up for past injustices and inequities, but D'Amato raises a new point that can be extended to other professions by arguing that gender and race create different ways of thinking that need to be represented. Examine the idea of affirmative action or quotas in a profession you are familiar with, taking into consideration D'Amato's argument.

Checks on Parental Power

Ellen Goodman

In a syndicated column published in 1981, Ellen Goodman reacts to a Supreme Court ruling, attacking the position taken by the Court and arguing the opposing view. Note the essay's appeals both to emotion and to reason.

1   First, consider the stories.

2   An 11-year-old retarded boy was brought to a mental hospital with a teddy bear under his arm. His parents were, they said, going on a two-week vacation. They never came back.

3   A 12-year-old "tomboy" and truant was committed to a mental hospital by her mother after school authorities threatened the woman with prosecution.

4   A 7-year-old boy's mother died one year, and he was committed the next year by his father—two days before the man's remarriage. The diagnosis: a reaction of childhood.

5   Consider, too, the story of one child committed because he had "school phobia," another because she was "promiscuous," a third and fourth because they were "difficult" or even "incorrigible."

6   Then, when you've heard the stories, listen to Justice Warren Burger insist that the "natural bonds of affection lead parents to act in the best interests of their children."

7   Last Wednesday the Supreme Court assured all parents—the confused and the pathologically indifferent as well as the caring and concerned—an equal right to put their kids in mental hospitals. Last Wednesday they denied all children—the odd and the unwanted as well as the ill—an equal right to a hearing before being institutionalized.

8   And they did it on a wish and a myth: that parents—and those bureaucratic "parents," state agencies—know best. It took seven years and four separate Supreme Court hearings to achieve this disappointing decision.

9   Lawyers from Pennsylvania and Georgia, and children's advocates, argued that minors deserve the same treatment adults have: a simple hearing before incarceration. They argued that children fac-

ing a mental institution deserved the same treatment as children facing a penal institution: a hearing.

But the justices, especially Burger and Potter Stewart, were convinced that these children didn't need any advocate other than their parents, or any check on parental power other than the institution's own medical team. In roughly 38 states, they left the fate of children up to parents and hospitals.   10

"That some parents may at times be acting against the interest of their child creates a basis for caution, but is hardly a reason to discard wholesale those pages of human experience that teach that parents generally do act in the child's best interest," wrote Burger.   11

The conflict was between the right of the parents to make decisions about bringing up their children, and the rights of children to their liberty, and to due process. Burger and Stewart, both ardent advocates of extreme parental supremacy, interpreted the Constitution to read, Families First.   12

I agree that most parents do want to act in the "child's best interest." But the law is not necessary to protect children from wise and sensitive parents. Nor is it made to "interfere" with families functioning smoothly on their own.   13

As David Ferleger, the Pennsylvania lawyer who argued this case, put it: "We all want to protect the integrity of a family where it exists. But when the family wants to incarcerate a member, it has already created a break. There is no longer a united family to protect."   14

At that point, the question is whether it's more important to protect a possible, and devastating, infringement of the child's liberty, or to protect the right of a parent or state guardian to dispose of that child's fate.   15

A family in stress may not have the information and emotional stability to make a good judgment. A state agency may not care. Nor can we trust the hospital for an impartial judgment. If surgeons have a bias toward surgery, institutional psychiatrists often have a bias toward institutional psychiatry. Psychiatry is hardly an infallible science, as Burger knows, and there are many children in hospitals now who are simply not mentally ill.   16

The justices compared signing a child into a mental hospital with signing him into a general hospital to have his tonsils out. But a tonsillectomy takes hours, not years. And it does less harm.   17

Parents obviously have and must have a wide range of decisions   18 over their children's lives. But they don't have absolute power and never have. They cannot refuse immunization for their kids or keep them uneducated. They cannot (at least yet) forcibly sterilize them, order them to become a transplant donor, commit incest or abuse them.

19 Nor should they have the right, without another impartial source, to deprive children of something equally as fundamental as their liberty, by putting them away in an institution. In this case (which bodes badly for other children's rights cases coming before the Court), the majority of the justices have sided with a parental power that is virtually unchecked.

20 Chalk one up for the folks who dropped off the boy with the teddy bear.

Thesis and Organization

1. What paragraphs introduce the essay? What elements do the examples in those paragraphs have in common?
2. What paragraphs focus on the Supreme Court's ruling? Which paragraph sums up the issues in the case?
3. What paragraphs present Goodman's analysis of the ruling? Which paragraph sets out her own position? What future actions are at stake? Is the essay's purpose to influence those actions directly or indirectly? How so?
4. Consult a handbook of grammar and usage for an explanation of the rhetorical paragraph. Do paragraphs 1 and 20 fit that explanation? How or how not? Evaluate the effectiveness of those paragraphs in providing a framework for the essay.

Technique and Style

1. Where in the essay does Goodman rely on emotional appeal? On logical appeal? Which predominates? Why might she have started with one and then gone to the other? In which category does the last paragraph fit?
2. What characteristics can you infer about Goodman as a person? What evidence can you cite for your assumptions? How would you describe Goodman's tone? In what ways is it in keeping with her persona? With the effect she wishes to have on her audience?
3. On what point or points does the author agree with Burger and Stewart? What effect does that agreement have on her credibility as a sound arguer?
4. Why might Goodman have chosen to quote from the Supreme Court

decision? Where does she quote and what effects does she achieve? Where does she paraphrase? How else does she use quotation marks and to what effect?

5. Where does Goodman fault the justices for a false analogy? How is her own analogy a correct one? Why might she have selected the examples she does?

Suggestions for Writing

Look around for concrete examples of a particular kind of abuse. For instance, leafing through a few days of newspapers may turn up examples of unprovoked violence, abandoned children, white-collar crime, political graft, or terrorist attacks. Using one category of examples, mull over their moral, political, or legal ramifications, figuring out what argumentative point you can make based on them. Or go about the assignment as a short research paper. Start with a recent Supreme Court decision with which you disagree and then work backwards through resource material to find examples that you can use for an emotional appeal.

Testing for AIDS

From the *New York Times*

At the time this essay was published, William Bennett was secretary of education and Gary Bauer a White House aide. The names and positions have changed, but the argument continues. The editorial was published in 1987.

1 Why not compel everyone to be tested for AIDS as the basis for halting further spread of the virus? That's a natural first thought to anyone who ponders the deadly epidemic. But it's only a first thought. That some senior administration officials argue for mandatory AIDS testing shows how late in the day they have arrived at step one.

2 William Bennett, the secretary of education, wants AIDS tests to be given to everyone admitted to the hospital or applying for a marriage license. Gary Bauer, a senior White House aide, says opponents of such tests are promoting "a bizarre type of enforced ignorance." The Public Health Service now says that all immigrants will be screened for AIDS virus.

3 There are at least six reasons for believing that advocates of general forced testing are opinionated, hasty or poorly informed.

4 **Lesson One: Don't drive victims underground.** Homosexuals and intravenous drug abusers, the principal victims, are not mainstream America. Living at the edge of social tolerance in many states, they face plenty of discrimination already. Their cooperation in changing their own behavior is crucial in slowing the disease's spread to other groups. Mandatory testing is the surest way to discourage them from contact with health authorities.

5 **Lesson Two: A consensus is not a conspiracy.** No one should lightly deny public health officials the tools they need to combat AIDS, including use of the AIDS antibody tests. What public officials want—for the reason cited above—is more voluntary testing, not mandatory testing. Mr. Bennett seems to believe that the federal public health agency has fallen under the influence of homosexuals who oppose mandatory testing for self-interested reasons. But the reason for agreement is not conspiracy. Both groups believe voluntary testing is the better way of halting AIDS.

Lesson Three: Why in hospitals? Hospital patients are pre-   6
dominantly the elderly and the very young, two categories least
likely to have AIDS. Why does Mr. Bennett propose to look there for
the virus instead of among high-risk groups? Because hospitals are
where testing is easiest. So too argued the drunkard who lost his
keys in the dark and explained he was searching for them under the
lamppost because the light was better.

Lesson Four: Like it or not, morals have changed. Many   7
states require a syphilis test for those seeking a marriage license. Mr.
Bennett can't understand why an AIDS test isn't given too. The
reason is that a minute proportion of known syphilis cases are
detected this way. New York recently dropped the syphilis test
because the results were not worth the cost, and because of suspicion that some couples nowadays have sex before marriage. The
same logic applies to AIDS, but there's another, far more cogent
reason.

Lesson Five: False alarms have grim consequences. The   8
two present tests for AIDS virus are highly specific but even in
conjunction are not totally accurate. The danger of "false positives"—diagnosing individuals as exposed to AIDS when they are
not—is probably minuscule with high-risk populations. But the
danger grows rapidly when screening large populations at low
risk.

According to a paper to be published shortly by Michael J. Barry   9
and colleagues at the Harvard School of Public Health, the two
standard AIDS tests would identify 28 true positives, 2 false nega-
tives and 11 false positives when applied to a low-risk population,
defined as 30 AIDS cases per 100,000 people. What those figures say
is that, for every 28 cases correctly diagnosed, the tests risk falsely
informing 11 individuals that they carry the virus of a deadly disease
and should never have children. Without guarantees of confidenti-
ality, the insurers, employers, landlords and classmates of these 11
individuals may also learn, and act, on the false information. What
a burden for mandatory testers to bear.

Lesson Six: AIDS makes a poor political football. Mr. Bauer   10
believes that public health officials have few qualms in urging explicit sex education for young children, offensive as that may be to
conservatives. But when it comes to testing, "the left's political
agenda takes over." He says, "Either this is potentially the Black
Death or it isn't." In fact, no one knows how widely AIDS will

spread, but it's prudent to take precautions. Teaching teenagers safe sex is an effective precaution—and mandatory testing is not.

11   AIDS is a medical issue. Those who politicize it, or see political motives where none exist, are seriously delaying national policy on AIDS and measures to save lives. The only known way to curb AIDS is to persuade people to change behavior. The administration still has not mounted a massive public education program of the sort already under way in several European countries. The secretary of education should be leading the charge for education about AIDS and voluntary testing. Mandatory testing should be his last thought, not his first.

Thesis and Organization

1. According to William Bennett, under what conditions should people be tested for AIDS? What arguments are used to show that mandatory testing of those groups is mistaken?
2. What do paragraphs 4, 8, and 9 indicate would be the effects of mandatory testing?
3. What political motivation do paragraphs 5 and 10 suggest? What does the author see as the effect of politicizing? What does the author favor as a national policy on AIDS?
4. Analyze the line of argument: Is the author arguing for a position or against one, or both? State the argument in one sentence.
5. Given the emotions evoked by the subject, you might expect the author to rely on emotional appeal. What examples can you find of appeal to emotion? To reason? To persona? Which appeal dominates?

Technique and Style

1. The essay appeared as an editorial in the *New York Times*. Who or what is its primary audience? Its secondary one?
2. Analyze paragraph 3 for its potential effect on the reader. What does it imply about the number of reasons that follow? Does the paragraph offend the very audience it intends to persuade? How or how not?
3. Where does the author use analogy to bolster the argument? What does the analogy imply about Bennett? Is it fair or false? What effect does it have on the argument?
4. What effects does the author achieve with the beginning of paragraphs 4–8 and 10? What does this device contribute to the essay's organization? The author's tone? What does it imply about Bennett? Why might the word *lesson* be appropriate?

5. The essay is also interesting for what it does not say. Why might explicit sex education offend conservatives? Why might mandatory testing offend liberals? What are some of the political charges that the essay avoids?

Suggestions for Writing

Consider a proposed or enacted regulation or law that affects you and take a stand on it. For example, you might think about recent changes in the drinking laws or in the 55 mph speed limit. Or perhaps your institution, workplace, or community has, or has proposed, rules or ordinances on smoking. Maybe a tuition hike or a new tax has been proposed.

*T*wo Views of Bias and the Media: Against All Odds, I'm Just Fine *and* A Case of "Severe Bias"

Brad Wackerlin and Patricia Raybon

Both of these essays appeared in Newsweek. *Brad Wackerlin's essay was published in a 1990 special issue devoted to "The New Teens." And Wackerlin is one. He graduated from high school in Illinois in 1990. Patricia Raybon's essay was published in the regular "My Turn" column in October 1989. Both writers address a similar subject but from their own particular perspectives. Wackerlin writes as a successful teenager and Raybon as a successful freelance writer and media relations consultant.*

▪ AGAINST ALL ODDS, I'M JUST FINE

Brad Wackerlin

1   What troubled times the American teenager lives in! Ads for Nike shoes urge us to "Just do it!" while the White House tells us to "Just say no." The baby boomers have watched their babies grow into teens and history has repeated itself: the punk teens of the eighties have taken the place of the hippie teens of the sixties. Once again, the generation gap has widened and the adults have finally remembered to remember that teenagers are just no good. They have even coined a name for their persecution of adolescents: "teen-bashing."

2   If what is being printed in the newspapers, viewed on television and repeated by adults is correct, it is against all odds that I am able to write this article. Adults say the average teenager can't write complete sentences and has trouble spelling big words. Their surveys report that I can't find Canada on a map. According to their statistics, my favorite hobbies are sexual intercourse and recreational drug use. It's amazing that I've found time to write this; from what they say, my time is spent committing violent crimes or just hanging

out with a gang. In fact, it is even more amazing that I'm here at all, when you consider that the music I listen to is supposedly "warping" my mind and influencing me to commit suicide.

Nonetheless, here I am. I write this article to show that a teenager   3
can survive in today's society. Actually, I'm doing quite well. I haven't fathered any children, I'm not addicted to any drugs, I've never worshiped Satan and I don't have a police record. I can even find Canada on a map along with its capital, Ottawa. I guess my family and friends have been supportive of me, for I've never been tempted to become one of those teenage runaways I'm always reading about. Call me a rebel, but I've stayed in school and (can it be true?!) I enjoy it. This month, I graduate from high school and join other graduates as the newest generation of adults. I'm looking forward to four years of college and becoming a productive member of society. I may not be America's stereotypical teen, but that only proves there is something wrong with our society's preconceived image of today's teenager.

My only goal in writing this article is to point out the "bum rap"   4
today's teenager faces. I feel the stereotypical teen is, in fact, a minority. The true majority are the teenagers who, day in and day out, prepare themselves for the future and work at becoming responsible adults. Our time is coming. Soon we will be the adults passing judgment on the teenagers of tomorrow. Hopefully, by then, we will have realized that support and encouragement have a far more positive effect on teenagers than does "bashing" them.

▓ A CASE OF "SEVERE BIAS"

Patricia Raybon

This is who I am not. I am not a crack addict. I am not a welfare   1
mother. I am not illiterate. I am not a prostitute. I have never been in jail. My children are not in gangs. My husband doesn't beat me. My home is not a tenement. None of these things defines who I am, nor do they describe the other black people I've known and worked with and loved and befriended over these 40 years of my life.

Nor does it describe most of black America, period.   2

Yet in the eyes of the American news media, this is what black   3

America is: poor, criminal, addicted and dysfunctional. Indeed, media coverage of black America is so one-sided, so imbalanced that the most victimized and hurting segment of the black community—a small segment, at best—is presented not as the exception but as the norm. It is an insidious practice, all the uglier for its blatancy.

4   In recent months, oftentimes in this very magazine, I have observed a steady offering of media reports on crack babies, gang warfare, violent youth, poverty and homelessness—and in most cases, the people featured in the photos and stories were black. At the same time, articles that discuss other aspects of American life—from home buying to medicine to technology to nutrition—rarely, if ever, show blacks playing a positive role, or for that matter, any role at all.

5   Day after day, week after week, this message—that black America is dysfunctional and unwhole—gets transmitted across the American landscape. Sadly, as a result, America never learns the truth about what is actually a wonderful, vibrant, creative community of people.

6   Most black Americans are *not* poor. Most black teenagers are *not* crack addicts. Most black mothers are *not* on welfare. Indeed, in sheer numbers, more *white* Americans are poor and on welfare than are black. Yet one never would deduce that by watching television or reading American newspapers and magazines.

7   Why does the American media insist on playing this myopic, inaccurate picture game? In this game, white America is always whole and lovely and healthy while black America is usually sick and pathetic and deficient. Rarely, indeed, is black America ever depicted in the media as functional and self-sufficient. The free press, indeed, as the main interpreter of American culture and American experience, holds the mirror on American reality—so much so that what the media says is *is,* even if it's not that way at all. The media is guilty of a severe bias and the problem screams out for correction. It is worse than simply lazy journalism, which is bad enough; it is inaccurate journalism.

8   For black Americans like myself, this isn't just an issue of vanity—of wanting to be seen in a good light. Nor is it a matter of closing one's eyes to the very real problems of the urban underclass—which undeniably is disproportionately black. To be sure, problems besetting the black underclass deserve the utmost atten-

tion of the media, as well as the understanding and concern of the rest of American society.

But if their problems consistently are presented as the *only* reality for blacks, any other experience known to the black community ceases to have validity, or to be real. In this scenario, millions of blacks are relegated to a sort of twilight zone, where who we are and what we are isn't based on fact but on image and perception. That's what it feels like to be a black American whose life-style is outside of the aberrant behavior that the media presents as the norm. 9

For many of us, life is a curious series of encounters with white people who want to know why we are "different" from other blacks —when, in fact, most of us are only "different" from the now common negative images of black life. So pervasive are these images that they aren't just perceived as the norm, they're *accepted* as the norm. 10

I am reminded, for example, of the controversial Spike Lee film, *Do the Right Thing,* and the criticism by some movie reviewers that the film's ghetto neighborhood isn't populated by addicts and drug pushers—and thus is not a true depiction. 11

In fact, millions of black Americans live in neighborhoods where the most common sights are children playing and couples walking their dogs. In my own inner-city neighborhood in Denver—an area that the local press consistently describes as "gang territory"—I have yet to see a recognizable "gang" member or any "gang" activity (drug dealing or drive-by shootings), nor have I been the victim of "gang violence." 12

Yet to students of American culture—in the case of Spike Lee's film, the movie reviewers—a black, inner-city neighborhood can only be one thing to be real: drug-infested and dysfunctioning. Is this my ego talking? In part, yes. For the millions of black people like myself—ordinary, hard-working, law-abiding, tax-paying Americans—the media's blindness to the fact that we even exist, let alone to our contributions to American society, is a bitter cup to drink. And as self-reliant as most black Americans are—because we've had to be self-reliant—even the strongest among us still crave affirmation. 13

I want that. I want it for my children. I want it for all the beautiful, healthy, funny, smart black Americans I have known and loved over the years. 14

And I want it for the rest of America, too. 15

I want America to know us—all of us—for who we really are. To 16 see us in all of our complexity, our subtleness, our artfulness, our enterprise, our specialness, our loveliness, our American-ness. That is the real portrait of black America—that we're strong people, surviving people, capable people. That may be the best-kept secret in America. If so, it's time to let the truth be known.

Thesis and Organization

1. Both essays personalize their arguments, yet Wackerlin begins with the general (1) and Raybon with the particular (1). Which is more effective and why?
2. Both writers introduce their essays with descriptions of situations. What are those situations?
3. What support do the writers provide for their charges of misrepresentation?
4. What do the writers declare as their purpose in writing the essays? What is the thesis of each?
5. Which essay better supports its major assertion and why?

Technique and Style

1. Both authors assert that the group each identifies with is misrepresented. How valid is the evidence each cites?
2. Who is guilty of this misrepresentation? To what extent is it conscious? Are there other reasons that the authors do not account for?
3. Both authors use themselves as evidence to disprove what they find is a widely held stereotype. To what extent, if any, are they generalizing from insufficient evidence (the fallacy also known as hasty generalization)?
4. What is each essay's primary argumentative appeal: Ethical? Emotional? Rational? A combination? Which essay's appeal do you find more effective?
5. What differences in paragraphing do you note in comparing the two essays? What reasons can you find for the differences?

Suggestions for Writing

Think about times when you or a group you identify with (or your city or state or even nation) has gotten a "bum rap." You may simply want to disprove it or you may want to go a step further and convey how it made you feel as well as argue that the image was unfair.

Two Views on Legalizing Drugs: Legalize Drugs? Not on Your Life *and* Yesterday's Drug War

Charles B. Rangel and Daniel Lazare

Alcohol is a drug with adverse effects but it's legal, so why not legalize marijuana? How about cocaine? Heroin? Everything? Charles B. Rangel tells us why. Daniel Lazare answers the question with historical precedent, citing our experience with Prohibition as an argument for legalization. Rangel was a Democratic congressman from New York and chair of the House Select Commission on Narcotics Abuse and Control at the time his essay was first published in the New York Times *(May 1988). Lazare's essay appeared in the* Village Voice *in January 1990.*

▓ LEGALIZE DRUGS? NOT ON YOUR LIFE

Charles B. Rangel

The escalating drug crisis is beginning to take its toll on many Americans. And now growing numbers of well-intentioned officials and other opinion leaders are saying that the best way to fight drugs is to legalize them. But what they're really admitting is that they're willing to abandon a war that we have not even begun to fight.   1

For example, the newly elected and promising mayor of Baltimore, Kurt Schmoke, at a meeting of the United States Conference of Mayors, called for a full-scale study of the feasibility of legalization. His comments could not have come at a worse time, for we are in the throes of the worst drug epidemic in our history.   2

Here we are talking about legalization, and we have yet to come up with any formal national strategy or any commitment from the administration on fighting drugs beyond mere words. We have never fought the war on drugs like we have fought other legitimate wars—with all the forces at our command.   3

Just the thought of legalization brings up more problems and concerns than already exist.   4

Advocates of legalization should be reminded, for example,   5 that it's not as simple as opening up a chain of friendly neigh-borhood pharmacies. Press them about some of the issues and questions surrounding this proposed legalization, and they never seem to have any answers. At least not any logical, well thought out ones.

6   Those who tout legalization remind me of fans sitting in the cheap seats at the ballpark. They may have played the game, and they may think they know all the rules, but from where they're sitting they can't judge the action.

- Has anybody ever considered which narcotic and psychotropic drugs would be legalized?
- Would we allow all drugs to become legally sold and used, or would we select the most abused few, such as cocaine, heroin, and marijuana?
- Who would administer the dosages—the state or the individual?
- What quantity of drugs would each individual be allowed to get?
- What about addicts: Would we not have to give them more in order to satisfy their craving, or would we give them enough to just whet their appetites?
- What do we do about those who are experimenting? Do we sell them the drugs, too, and encourage them to pick up the habit?
- Furthermore, will the government establish tax-supported facili-ties to sell these drugs?
- Would we get the supply from the same foreign countries that support our habit now, or would we create our own internal sources and "dope factories," paying people the minimum wage to churn out mounds of cocaine and bales of marijuana?
- Would there be an age limit on who can purchase drugs, as exists with alcohol? What would the market price be and who would set it? Would private industry be allowed to have a stake in any of this?
- What are we going to do about underage youngsters—the age group hardest hit by the crack crisis? Are we going to give them identification cards? How can we prevent adults from purchasing drugs for them?
- How many people are projected to become addicts as a result of the introduction of cheaper, more available drugs sanctioned by government?

Since marijuana remains in a person's system for weeks, what   7
would we do about pilots, railroad engineers, surgeons, police,
cross-country truckers and nuclear plant employees who want to
use it during off-duty hours? And what would be the effect on the
health insurance industry?

Many of the problems associated with drug abuse will not go   8
away just because of legalization. For too long we have ignored the
root cause, failing to see the connection between drugs and hope-
lessness, helplessness and despair.

We often hear that legalization would bring an end to the blood-   9
shed and violence that has often been associated with the illegal
narcotics trade. The profit will be taken out of it, so to speak, as will
be the urge to commit crime to get money to buy drugs. But what
gives anybody the impression that legalization would deter many
jobless and economically deprived people from resorting to crime to
pay for their habits?

Even in a decriminalized atmosphere, money will still be needed   10
to support habits. Because drugs would be cheaper and more available, people would want more and would commit more crime.
Does anybody really think the black market would disappear? There
would always be opportunities for those who saw profit in peddling
larger quantities, or improved versions, of products that are forbidden or restricted.

Legalization would completely undermine any educational effort   11
we undertake to persuade kids about the harmful effects of drugs.
Today's kids have not yet been totally lost to the drug menace, but
if we legalize these substances they'll surely get the message that
drugs are OK.

Not only would our young people realize that the threat of jail   12
and punishment no longer exists. They would pick up the far more
damaging message that the use of illegal narcotics does not pose a
significant enough health threat for the government to ban its use.

If we really want to do something about drug abuse, let's end this   13
nonsensical talk about legalization right now.

Let's put the pressure on our leaders to first make the drug prob-   14
lem a priority issue on the national agenda, then let's see if we can
get a coordinated national battle plan that would include the de-
ployment of military personnel and equipment to wipe out this
foreign-based national security threat. Votes by the House and more

recently the Senate to involve the armed forces in the war on drugs
are steps in the right direction.

15   Finally, let's take this legalization issue and put it where it belongs—amid idle chitchat as cocktail glasses knock together at social events.

■ YESTERDAY'S DRUG WAR

Daniel Lazare

1   *Plus ça change. . . .* The great historical precedent for the current
drug war is, of course, Prohibition. The war on booze backfired in
essentially the same way the war on drugs is boomeranging today.
Besides fostering an unprecedented wave of gang violence, Prohibition promoted immoderate use by tilting the market away from
softer substances to harder ones.

2   During Prohibition, beer drinking declined in much the same
way pot smoking is declining today: the reason wasn't changing
taste, but the effect of government interdiction on supply and demand. Bootleggers refused to risk their lives for something that was
95 percent water and hops. According to data collected in the late
1920s by Irving Fisher, the famous Yale economist, a glass of beer
grew to be twice as expensive as a shot of bathtub gin—meaning, in
effect, that Prohibition wound up pushing drinkers toward the hard
stuff. The day of having a brew or two with friends was past. The
age of getting blind, blotto, buried, canned, etc., had arrived.

3   The upshot was a wave of drunkenness that left ordinary people
aghast. As one witness observed: "Everybody drank as if there
would never be another drink. If you opened a bottle, you killed it."
With supplies unpredictable, bingeing became the norm. "Eat, drink,
and be merry," went the doggerel of the day, "for tomorrow, it may
be prohibited by law." In Chicago, a Croatian immigrant complained
that when working men get their hands on liquor, "they take one
drink, then two, then another because they know it will be long
before they can have more, and end up by spending their whole pay
and then getting very sick."

4   With repeal, however, the nature of alcohol consumption was
transformed. People who would have killed for rotgut whiskey now

breezed passed liquor stores. In a freer, more tolerant atmosphere, alcohol returned to being ordinary. Drinking increased but there's no evidence that drunkenness did. Some people had difficulty coping with the new freedom—and alcoholism remains a scourge—but taken as a whole, the social cost of drinking—as measured by corruption, enforcement expenditures, and the sheer loss of lives—went down.

Hopefully, legalization would transform the demand for drugs in much the same way. Instead of the desperate desire to get as high as possible in the shortest period of time, people might grow to use drugs more carefully, discriminately, and wisely. Certainly, they couldn't use them any *less* wisely than they do under today's overwrought conditions.   5

Legalization would undercut the drug lords (or at least force them to go legit). By introducing free and open competition, it would bring profits and prices down to normal business levels. Sidewalk dealers, suddenly legitimized, would have no more reason to settle their disputes with Uzis than do liquor salesmen. Whatever reasons black and Latino kids have to quit school, the desire to make big money selling crack would not be among them. And junkies would no more have to rob and steal than would a wino trying to rustle up the fistful of change needed to purchase a bottle of MD 20/20. With drugs subject to pure food and drug laws, overdoses and poisonings would decline.   6

Instead of expending vast sums for cops, prosecutors, judges, prison guards, etc., society would be able to finance noncoercive drug treatment by taxing hitherto forbidden substances. With the destigmatization of drugs would come a form of junkie liberation—freedom to come out of the shadows, take jobs, demand services, and organize politically against police harassment and the scourge of AIDS.   7

Thesis and Organization

1. At what point in each essay is the thesis clear? Which placement is the more effective and why?
2. Both authors use cause and effect as a way to organize their essays. Which one uses it more effectively and why?
3. Both authors also rely on example to support their assertions. Which is the more effective and why?

4. What counterarguments does each author address? Which author does it better?

5. Look up the terms listed under *Logical fallacies* in the Glossary (page 309). Do any of those fallacies apply to either author?

Technique and Style

1. Rangel's point of view is the first-person plural *we,* while Lazare opts for an objective position, avoiding all pronouns. Which is the more effective and why?

2. Which writer deals more fairly with opposing views? What evidence can you use to support your opinion?

3. Compare the two essays from the perspective of diction. What differences do you notice? What reasons can you think of for the writers' choices? Which do you find more persuasive and why?

4. How would you characterize each of the writers? Which persona do you find the more appealing?

5. Analyze each essay from the perspective of argumentative appeal. What appeal dominates each essay? Considering *only* the authors' support for their assertions, their use of appeals, and their writing style, which do you find more persuasive?

Suggestions for Writing

Consider "victimless crimes" (sometimes called "willing-victim" crimes) such as prostitution, gambling, various sexual acts between consenting adults, and pornography. Choose one of those topics or another and rethink whether or not it should be legalized.

*H*andgun Control: Pro and Con

Pete Shields and J. Warren Cassidy

In the 1986 debate that follows, two opposing groups square off, each represented by a person who knows how to lobby: N. T. "Pete" Shields chairs Handgun Control Inc., an advocacy group based near Capitol Hill; J. Warren Cassidy is the executive vice president of the National Rifle Association. With the attempted assassination of then President Reagan that resulted in the crippling of James Brady, his press secretary, the proposal for a waiting period for the purchase of handguns has been known as the Brady amendment.

▨ PRO

Pete Shields

Five years ago last month, when John Hinckley, Jr., used a handgun to shoot President Reagan, James Brady and two law enforcement officers, Americans were reminded again that our nation's handgun laws are dangerously weak. While we mourned the tragedy, we once again looked for answers to the nation's handgun violence problem. And just as in years past, the answer was obvious. With stronger laws to keep handguns out of the wrong hands, this tragedy could have been prevented.

Twenty thousand Americans were killed with handguns last year. Hundreds of thousands more were injured. One child a day dies in a handgun accident. And every so often, our nation's leaders are the targets.

Since President Reagan was shot, Congress has not acted to strengthen our federal handgun laws. Instead, our politicians have watched as more Americans have fallen victim. The lessons of yet another handgun tragedy have been ignored.

Twelve years ago last week, my 23-year-old son, Nick, was murdered by someone using a handgun—the last victim of the "Zebra Killings," a wave of senseless, brutal attacks that plagued San Francisco for more than a year.

Since my son's murder, I have worked for passage of federal laws

1

2

3

4

5

to keep handguns out of the wrong hands: the hands of felons, of drug and alcohol abusers, of children and of the mentally incompetent. But Congress has refused to act, and the price we've paid is staggering.

6   More Americans were killed here at home with handguns than died in the war in Vietnam. More Americans are killed with handguns each week than lost their lives in the bombing of the Marine barracks in Beirut. As many Americans die each year by handgun fire as are killed by drunk drivers.

7   Yet Congress has done little to stop the violence.

8   Handgun Control Inc. believes that commonsense improvements to existing law can prevent handgun crime and make it easier to jail those who do commit crimes with handguns. Rather than ban or confiscate handguns, we believe that there is a responsible middle ground: legislation that protects the law-abiding gun owner and gives police the tools they need to fight violent crime.

9   Such measures include licensing those who wish to carry handguns; prohibiting the manufacture of snub-nosed handguns; requiring mandatory safety training for handgun purchasers; tightening record-keeping requirements of gun manufacturers; and requiring tough, mandatory sentences, with no parole, for those who use guns to commit crimes.

10   The centerpiece of this agenda is a waiting period and background check for handgun purchases to allow law enforcement time to ensure that individuals purchasing handguns are not convicted felons, fugitives from justice or criminally insane. Such a measure could have a strong impact on our nation's violent crime.

11   Current law prohibits felons and other unqualified persons from purchasing handguns, but the law contains a glaring loophole. It does not require verification of a purchaser's eligibility; only that the purchaser signs a form on which he affirms he is not prohibited from purchasing a handgun. An "honor system" does little to prevent proscribed persons from obtaining handguns, since a criminal certainly will lie when signing this form. In fact, a recent study performed under a grant from the Justice Department found that at least one in five career criminals purchases his handgun from a licensed dealer simply by lying on the federal form.

12   In 1981 the Reagan administration's Task Force on Violent Crime addressed this loophole in federal gun laws and recommended that "a waiting period be required for the purchase of a handgun to

allow for a mandatory records check to ensure that a purchaser is not in one of the categories of persons who are proscribed by existing federal law from receiving a handgun."

The International Association of Chiefs of Police, the Fraternal   13
Order of Police, the National Troopers Coalition, the Police Executive Research Forum, the National Organization of Black Law Enforcement Executives, and the Police Foundation support a waiting period for handgun purchases. Police chiefs from more than 400 of America's towns and cities believe a waiting period will help reduce the number of handguns that fall into criminal hands.

Even the National Rifle Association, until the late 1970s, said, "a   14
waiting period could help in reducing crimes of passion and in preventing people with criminal records or dangerous mental illness from acquiring guns." And more recently, the NRA's executive vice president, G. Ray Arnett, has indicated that he believes background checks are appropriate for those wishing to carry handguns.

Statistics clearly prove that these laws work. Police in Palm Beach   15
County, Florida, credit an ordinance enacted last year requiring a 7- to 14-day waiting period for handgun purchases with reducing homicides by 60 percent in the first quarter of 1985. In the 19 years New Jersey has required a background check for handgun purchases, 10,000 convicted felons have been caught attempting to buy handguns.

California reports that in 1981, 1,200 prohibited persons were   16
stopped. The chief of police in Columbus, Georgia, says that the city's three-day waiting period catches two felons a week trying to buy guns.

Conversely, in South Carolina, where there is no waiting period,   17
police estimate that 300 to 350 guns each year are sold to people convicted of serious crimes, those who have been treated for mental disorders, or those who are otherwise proscribed from handgun ownership.

Clearly, places that require this commonsense step make it far   18
more difficult for criminals to buy handguns. But we must have these laws on the federal level to be truly effective.

The case of John Hinckley, Jr., exemplifies the need for a waiting   19
period. Hinckley walked into a Texas pawnshop, purchased a handgun, and a few minutes later was on his way to shoot the president, just because he though it would make a popular actress fall in love with him!

20   Had a waiting period and background check been law in Texas, John Hinckley would have been stopped. He lied about his address and used an old Texas driver's license to purchase that handgun. He was not a Texas resident. In fact, had police been given the opportunity to discover his lies, John Hinckley would have been in jail (lying on the federal form is a felony offense) instead of on his way to Washington.

21   Yet our nation continues to allow such tragedies to occur because Congress refuses to put any barriers in the criminal's path. By ignoring the success of reasonable laws we are, in effect, arming the very criminals we are trying to stop.

22   Measures to keep handguns out of the wrong hands can make a difference. Earlier this month, when the House passed the McClure-Volkmer Bill, Congress moved one step closer to recognizing that fact. Though many proclaimed a victory for the National Rifle Association, it was a hollow victory. Congress did not give the gun lobby what it wanted.

23   When the McClure-Volkmer bill was first introduced, the NRA described the bill as "the first step toward the repeal of the 1968 Gun Control Act." The bill allowed mail-order gun sales; repealed all curbs on interstate weapons sale and transport; prohibited unannounced inspections of gun dealers; and nullified state and local handgun carrying laws. But none of those provisions was in the bill passed by the House.

24   Just last week, House members stating that they must part company with the NRA, voted to maintain existing gun control laws. The House also voted to ban machine guns and the kits used to convert semiautomatic weapons into machine guns. The bill now contains a ban on the importation of parts for snub-nosed handguns.

25   Most important, our representatives struck at the central core of NRA philosophy by denying the NRA's argument that controlling inanimate objects will not help reduce crime.

26   By recognizing the distinction between handguns and long guns, by banning machine guns, Congress agreed with responsible Americans that we must try to keep dangerous weapons out of the wrong hands.

27   With such gains for handgun control and crime control advocates, it is likely that new laws ultimately will be enacted to protect our citizens and our police. By refusing to support the NRA's whole-

sale attempt to repeal our nation's handgun control laws, Congress has held the line against the gun lobby onslaught.

Despite the work of NRA leaders in Washington, responsible gun owners share a common goal with those who do not own guns—a safe America, a nation where our children can enjoy their parks and playgrounds, a time when our family restaurants and shopping malls are no longer shooting galleries. Passage of rational, commonsense handgun laws will bring us closer to that day.   28

■ CON

J. Warren Cassidy

"Gun control is being able to hit your target."   1

That dig at the antigun crowd has become a favorite of many gun owners. But gun control, whether it be in the form of registration, licensing, waiting periods, background checks or outright bans, is no joke to the more than 60 million law-abiding gun owners, sportsmen and gun collectors in this country.   2

To claim that such schemes are implemented to reduce crime and "keep guns out of the wrong hands" is ignorant at worst and naive at best. Controlling handguns will not deter people bent on crime from committing their heinous acts, nor will it reduce the availability of guns to the criminal population.   3

In fact, a recent survey of incarcerated felons conducted by the National Institute of Justice found that 88 percent of criminals secure their guns through illegal channels on the black market, stealing or borrowing from fellow criminals.   4

A study done by the Justice Department found that "there is no conclusive evidence that restrictive gun laws either impair the access of criminals to firearms or reduce the amount of violent crime."   5

Cities with the most restrictive gun laws—New York, Washington, D.C., and Chicago for example—consistently have ranked among the ten most violent cities in America, according to the FBI's Uniform Crime Reports.   6

But whatever the statistics prove, however they are manipulated, the simple truth is that handgun controls may be imposed only upon   7 those who would submit to them: law-abiding citizens. Criminals, by definition, are lawbreakers, so no matter how many handgun control laws are enacted, criminals will continue to get guns by breaking those laws.

8   Gun control advocates claim that their simple and moderate proposals will help reduce the likelihood of a criminal getting a gun.

9   A look at their "simple" schemes proves otherwise. One of the proposals most often suggested by antigun groups is registration. But according to the 1968 U.S. Supreme Court ruling, *Haynes* v. *U.S.,* persons with felony records are "exempt" from firearms registration, because to require a felon to register what is already deemed illegal for him to possess (federal law prohibits convicted felons from possessing, receiving, or transferring any firearm) would be a violation of the constitutional guarantee of the Fifth Amendment against self-incrimination.

10   Waiting periods and background checks are two other favorites of those opposed to the private ownership of handguns. Advocates of these controls say that they will weed out criminals attempting to buy guns and reduce so-called "crimes of passion."

11   But the evidence proves that waiting periods and background checks do not affect criminals. As Professor Philip J. Cook of Duke University wrote in the *Annals of the American Academy of Political and Social Sciences:* "There has been no convincing empirical evidence that a police check (and accompanying waiting period) of handgun buyers reduces violent crime . . . we suspect that most felons and other ineligibles who obtain guns do so not because the state's screening system fails to discover their criminal record, but rather because these people find ways to circumvent the screening system entirely."

12   "Crimes of passion" would not abate simply because a waiting period existed. "Few homicides could be avoided merely if a firearm were not immediately present," said Marvin Wolfgang, a criminologist who studied homicides in Philadelphia and published his findings in *Patterns in Criminal Homicide.* "The offender would select some other weapon to achieve the same destructive goal."

13   Studies indicate that there is a "slow buildup" to "passion" killings, that in 90 percent of spouse slayings the police had been called to the scene on at least one prior occasion, and in 50 percent of such murders the police had been called at least five times.

14   Other studies show that the majority of domestic homicides are

justifiable killings committed by women defending themselves against men under the influence of drugs or alcohol or both. Statistics also show that argument-precipitated murders generally occur from 10 P.M. to 3 A.M. Not a gun shop in the country is open during those hours.

The handgun murder of former Beatle John Lennon and the attempted assassination of President Reagan provoked a strong cry for waiting periods and criminal background checks. But Lennon's murderer purchased his handgun in Hawaii, which has a permit-to-purchase-and-registration system. And Reagan's assailant legally purchased the gun he used in Texas, and his purchase would have been legal under any "waiting period" scheme ever devised. Obviously, the waiting period didn't stop him from purchasing a handgun.   15

After Lennon was murdered, the call for gun control was great, but those not caught in the emotionalism of the moment could see the real problem, and it wasn't guns. The *Wall Street Journal* wrote in an editorial following the death of Lennon: ". . . the sudden hue and cry for more gun control at such times is a kind of cop-out, the sort of cop-out that is part of the problem in America. The country knows that something is wrong. Too many are turning to crimes of violence. The notion that this can be changed by controlling guns, we worry, may be an excuse for avoiding the hard work of making our decrepit criminal justice system start to function, and the even harder work of buttressing what used to be called the nation's moral fiber."   16

While the effects of gun registration, licensing and waiting periods and background checks on crime are sure to be debated as long as there are guns, one fact cannot be overlooked: such schemes have been used to harass law-abiding gun owners and, in some cases, to deny them access to guns.   17

In New Jersey, for one year the state police refused to issue any gun permits because the FBI was refusing to do fingerprint checks for civil matters. The mayor of Gary, Indiana, once ordered his police chief to refuse to provide handgun application forms to citizens, and "lost" applications are a common occurrence in jurisdictions that have gun control.   18

Registration, licensing, waiting periods and background checks also cost money. Added paperwork costs to gun dealers are passed to buyers, and police administrative fees for conducting checks and   19 processing applications are passed to all taxpayers. Such measures also redirect limited law enforcement resources away from crime fighting. (Besides, criminals don't register their guns, get them licensed or undergo criminal background checks.)

20   Laws banning the sale and possession of handguns, such as those in Evanston, Morton Grove and Oak Park, Illinois—all suburbs of Chicago—not only have failed to reduce crime, but also have increased the likelihood that unarmed citizens will become the victims of crime. And such laws penalize law-abiding citizens not because they misuse a firearm or commit a crime, but simply because they choose to possess a handgun for self-protection, target shooting or hunting.

21   Dr. David J. Bordua, a University of Illinois professor of sociology who studies gun control and gun ownership, conducted interviews on the subject of handgun bans with criminals convicted of armed robbery. Said Bordua: "[They] unanimously agreed that the handgun ban in Morton Grove would do absolutely nothing to curb crime, but it would make things easier for them."

22   Bordua's findings have been almost prophetic. Since Morton Grove became the first U.S. municipality to ban the sale and possession of handguns in 1981, its rates of occurrence for robbery and burglary increased 33 and 47 percent, respectively, through 1984.

23   Again, statistics can be debated, but what happened to Oak Park, Illinois, gas station owner Donald Bennett points out both the uselessness of a ban and the stupidity of such laws.

24   Bennett's gas station had been held up three times in six years, so he and his employees decided to carry guns while at work. But in 1984 the village of Oak Park banned the sale and possession of handguns.

25   Bennett and his employees disarmed the day the law took effect. Two days later the station was robbed.

26   The fourth time Bennett was robbed he took action. As two armed men fled with the station receipts and some jewelry last March 26, Bennett grabbed a .45-caliber pistol beneath the seat of his truck and fired at their car. The robbers got away, and Bennett was charged with unlawful possession of a handgun. The maximum penalty for such an offense is $2000 and/or six months in jail.

27   The Oak Park ban did not stop the robbery of Donald Bennett's gas station, but it did make a criminal of Bennett, who told the *Chicago Tribune:* "The way I feel about this is you're better off

being a criminal than an honest citizen, because criminals have more rights. They take guns away from the good people and the only ones that have them left are the thieves and the police."

So, gun control is no joke to Donald Bennett, and no joke to   28
millions of people who want to be able to defend themselves against criminal attack.

Ultimately, the fight over gun control comes down to controlling   29
the rights of law-abiding citizens to be secure in their persons and properties, and the misguided efforts of some people who believe that by controlling guns they can control the actions of people.

But gun control is not crime control, it's only being able to hit   30
your target.

Thesis and Organization

1. Each writer introduces his argument by spelling out causal relationships, Shields in paragraphs 1–7 and Cassidy in paragraphs 1–5. What are the arguments? What basic premise does each introduction establish?
2. Both essays focus primarily on requiring a waiting period and background check. Trace each writer's reasons for and against these measures and then, in one sentence, state each author's full position.
3. What other measures does Shields mention? Cassidy? What differences do you note? Does either author beg the question?
4. Think about the essay in terms of problem and solution. Both address the problem of violent crime. You will have noted Shields's solution in answering question 3. What solutions does Cassidy bring out? Which author's focus on problem/solution is more effective and why?
5. Analyze the two writers' concepts of audience. Do the essays address the same audience or different ones? What are the characteristics of the audience(s)?

Technique and Style

1. Both essays open dramatically and then return to that opening. Analyze each author's use of his opening paragraph to determine who uses the technique better.
2. Where in the essay does each author refer to the opposition? What qualities does the author attribute to the opposition? To what extent can the writers be accused of name-calling?
3. Both authors rely heavily on emotional appeal. Find two examples of each author's use of this device and analyze them for their effect. To what extent are the authors' appeals legitimate?
4. Both authors also rely heavily on an appeal to reason. Find two exam-

ples of each author's use of this technique and analyze them for their validity. What holes can you find? To what extent are the authors' appeals legitimate?

5. John Hinckley, Jr., turns up as an example in both essays. Compare the writers' use of this example to see what differences you find. What generalization does each writer draw from the example? Test each for its validity.

Suggestions for Writing

List as many emotionally charged issues as you can: abortion, euthanasia, use of nuclear weapons, capital punishment, chemical warfare. Select one of the issues that interests you and write down all the reasons you can think of for both pro and con positions. Separate the reasons into false and fair ones and you're on your way to a paper that can use this debate guideline for development.

Exploring the Topic

1. **What position do you want to take toward your subject?** Are you arguing to get your audience to adopt your conviction or to go further and take action? What is your conviction? What action is possible?

2. **How is your audience apt to respond to your conviction if you state it baldly?** How much background do they need you to provide? Do you need to use definition? What arguments can the reader bring against your assertion?

3. **What examples can you think of to illustrate your topic?** Are all of them from your own experience? What other sources can you draw upon?

4. **How can you appeal to your readers' emotions?** How can you use example, description, and narration to carry your emotional appeal?

5. **How can you appeal to your readers' reason?** How can you use example, cause and effect, process, comparison and contrast, analogy, or division and classification to strengthen your logic?

6. **What tone is most appropriate to the kind of appeal you want to emphasize?** Does your persona fit that tone? How can you use persona to support your argument?

Drafting the Paper

1. **Know your reader.** Estimate how familiar your reader is with your topic and how, if at all, the reader may react to it emotionally. Keeping those ideas in mind, review how the various patterns of development may help you contend with your audience's knowledge and attitudes, and decide whether your primary appeal should be to emotion or reason. Description, narration, and example lend themselves particularly well to emotional appeal; process, cause and effect, comparison and contrast, analogy, example, and division and classification are useful to rational appeal. Use definition to set the boundaries of your argument and its terms as well as to clear up anything the reader may not know.

2. **Know your purpose.** Depending on the predominant appeal you find most appropriate, your essay will tend toward persuasion or argument; you are trying to get your reader not only to understand your major assertion but also to adopt it and perhaps even act on it. Short of that, a successful writer of argument must settle for the reader's "Well, I hadn't thought of it that way" or "Maybe I should reconsider." The greatest danger in argumentative writing is to write to people like yourself, ones

who already agree with you. You need not think of your audience as actively hostile, but to stay on the argumentative track, it helps to reread constantly as you write, playing the devil's advocate.

3. **Acknowledge the opposition.** Even though your reader may be the ideal, someone who holds no definite opposing view and indeed is favorably inclined toward yours but hasn't really thought the topic through, you should bring out one or two of the strongest arguments against your position and demolish them. If *you* don't, the reader may, and there goes your essay. The ideal reader is also the thinking reader who says, "Yes, but. . . ."

4. **Avoid logical pitfalls.** Logical fallacies can crop up in unexpected places; one useful way to test them is to check your patterns of development. If you have used examples, does your generalization or assertion follow? Sometimes the examples are too few to support the assertion, leading to a hasty generalization; sometimes the examples don't fit, leading to begging the question or arguing off the point or misusing authority; and sometimes the assertion is stated as an absolute, in which case the reader may use an example as the exception that destroys your point. If you have used analogy, double-check to see that the analogy can stand up to scrutiny by examining the pertinent aspects of the things compared. If you have used cause and effect, you need to be particularly careful. Check to see that the events you claim to have a causal relationship are not related instead by a temporal one, or else you fall into the *post hoc, ergo propter hoc* fallacy. Also examine causal relationships to make sure that you have not merely assumed the cause in your statement of effect. If you claim that "poor teaching is a major cause of the high dropout rate freshman year in college," you must prove that the teaching is poor; if you don't you are arguing in a circle or begging the question. Non sequiturs can also obscure cause-and-effect relationships when an element in the relationship is missing or nonexistent. The reader's response is "It does not follow," in Latin *non sequitur*. Definition also sets some traps. Make sure your definition is not only fully stated but also commonly shared and consistent throughout. (All of the logical fallacies referred to in this section are defined more fully in the Glossary of Terms.)

5. **Be aware of your persona.** The ethical appeal, the rational appeal, and the emotional appeal are fundamental concepts of argument, and it is the persona, together with tone, that provides the ethical appeal. To put it simply, you need to be credible. If you are writing on an issue you feel strongly about and, for example, are depending primarily on an appeal to reason, you don't want to let your dispassionate, logical persona slip and resort to name-calling (formally known as arguing *ad hominem* or *ad populem*). That's obvious. Not so obvious, however, is the same slip

in diction or tone that reveals the hot head behind the cool pen. Your reader may feel manipulated or use the slip to discount your entire argument, all because you lost sight of the ethical appeal. Tone should vary, yes, but never to the point of discord.

6. **Place your point where it does the most good.** Put each of your paragraphs on a separate piece of paper so that you can rearrange their order as you would a hand of cards. Try out your major assertion in different slots. If you have it at the beginning, try it at the end and vice versa. Or extend the introduction so that the thesis comes closer to the middle of the paper. See which placement carries greater impact. You may want to organize your material starting with examples that lead up to the position you wish to attack and to the conviction you are arguing for; in that case your thesis may occur somewhere in the middle third or at the end of the paper. On the other hand, you may want to use deduction, starting with the opposition, stating your position, and then spending 90 percent of the remaining essay supporting your case. Remember that you want to win over your reader, so put your thesis where it will do the greatest good.

Glossary of Terms

Active voice See *Voice.*

Ad hominem A logical fallacy in which the argument is directed at the person, not the view held by the person. Name-calling.

Ad populem A logical fallacy in which the argument is directed at the group the opponent belongs to, not the views held by the opponent. Name-calling.

Aim See *Purpose.*

Allusion A reference to a real or fictitious person, place, or thing. An allusion is a concise form of association that carries the meaning of the thing alluded to and uses it to enhance the writer's own meaning.

Analogy One of the patterns used to develop an idea. Analogy examines a topic by comparing it point by point to something seemingly unlike but more commonplace and less intricate. Analogy extends a metaphor, concentrating on one subject; comparison and contrast explores the similarities and differences of two or more subjects within the same class.

Antithesis The use of opposite words or phrases to emphasize contrasting ideas that are usually stated in balanced or parallel terms.

Argumentative appeals The three classical appeals central to argument: *logos,* the appeal to reason; *pathos,* to emotion; and *ethos,* to the writer or speaker's persona. For a fuller discussion, see Chapter 10.

Argumentative writing One of the four major purposes of writing. Argument attempts to move the reader to action or to adopting the writer's conviction. Many teachers distinguish between argumentative and persuasive writing: argumentative writing appeals primarily to reason, persuasive writing to emotion.

Assertion   A statement that is debatable, as opposed to a fact. Sometimes the author's major assertion appears in the essay's title (Robert Keith Miller's "Discrimination Is a Virtue"), sometimes in a key sentence. Often, however, the reader deduces the writer's assertion by considering the essay's most important statements, most of which appear as topic sentences.

Audience   The intended readership for a given work. The audience can be general, as in Lewis Thomas's "The Ilks"; specific, as in Sara Paretsky's "Soft Spot for Serial Murder"; or multiple, as in Robert C. Maynard's "Of Prophets and Protestors." No matter what the audience, a writer should keep in mind A. D. Van Nostrand's summary of the "Common Reader": a person who does not know the thesis, is impatient, shares the writer's level of maturity and education, and knows something about the subject.

Balanced sentence   See *Sentence*.

Begging the question   A logical fallacy in which the major line of argument is dodged and a lesser line taken up instead.

Cause and effect   One of the patterns used to develop an idea. Cause and effect examines the topic to discover, explain, or argue why a particular action, event, situation, or condition occurred.

Chronological organization   See *Organization*.

Classification   One of the patterns used to develop an idea. Classification examines a class of things according to shared characteristics, grouping the things according to a similar feature.

Coherence   Literally the quality of sticking together. To communicate ideas clearly to the reader, the writer must present material in a logically integrated, understandable, and consistent manner; in short, words, phrases, clauses, sentences, and paragraphs must relate to each other. Coherency can be achieved by using appropriate transitions, logical sequences, and interlocking ideas.

Comparison and contrast   One of the patterns used to develop an idea. Comparison and contrast examines two or more subjects by exploring their similarities and differences. Similarities are usually developed through literal and logical comparisons within similar categories: small cars such as Ford Escort and Honda Civic, popular music such as rock and reggae. Figurative comparisons usually come under analogy. In contrasting subjects, differences fall into two categories: differences in kind, such as Yale has a football team and the University of Chicago does not; or differences in degree, such as the University of Michigan has a better football team than the University of Texas.

Complex sentence   See *Sentence.*

Compound sentence   See *Sentence.*

Compound-complex sentence   See *Sentence.*

Conflict   An element essential to narrative. Conflict involves pitting one force against another: a rat against traffic in "Tale of the Rodent," a student against the educational system in "Angels on a Pin," a woman against a potential mugger in "I Have a Gun."

Connotation   The meanings associated with and suggested by a word that augment its explicit denotative or dictionary definition. The words *home* and *domicile* have a similar denotative value, but they differ radically in their connotations.

Cumulative sentence   See *Sentence.*

Declarative sentence   See *Sentence.*

Deductive reasoning   The method of argument whereby the author first gives the assertion and then explores the reasoning behind it. Charles B. Rangel's and Pete Shields's essays both are organized deductively.

Definition   One of the patterns used to develop an idea. Definition examines a word or phrase by exploring its meaning, determining its essence. Simple definition employs synonyms, antonyms, and etymology; extended definition may use classification, comparison, description, and example as well as other patterns in order to expand upon the connotations of a word or phrase.

Denotation   See *Connotation.*

Description   One of the patterns used to develop an idea. Description explores the subject by breaking it down into parts in order to better understand the whole. It draws upon the senses to paint vivid images usually set in time and space, employing repetition, enumeration, spatial development, perspective, and imagery. Description can be classified according to what is described—a person, place, or thing—or according to how it is described—subjectively or objectively.

Detail   A precise description—"Six feet four inches" instead of "tall," for example.

Diction   The writer's choice of words. The level of diction (colloquial, slang, informal, technical, formal) along with denotation, connotation, and sound determine the writer's judgment of a word's appropriateness to the work's audience and the writer's purpose.

Division   The process of separating, usually associated with classification. First a subject is divided into groups, then examples can be sorted out—classified—into the groups or categories.

Dramatic organization   See *Organization.*

Either-or Reasoning   A logical fallacy in which the central term is claimed to be either one thing or another, omitting any possibility of middle ground. A writer who argues that a person is a believer in either democracy or communism is guilty of either-or thinking.

Ethos   See *Argumentative appeals.*

Example   One of the patterns used to develop an idea. Example explores an assertion by illustrating it, showing how the assertion applies in particular instances. Example is used to provide evidence to support generalizations.

Exclamatory sentence   See *Sentence.*

Expository writing   See *Informative writing, Purpose.*

Expressive writing   One of the four major purposes of writing. Expressive writing emphasizes the author's feelings or attitudes toward the subject.

Fallacy   See *Logical fallacies.*

False analogy   A logical fallacy in which the analogy does not hold true. Ellen Goodman, in "Checks on Parental Power," accuses Justices Burger and Stewart of using false analogy when they "compared signing a child into a mental hospital with signing him into a general hospital to have his tonsils out."

Hasty generalization A logical fallacy in which a conclusion is reached on the basis of inadequate examples or sampling. If Patricia Raybon had not made a connection between her experience and that of other black Americans, she would have been guilty of hasty generalization.

Imperative mood See *Mood*.

Imperative sentence See *Sentence*.

Indicative mood See *Mood*.

Inductive reasoning The method of argument whereby the author first presents information and then moves from explanation and evidence to a logical conclusion. Patricia Raybon and Ellen Goodman use inductive reasoning in their argumentative essays.

Informative writing (expository writing) One of the four major purposes of writing. Informative writing attempts to further the reader's understanding about the topic.

Interrogative sentence See *Sentence*.

Irony A statement or action in which the intended meaning or occurrence is the opposite of the surface one. Shana Alexander, for instance, cites a judgment that the funerary customs among tribes in New Guinea are "bizarre in the extreme" and then contrasts them with a technological society's high-rise mortuary. The ironic juxtaposition raises questions as to which is the more "bizarre."

Journalistic questions The traditional questions: *who, what, where, when, why,* and *how.*

Logical fallacies Errors in reasoning. See *Ad hominem, Ad populem, Begging the question. Either-or reasoning, False analogy, Hasty generalization, Misusing authority, Non sequitur, Post hoc, propter hoc, Shift in definition, Straw man.*

Logos See *Argumentative appeals*.

Loose sentence See *Sentence*.

Metaphor   An implied but direct comparison in which the primary term is made more vivid by associating it with a quite dissimilar term. Rick Telander, for instance, explores the mascot as metaphor in "Fight! Fauna Fight!"

Middle premise   See *Syllogism.*

Misusing authority   A logical fallacy in which a person's skill or knowledge in one area is assumed to exist in another. A successful baseball player may be a valid authority on makes of baseball gloves, for instance, but not on after-shave lotion.

Modes   Common patterns of thought used to explore, develop, and organize a topic. The various modes or patterns can be classified according to their function: those that sequence information are narration, process, and cause and effect; those that compare are analogy and comparison and contrast; and those that divide are classification, description, definition, and example.

Mood   An aspect of the verb that reveals the attitude of the writer. The indicative mood states fact or asks a question; the subjunctive mood states a matter of possibility, desire, contradiction, or uncertainty; the imperative mood states a command or request.

Name-calling   See *Ad hominem* and *Ad populem.*

Narration   One of the patterns used to develop an idea. Narration explores a topic by presenting a story or account of an experience bounded by time and space. Whereas cause and effect emphasizes *why,* and process emphasizes *how,* narration emphasizes *what.* Narration can be factual, grounded in an actual event, or fictional, grounded in the imagination.

Non sequitur   A logical fallacy in which the causal relationship claimed does not follow: "The essay was published in the *New York Times,* so it must be accurate."

Organization   The manner in which a paragraph or essay is put together. Essays are usually organized by several principles: the various modes, and chronological, dramatic, and spatial order. Chronological order is determined by time, dramatic order by emotional effect, and spatial order by physical location.

Paradox   A statement that appears to be contradictory yet may in fact be true; an apparent contradiction.

Paragraph A cohesive unit of thought or emphasis set off by indention. Most paragraphs develop a controlling assertion or topic sentence, explicit or implied, and therefore run to 150 words or so; other shorter paragraphs function as transitions or as rhetorical devices.

Paragraph block A group of paragraphs that taken together develop a controlling assertion or topic sentence. William Raspberry's "The Handicap of Definition" illustrates paragraph blocks.

Parallelism The repetition of words or grammatically similar phrases, clauses, or sentences to emphasize coherence.

Parody An exaggerated imitation that treats a serious subject in an absurd manner, ridiculing both form and content. James Gorman's "Man, Bytes, Dog" is a parody.

Passive voice See *Voice*.

Pathos See *Argumentative appeals*.

Patterns of organization Common patterns of thought used to explore, develop, and organize a topic. The various patterns can be classified according to their function. Those that sequence material are cause and effect, process, and narration; those that compare are analogy and comparison and contrast; those that divide are classification, description, definition, and example. Patterns of organization are also called modes.

Periodic sentence See *Sentence*.

Persona The mask or character assumed by the writer to engage the intended audience. While the most obvious persona is an ironic one (as in the case of James Gorman), to achieve credibility, focus, and emphasis, all writers assume personas to greater or lesser degrees.

Persuasive writing See *Argumentative writing* and *Purpose*.

Point of view The perspective from which the work is related. In nonfiction, point of view usually refers to the writer's use of personal pronouns (*I, you, he, she, we they,* etc.); in fiction, point of view is usually further divided into first person, limited omniscient, omniscient, and objective.

Post hoc, propter hoc   A logical fallacy in which a temporal relationship is mistaken for a causal one: if all your lights went out just as you plugged in your new television set and you then assume you are the cause of the power failure, you must be in a *post hoc* trap.

Process   One of the patterns used to develop an idea. Process examines the topic to discover the series of steps or acts that brought or will bring out a particular result. Whereas cause and effect emphasizes *why* and depends primarily on analysis, process emphasizes *how* and depends primarily on classification. For example, the topic "leaving the teaching profession" can be developed by cause and effect, explaining *why* by providing an analysis of the various reasons that lay behind the decision, or by process, explaining *how* by showing the steps that were involved, steps that may be put in categories such as first doubts, the brink of decision, and tidying up. Process can be further divided into historical, practical, and scientific: historical process deals with topics such as how the United States will carry out foreign policy or how Levi's became big business; practical process deals with topics such as how to make butter; scientific process deals with topics such as how the body reacts to starvation.

Purpose   The intention that drives the text; its function. Most written work can be classified into one of four categories according to its purpose: expressive writing, such as journal entries and diaries that analyze, record, relate the writer's feelings and ideas; informative or expository writing, such as explanations and analyses that further the reader's understanding about the topic; persuasive or argumentative writing, such as narratives, descriptions, and analyses that try to move the reader to action or to share the writer's conviction; and literary writing, such as poems, plays, short stories, and novels that create fictional worlds out of the interplay of language. In general, expressive writing emphasizes the writer, informative writing the subject, persuasive writing the reader, and literary writing the language itself.

Sarcasm   A caustic or sneering remark or tone that is usually ironic as well.

Satire   The use of wit, sarcasm, irony, and parody to ridicule or expose some folly or evil.

Sensory detail   Detail relating to one or more senses. See *Detail*.

Sequence   See *Organization.*

Sentence   One or more words that convey meaning. In grammar, sentences can be classified as simple, compound, and compound-complex. A simple sentence has one main clause and no subordinate clauses; a complex sentence has a main clause and a subordinate clause; a compound sentence has two or more main clauses and no subordinate clause; and a compound-complex sentence has two or more main clauses and one or more subordinate clauses.

In rhetoric, sentences can be classified as declarative, stating facts; as interrogative, asking questions; as imperative, giving commands; and as exclamatory, expressing feeling.

Also in rhetoric, certain types of sentences achieve certain effects; the cumulative or loose sentence, in which the main clause comes first, occurs most frequently and allows for modification without sacrificing clarity; the less used periodic sentence, in which the main clause comes last, achieves dramatic tension; and the balanced sentence, in which phrases are parallel, usually emphasizes contrast.

Shift in definition   A logical fallacy in which the meaning of a term central to the argument is changed. A person who shifts the definition of lying from intention to deceive to the far narrower meaning of verbal untruth is guilty of a shift in definition, a form of *begging the question.*

Simile   A stated but removed comparison in which the primary term is made vivid by associating it with a quite dissimilar one. Simile differs from metaphor in that simile uses a term of comparison such as *like* or *as,* as in Bruce Berger's description of deck shoe treads that leave footprints "like postage cancellations."

Simple sentence   See *Sentence.*

Spatial organization   See *Organization.*

Straw man   A logical fallacy in which the argument is shifted to an insignificant or unrelated point, which is then attacked and destroyed in hopes that some of the destruction will carry over to the main point. The use of an extreme example is a popular form of straw man argument.

Subjunctive mood   See *Mood.*

Syllogism   A form of deductive reasoning composed of a major premise, a minor or middle premise, and a conclusion: All Labrador retrievers are gentle; Beartrap is a Labrador retriever; therefore Beartrap is gentle. Note that a syllogism can be logical but false, as above.

Syntax   The way in which words are put together to form phrases, clauses, and sentences; the grammatical relationship between the words.

Thesis   A statement about a subject that accounts for the relevant information about it; a statement or assertion of the subject's significance. An essay's thesis is its umbrella statement, the assertion at the highest level of generality under which all the essay's other assertions fit.

Tone   A writer's attitude toward the subject and the audience. An author's tone can be contemplative (Peter Steinhart), intense (Patricia Raybon), tongue-in-cheek (James Gorman), and so on.

Topic sentence   A statement of the topic of a paragraph and an assertion about the topic. A topic sentence is to the paragraph what the thesis is to the essay. Whether implicit or explicit, the topic sentence conveys the paragraph's controlling idea.

Transition   A word, phrase, sentence, or paragraph that carries the reader smoothly from point A to point B. Some transitions, such as time markers and semantic guideposts—*therefore, however, but,* and so on—are overt; others are more subtle—a repeated word or phrase, a synonym for a key term, a shift in tense. All, however, provide coherence and unity.

Voice   In grammar, forms of the verb. If the subject performs the action, the verb is in the active voice; if the subject is acted upon, the verb is in the passive voice: "I bit the dog" versus "The dog was bitten by me."

In rhetoric and composition, voice refers to the reader's sense of the writer as a real person. A writer's voice is a combination of tone and persona.

Wordplay   A clever phrasing of words, a pun.

Acknowledgments

Chapter 1

From *A Country Year: Living the Questions* by Sue Hubbell. Copyright © 1983, 1984, 1985, 1986 by Sue Hubbell. Text and title "Where I Live" reprinted by permission of Random House, Inc.

"El Hoyo" by Mario Suarez for *Arizona Quarterly,* Summer 1947, vol. III, no. 2. Copyright © by the Arizona Quarterly. Reprinted by permission.

From "At 85, Frightened by a Loss of Power" by J. Merrill-Foster, *The New York Times,* January 31, 1988. Copyright © by The New York Times Company. Reprinted by permission.

"Cyclone" by Peter Schjeldahl. Copyright © 1988 by Harper's Magazine. All rights reserved. Reprinted from the June issue by special permission.

"The Vibram Stomp" from *The Telling Distance* by Bruce Berger. Copyright © 1990 by Bruce Berger. Reprinted by permission of the author.

Chapter 2

"Tale of the Rodent" by Roger Starr, *The New York Times,* August 2, 1981. Copyright © 1981 by The New York Times Company. Reprinted by permission.

"Bad Luck Bob and His Dog" by Al Martinez from *Ashes in the Rain,* A TQS Book. Copyright © 1989 by TQS Publications, Berkeley, CA. Reprinted by permission of the author.

"Living an Adventurous Life" from *Plaintext* by Nancy Mairs. Copyright © 1986 The University of Arizona Press. Reprinted by permission.

"I'm Frightened, Angry and Ashamed: I Have a Gun" by Tania Nyman, *The Times-Picayune,* April 21, 1990. Reprinted by permission of The Times-Picayune Publishing Corporation.

"Angels on a Pin" by Alexander Calandra from *Saturday Review,* December 21, 1968. Copyright © 1968 by Saturday Review. All rights reserved. Reprinted by permission.

Chapter 3

Excerpts for *Doublespeak* by William Lutz. Copyright © 1989 by Blonde Bear, Inc. Reprinted by permission of HarperCollins Publishers.

"Rambos of the Road" by Martin Gottfried. Appeared in *Newsweek,* September 8, 1986. Reprinted by permission of the author.

"Here Be Beasties" by Angus McGill, (London) *Evening Standard,* November 6, 1990.

"TV's War Coverage Is Packaged Like a Miniseries" by Kathleen J. Turner, *The Times-Picayune,* January 23, 1991. Reprinted by permission of The Times-Picayune Publishing Corporation.

"Mom, Dad and Abortion" by Anna Quindlen, *The New York Times,* July 1, 1990. Copyright © 1990 by The New York Times Company. Reprinted by permission.

"Learning to Hear the Small, Soft Voices" by Michael Gorra, *The New York Times,* May 1, 1988. Copyright © 1988 by The New York Times Company. Reprinted by permission.

Chapter 4

"Fight! Fauna, Fight!" by Rick Telander, *National Wildlife,* February–March 1989. Copyright © 1989 by the National Wildlife Federation. All rights reserved. Reprinted by permission.

"The Roots of Rock" by Penelope Green, *The New York Times,* January 20, 1991. Copyright © 1991 by The New York Times Company. Reprinted by permission.

"The Plot Against People" by Russell Baker, *The New York Times,* June 18, 1968. Copyright © 1968 by The New York Times Company. Reprinted by permission.

"Life Without Cable" by Jeff Greenfield. Reprinted with permission from TV Guide® Magazine and the author. Copyright © 1987 by News America Publications Inc.

Chapter 5

"Fashions in Funerals" from *Talking Woman* by Shana Alexander, pp. 120–121. Copyright © 1976 Shana Alexander. Reprinted by permission.

"That Lean and Hungry Look" by Suzanne Britt, *Newsweek,* October 9, 1978. Copyright © 1978 Suzanne Britt. Reprinted by permission of the author.

"On to Disneyland and Real Unreality" by Toni Morrison. Reprinted by permission of International Creative Management.

"Man, Bytes, Dog" by James Gorman. Originally appeared in *The New Yorker.* Copyright © 1984 James Gorman. Reprinted by permission of The New Yorker.

"Of Prophets and Protesters" by Robert C. Maynard. Copyright © 1989 Universal Press Syndicate. Reprinted with permission. All rights reserved.

Chapter 6

"The Writer" by Perry James Pitre. Reprinted by permission of the author.

"Changing How We 'Grow' Students" by Albert Shanker. Copyright © 1989 by Albert Shanker. Reprinted by permission.

"The Iks," copyright © 1973 by The Massachusetts Medical Society, from *The Lives of a Cell* by Lewis Thomas. Used by permission of Viking Penguin, a division of Penguin Books USA Inc.

"My Brother Shaman" from *Taking the World in for Repairs* by Richard Selzer (New York: William Morrow & Company, 1986). Copyright © 1986 by Richard Selzer. Reprinted by permission of Georges Borchardt, Inc., for the author.

Chapter 7

"Making the Grades: How to Cram" by Jill Young Miller, *Campus Voice,* Fall 1987. Copyright © 1987 Jill Young Miller. Reprinted by permission of the author.

"You Sure You Want to Do This?" by Maneka Gandhi, Third World Network Features.

"The Tennis Shirt" by John Berendt, *Esquire,* October 1986. Copyright © 1986 John Berendt. Reprinted by permission of the author.

"Death by Fasting" by Joan Stephenson Graf from *Science 81,* November 1981, vol. 2, no. 9. Copyright © 1981 by American Association for the Advancement of Science. Reprinted by permission.

"A Nation of Beachwalkers" by Peter Steinhart, in *Audubon* magazine, March 1989, pp. 10–12. Reprinted by permission of the author.

Chapter 8

"Censoring Sex Information: The Story of *Sassy*" by Elizabeth Larsen, *Utne Reader,* July/August 1990. Copyright © 1990 by LENS Publishing Co. Reprinted by permission.

"Black Men and Public Space" by Brent Staples. Reprinted by permission of the author.

"Pain, not Pleasure, Now the Big Sell" by George Felton. Reprinted by permission of the author.

"How an Era Empowered Students" by Constance L. Hays, *The New York Times,* January 10, 1989. Copyright © 1989 by The New York Times Company. Reprinted by permission.

"Father and Child" by Shelley Moore, *The Crisis,* 1987. Reprinted by permission of Crisis Publishing Company.

Chapter 9

"O the Porch" from *We Are Still Married* by Garrison Keillor. Copyright © 1982, 1989 by Garrison Keillor. Reprinted by permission of Viking Penguin, a division of Penguin Books USA, Inc., and Ellen Levine Literary Agency.

"Let It Beep" by Craig Stoltz. Reprinted by permission of the author.

"Gleanings: The Best of the Rest" by Kurt Andersen, *Rolling Stone,* May 18, 1989. By Straight Arrow Publishers, Inc. © 1992. All rights reserved. Reprinted by permission.

"Discrimination Is a Virtue" by Robert Keith Miller, *Newsweek,* July 21, 1980. Copyright © Robert Keith Miller. Reprinted by permission.

Index of Authors, Titles, and Rhetorical Terms